ARSEN.
THE FRENCH CONNECTION
How The Arsenal became L'Arsenal.

By FRED ATKINS

First edition published by GCR Books, 2012.
Second edition, published by Amazon KDP 2016.
Copyright © Fred Atkins

For Tom, Jack, Allen and Tom Atkins, for May "Supernanna" Atkins, the head of this Arsenal supporting family and for her father Bill Carter, who was a cartridge inspector at the Royal Arsenal in Woolwich – and who thought football was "22 men running around after a ball."

PREFACE TO THE SECOND EDITION

This book was first published in 2012 and when it first came out the reviewers were largely kind. Even when they weren't, such as when "When Saturday Comes" decried the "puerile jibes about Sir Alex Fergsuon", I wore the criticism as a badge of honour.

When "The French Connection" came out a civil war was breaking out between the pro-Wenger "Arsene Knows Best" camp and the Wenger Out brigade.

The Gingers 4 Limpar website suggested buying it as a Christmas present for your anti-Wenger mates "for a laugh" to see how they'd react.

Re-reading the book four years down the line, I was tempted to make a few revisions, although not to the chapter on Wenger. In the mean time Nicolas Anelka has somehow managed to make himself look even more cretinous, the chapter on the prodigal Mathieu Flamini may seem unduly harsh and the section on Samir Nasri unduly generous, but the text remains largely unaltered, with the information correct as of the autumn of 2012.

The exception was a fate-temptingly naïve post-script to the chapter on Abou Diaby I wrote in the immediate aftermath of a stellar performance at Anfield, which has been cut from this edition.

For the record the 23 French players referred to in the chapter on Arsene Wenger have become 27: Olivier Giroud, Yaya Sanogo, Mathieu Debuchy and Jeff Reine-Adelaide all joined, while Flamini rejoined the club from AC Milan.

CONTENTS

Foreword by Gilles Grimandi
Introduction
1 The Factory of Death
2 Bigotry, a Dutch Airman and Didier Six
3 The Alsatian
4 Just Because You're Paranoid
5 Windows
6 Patrick Vieira
7 Remi Garde
8 Nicolas Anelka
9 EmmanuelPetit
10 Gilles Grimandi
11 David Grondin
12 Jeremie Aliadiere
13 Robert Pires
14 Sylvian Wiltord
15 Pascal Cygan
16 Gael Clichy
17 Mathieu Flamini
18 Abou Diaby
19 William Gallas
20 Bacary Sagna
21 Lassana Diarra
22 Samir Nasri
23 Mikael Silvestre
24 Francis Coquelin
25 Gilles Sunu
26 Laurent Koscielny
27 Sebastien Squillaci
28 Thierry Henry
Appendices

FOREWORD: BY GILLES GRIMANDI

We're now living in a virtual world but for all the importance of twitter and facebook, I personally still want to believe that face-to-face encounters are the most important kind.

The two most significant things to happen in my professional life were when I met Arsene and when I signed for Arsenal, where I experienced the passion England has for football.

The alchemy created by Arsene Wenger and Arsenal is exceptional: they stand for longevity, loyalty, professionalism, honesty and a belief in attractive football.

Arsenal is now the model that all clubs operating under normal financial conditions want to follow. The club is admired throughout France and because of its huge profile there, young players all over the country aspire to wear the red and white shirt.

Almost without exception all players that have played for Arsenal, even those that have left for better conditions, retain a huge admiration and passion for the club that they were unable to find elsewhere.

I am very proud to have worn this shirt and to still be working for the club - and I believe we will have great success in the future. I'm far from the most talented player to have represented Arsenal but I'm happy to have made some contribution towards the club's success.

The start of my Arsenal career wasn't easy but I have wonderful memories of playing at Highbury. Fans always remember me for the incident with Diego Simeone and my tackle on Edgar Davids and while I'm not proud of either incident, that was part of my character. Some may also remember my goal against Crystal Palace although I have to confess that I was trying to cross and not to score!

After a 13-year association with Arsenal I've become very attached to the club and have an enormous admiration for Arsene Wenger and all that he has achieved. My meetings with Arsenal and Arsene remain the most important in my football life and, naturally, as a Frenchman, I'm pleased that there has been a large French influence on the club's recent history which you can read about in this excellent book.

I'm sure we'll soon be writing a new, successful chapter - and that we will keep giving joy to everyone, from England, France and everywhere else, that loves this great club.

Gilles Grimandi, August 2012.

"We don't like them and it's better to say that than be hypocritical. We have a bit of trouble with the English. We respect them, well, in my case at least I respect them, but you couldn't say we have the slightest thing in common with them.

"We appreciate our Italian cousins with whom we share the same quality of life, we appreciate the Celts and their conviviality ... and then among all these nations we have one huge thing in common: we don't like the English.

"This insular country who always drape themselves in the national flag, their hymns, their chants, their traditions. They are people who one regards as a very proud people."

Marc Lievremont, France national Rugby coach, February 2011.

"David Cameron is like a man who goes to a wife swapping party without his wife."

Unnamed French government official, December 2011.

"You're a big-nosed French twat!"

Paul Merson to David Ginola, Parc des Princes 1994

INTRODUCTION

IT'S March 29, 1994 and Arsenal are playing Paris St. Germain in the Parc des Princes, in the semi-final of the European Cup Winners Cup.

Paul Merson has been handed the task of marking David Ginola at a corner.

The tie is 49 minutes into its first leg and Arsenal, reputed to be the most obdurate, dour and defensive side in England have sent a shockwave through the ground by conjuring a fluent, attacking display against a team soon to become the champions of France.

They lead 1-0 thanks to a 35th-minute header from Ian Wright, but there's a problem. On the left flank Ginola has been causing Lee Dixon so many problems his captain Tony Adams has repeatedly had to bail him out of trouble and Adams, with George Weah to deal with, has problems of his own.

Ginola's already healthily-sized ego is feeding off the adoration of the Parisian crowd, but his pouting and hair-flicking also draws the derision of his opponents and Merson and his team mate Steve Bould are baiting the self-regarding future Shampoo salesman.

Merson, giggling, calls Ginola a "big-nosed French twat" when he and Bould should be concentrating on marking him. As Valdo's cross swings into the box, Ginola finds a yard of space and with a flick of his forehead glances the ball into David Seaman's net at the near post.

Ginola peels off to celebrate, but after a couple of seconds he checks his run and begins showering Merson with abuse.

Merson ignores him, knowing he can expect far worse from his manager George Graham when he returns to the dressing room.

300 miles to the east, in a university building in Strasbourg, a small group of English-speaking students are experiencing a similar feeling.

In the television room of the Robertsau hall of residence, I am with a group of half a dozen friends who are more desperate to win this match than any World Cup final, even though I am the only Arsenal supporter among them.

Our group includes an Irishman and a law student from Derbyshire, both of whom have only a passing interest in football. There is a Scotsman called Bruce, whose devotion to Rangers is second only to his devotion to the bottle, but who, less stereotypically, is a passionate supporter of both the Union and any side representing the UK. Bruce has spent his months in France cultivating a deep-seated Francophobia instead of studying.

Within a month of this game Bruce will sit in an exam having done minimal revision, write: "Je suis un poisson," on his paper in honour of the Red Dwarf character Arnold Rimmer and walk out of the hall.

Bruce's desperation for an Arsenal win shocks me. Two months beforehand I made the mistake of watching a Calcutta Cup game with him.

Although the television room was supposedly isolated from the residential areas, we were receiving complaints even before he'd finished his eulogistic rendition of "Flower of Scotland" (to this day he remains the only Scot I have ever met who actually knows the words in their entirety.)

With around a minute to go there were further complaints when he celebrated what he assumed would be the winning penalty and when Jon Callard subsequently kicked England to victory in the dying seconds his anguish was so acute he looked like a rabid cat in its death throes.

Yet this isn't the only unusual alliance in the room and the appetite for this fixture has also surprised me.

French football is neither particularly well known, nor well regarded in England. Matches are not televised and newspapers list their results but otherwise give the league no coverage at all.

Yet French people with little interest in football and no interest in the French domestic league regard European competition as a matter of national prestige and support their clubs in Europe in the same way a British sports fan with no particular interest in athletics will suddenly become engaged by Kelly Holmes or Steve Ovett at the Olympics.

This tie means more to me than any North London derby ever will. There are probably around 300 people crammed into this mini-auditorium and while a clear majority are supporting PSG, a significant number of black Africans cheer when Wright heads in Paul Davis's cross for the Arsenal goal.

One pumps his fists and cries: "Ca c'est Wright!"

The sentiment is pro-Wright, anti-French and anti-PSG all at once.

Expats often have complicated relationships with their host nation and while many Africans may love France for giving them a home, some also resent the way they can never feel entirely integrated.

PSG also polarise opinions. They are a relatively new club, created in 1970 and the only side from the capital in the top flight.

The 93-94 crop is the best in the club's brief history.

In addition to Ginola, Weah and Valdo they have the captain of the Brazilian national team Rai, who has been left out tonight due to UEFA's "three foreigners" rule, plus Paul Le Guen, who will go on to win three titles as the coach of Lyon.

Undefeated in 35 league games, they will romp to the French title and should go on to dominate the domestic scene for years to come.

But they don't. Something goes wrong. In the second leg at Highbury a fortnight later they squander a host of chances and lose 1-0 to an early goal from Kevin Campbell.

The crowd for this match in the Robertsau television room is around a third of that for the first leg, with many people assuming incorrectly that the tie is already over - during a fraught second half the French transmission will break down for half an hour, prompting Bruce to yell: "Only in fucking France! Even Border TV, who are shite, could show this!"

Although they win the league title that year and the Cup Winners Cup in 1997, PSG enter a period of relative decline.

And a side from a great European capital will capture the imagination of the French public, but that team is Arsenal.

The Arsenal side that defeats PSG is almost entirely English. Its only foreigner is John Jensen, a Dane whose style of play seems more suited to a pub kick around than a European final.

Yet within two and a half years Arsenal will employ a French manager. By 1998 the Gunners will have a quartet of French players on their books and will win their first double since 1971.

A year later a French team will beat England 2-0 at Wembley in a game that features so many Gunners the Daily Mirror will use the headline "The Arsenal 0, L'Arsenal 2."

By the year 2000 English players will be outnumbered by French players in the first team and by 2008 the English will temporarily become an endangered species. When, on November 1 2011, Arsenal play without a French player (ironically in a Champions League game with Marseille) it is the first time they have fielded a team for a fully competitive fixture without a French player since a UEFA cup tie with Borussia Monchengladbach on September 10 1996.

The team on that occasion consisted of nine Englishmen, a Welshman and a Dutchman, with English and Dutch subs:
Seaman
Dixon, Keown, Linighan, Keown, Winterburn
Platt, Merson,
Wright, Bergkamp, Hartson
Subs: Bould, Helder

In the next 15 years Arsenal will play just two nominally competitive games without a French player and on both occasions the manager, Arsene Wenger, deliberately fields what is in effect a reserve team. The first is for a 4-2 defeat at Newcastle on May 14 2000, the final day of the 1999-2000 English League season, with Arsenal resting the entire first team squad ahead of the UEFA cup final with Galatasaray. The second is for a League Cup tie with Wigan on November 11 2008, a 3-0 win (with Francis Coquelin an unused sub) in a competition that for over a decade Wenger used in the same way a scientist might use laboratory mice, conducting risky experiments he wasn't prepared to do when it really mattered.

The Marseille tie was therefore a significant landmark, the line-up reflecting just how internationalised the game had become and also perhaps the end of an era.

Szczesny
Jenkinson, Vermaelen, Mertesacker, Santos
Song, Arteta, Ramsey
Walcott, Gervinho, Park
Subs: Rosicky, Arshavin, Van Persie

14 players were used from 13 different countries: Poland, England, Belgium, Germany, Brazil, Cameroon, Spain, Ivory Coast, South Korea, the Czech Republic, Russia and Holland. The right back Carl Jenkinson has dual-nationality as his mother is Finnish and the unused subs included a Polish keeper in Fabianski, the Swiss Johan Djorou, Israel's Yossi Benayoun and a Frenchman with Polish ancestry in Laurent Koscielny.

In all, from 1996 to 2011 Arsenal will use 23 French players in their first team, although such is the ethnic diversity of the French population, only four of these would be deemed fully French under the quasi-fascist agenda of the extreme right-wing politician Jean Marie Le Pen.
12 of these players, a slight majority, are black or of mixed race. Patrick Vieira and Bacary Sagna's familes are from Senegal. Nicolas Anelka, Sylvain Wiltord and Gael Clichy's from Martnique, while Thierry Henry and William Gallas's hail from Guadeloupe. Abou Diaby has Ivorian origins, Lassana Diarra's ancestry is Malian, Gilles Sunu's father played for Togo and Francis Coquelin's family are from La Reunion, where one of Arsenal's white French players, David Grondin, also has family connections.
Even the 11 white players would still provoke the ire of Le Pen and his ideologically stunted followers. Aside from Grondin, Gilles Grimandi had Italian grandparents, Mathieu Flamini's father is Italian, Samir Nasri's family are from Algeria and Laurent Koscielny's paternal grandfather is from Poland.
Sebastien Squilacci's Italian-sounding name comes from his Corsican

ancestry, making him a borderline case for the kind of white-collar lunatic that used to teach me international relations when I was studying in France. Robert Pires, who said he would refuse to play for the French national team if Le Pen were elected president in 2002, was born in Reims, to a Portuguese father and a Spanish mother.

That leaves Emmanuel Petit, Remi Garde, Jeremie Aliadiere and Pascal Cygan and given the historical patterns of migration around Europe it would be a surprise if they didn't have some kind of foreign ancestry somewhere down the line.

The idea that the French were all descended from Asterix the Gaul, as a sizable minority of inadequates living in metropolitan France would have you believe, is a myth.

Wenger's 23 could play for a total of 14 other countries and the manager himself is from Alsace, a region of France that has been part of Germany for much of its history, the nation his father was forced to serve during the Second World War.

The assimilation of players from such a variety of backgrounds might seem remarkable, but again history suggests people from different ethnic backgrounds have no difficulty living and working alongside each other, provided the ideologies that imply they are somehow different and inferior aren't allowed to take root.

Witness the Yugoslavian general who wept as he remembered his team Red Star Belgrade side ripping Bayern Munich apart in 1991, a team of seven Serbs, two Macedonians, the brilliant Montenegrin Dejan Savicevic and the Croat Robert Prosinecki. These players would soon find themselves on opposite sides in an utterly futile civil war that, as a side issue, also destroyed Yugoslavia as a footballing force.

Compare and contrast this with France, where the successful integration of so many disparate elements produced the rainbow "Black, Blanc et Beur" coalition that won the World Cup in 1998 and that helped transform Arsenal from an almost entirely English team, into a diverse gang who became a major force in European football.

The 23 have other shared characteristics. All were born in France, with the exception of Vieira, who moved to the outskirts of Paris as a child. The other 22 are almost all second or third generation immigrants and all were educated under the French system.

They are generally men of above average intelligence, in the case of the legally-trained Flamini significantly so, and certainly by comparison to their English counterparts, among whom Frank Lampard's qualification in GCSE Latin is a thing of wonder. (Wenger's most successful English signings,

Theo Walcott and Alex Oxlade-Chamberlain, speak noticeably more correct English than the average professional).

All speak English to at least some degree, many to an advanced level and some are polyglots, fluent in two or three other languages like Vieira, or Pires, who is fluent in Spanish and Portuguese because of his parents, but who is reluctant to speak English, even though he is far from inarticulate.

There are other factors. While the English academy system stresses the importance of education as a safety net for aspiring footballers, there is little or no academic culture among young players, who are often poorly read, monoglot and inarticulate even in their native language.

Glenn Hoddle, whose English is only on nodding terms with the basic rules of grammar, spent four seasons at Monaco and somehow managed not to pick up any French at all, while Chris Waddle was at least willing to try during his time with Marseilles but still sounded like a GCSE student who'd been forced to study a language against his will as he stumbled his way through the oral exam.

The favoured newspaper of the English professional, and indeed the English in general, is the Sun, the market leader among a predominantly regressive right-wing media that actively helps promote and perpetuate insularity and ignorance with its unashamed Europhobia and in some cases overt anti-muslim agenda.

While this hasn't yet succeeded in turning England into a nation of morons, there's an engrained and unapologetic revulsion for studying among a certain kind of English football prodigy and while some of Arsenal's French players confess to being similarly disinterested by their schoolwork, they at least don't try to wear this as a badge of honour.

The 23 generally come from stable family backgrounds, with married parents (Vieira is again an exception, although the strength of his extended family compensated for an absentee father) and most were at least reasonably affluent.

While there is plenty of pejorative commentary about the banlieues, the suburbs where a number of Arsenal's French players were raised, much of the criticism is exaggerated and the standard of living here is higher than in the equivalent inner city areas of, for example, London.

The only one of the 23 to have experienced genuine poverty was Vieira (again) when he was in Senegal and although France lags behind England in the availability of grass pitches, the least affluent areas still have dirt or gravel pitches and even small villages have some kind of municipal stadium.

Yet all 23 gravitated towards London, where its estimated anything between 250,000 and 400,000 French people now live.

Some, like Anelka, were mere teenagers when they emigrated, while Squillaci was the oldest at 30, but all 23 chose to uproot themselves because were looking for something they couldn't find enough of in their homeland, be it money, glory or the adulation of the fans in a land where the culture of watching the game is so much more engrained.

In his book "The Football Men" the author Simon Kuper postulates that footballers are all essentially businessmen, with the most successful of them becoming effectively human corporations.

Their sole motivation is to make as much money as they can during a playing career and any attachment they feel to a particular club is fleeting, incidental and in some cases entirely feigned.

As harsh as that may sound there is definitely an element of truth to this for most, if not all, professional players in England and in some cases, most obviously that of Nicolas Anelka, it seems to be both fair and entirely accurate.

Fernando Torres was honest enough to admit this when he signed for Chelsea, a club whose success has been built almost entirely at the behest of a man who, in common with some of his players, apparently sees it as a vehicle for his personal ambitions.

Others however, do appear to develop genuine and binding emotional ties with particular clubs, like Zola at Chelsea and Cantona at Manchester United, footballers whose qualities as both players and men transcended club loyalties.

Of the Arsenal 23 some, like Mathieu Flamini and William Gallas appeared to be there because Arsenal were the right club at the right time to further their own personal interests.

Others, like Henry and Vieira, became authentic club legends. Even though both ultimately left, again to pursue their own interests, the bonds they formed were not broken by their decisions to leave because the efforts they made when their interests coincided with Arsenal's yielded so many rewards. The same could not be said of Samir Nasri, whose affection for the club appeared genuine, but who left for economic reasons before he ever had the chance to be mentioned in the same breath.

In the case of one man at least however, the idea of being a corporation is anathema.

Arsene Wenger's vision for Arsenal went well beyond the accumulation of personal wealth. As well as he was undoubtedly paid, Wenger would have earned far more had he put himself on the market and accepted one of the myriad offers made to him by the likes of Real Madrid.

Wenger saw Arsenal as his chance to create a great European footballing power, playing some of the most exhilarating football the game has ever seen.

This is the story of how the Arsenal became l'Arsenal.

1) THE FACTORY OF DEATH

The Royal Arsenal was a factory of death, a sprawling site dedicated to the mechanics of killing and maiming, (the defence industry as its apologists still refer to it), located on the banks of the Thames a couple of miles east of Greenwich.

The weaponry they produced allowed Britain to conquer a third of the globe and for much of its existence the enemies in the sights of the guns they produced were usually French.

It was here, in 1886, that munitions workers assembled at a pub called the Royal Oak to form Dial Square FC, soon to become Royal Arsenal and then Woolwich Arsenal.

By the time Dial Square FC was formed Britain's enmity towards the French was fading, to be replaced by a historically improbable alliance by the time the club had decamped to Highbury in 1913.

The Royal Arsenal has now been turned into a museum, plus a mixture of unaffordable housing and spirit-crushing industrial estates.

Unlike at Highbury, where the former East and West stands remain in perpetuity, there are almost no traces of the football club, apart from a plaque at Woolwich Station and a few bits of terracing from the Invicta Ground in Hector Street, which are now part of a row of back gardens.

Arsenal's other former home, the Manor Ground, is now the kind of industrial estate that offers the casual visitor a glimpse of what a nuclear winter might look like, full of warehouses, pallets, plastic bags and litter.

It's a soul destroying place, though there are other, more vivid connections to the Arsenal nearby.

Barely a mile down the road to the south west Ian Wright was born in Woolwich hospital, while a similar distance to the east lies the bleakly futuristic settlement of Thamesmead, a startlingly godless, greying cubist wasteland where the reclusive American film director Stanley Kubrick, an improbably devoted Arsenal supporter, filmed "A Clockwork Orange", banned for the best part of three decades for its depictions of ultra-violence.

During these formative years visiting teams looked forward to visits to Arsenal's Manor Ground with all the relish of a single female planning a midnight stroll through one of Kubrick's tunnels.

A violent, brutal team, backed by equally unpleasant hordes of droogs on the sidelines, the Arsenal of the pre-war era were precisely the kind of team their modern equivalent would come to despise and it's fascinating to imagine how Arsene Wenger's side, who are said with only partial justification to fear the bear pits of the modern north, would have coped with the painfully slow journey to Plumstead and the cauldron of spite that awaited them there.

Kubrick was said to have regretted the transformation Arsenal made under Wenger.

For him the influx of foreign players he witnessed in the three years before his death in 1999 somehow diluted the qualities he admired in the team.

Younger Arsenal fans would find it difficult to understand just how their team was reviled, even 20 years ago.

The very qualities that Wenger's Arsenal are perceived to lack - "bottle," physicality, psychological resilience and a willingness to get your retaliation in first, were precisely those that made the club pariahs under George Graham.

2) BIGOTRY, A DUTCH AIRMAN AND DIDIER SIX

Given the proximity of France and England - just 22 miles separate the countries at the channel's narrowest point – it seems surprising only two professionals had played in England before Didier Six signed for Aston Villa in 1984.

Georges Crozier, who played twice for the national team, spent two years with Fulham, then in the Southern League from 1904 to 1906, while Eugene Langenove joined Walsall in 1922, becoming the first Frenchman to play in the Football League.

But even in the interwar era, Arsenal were more forward-thinking than many clubs. Having decamped to Highbury, the enlightened regime of Herbert Chapman Arsenal tried to sign an Austrian keeper Rudy Hiden in 1930, only to find that once he'd arrived at Dover he was denied a work permit, specifically because he was foreign.

Undeterred Chapman instead signed Gerrit Keizer, a Dutch international who had played for Ajax before coming to England to improve his English and had joined Margate, Arsenal's unofficial nursery club.

Chapman brought him to Highbury in 1930 and he made 13 appearances as Arsenal won their first ever league title.

As a Dutchman, Keizer was from a less politically sensitive country than Hiden, but the move still outraged the Ministry of Labour and the FA, which in 1931 passed a rule that barred foreign players unless they had been resident in Britain for two years.

This now seems like a backward and xenophobic step, effectively a form of protectionism designed to "stop foreigners taking British jobs" as the political cliché would have it.

They were too late to thwart Keizer, who had already been in England long enough to qualify as a resident, but his haphazard goalkeeping, exemplified during a 4-2 defeat at Derby when he was at fault for at least two goals, saw him fall out of favour with Chapman and he joined Charlton and then QPR.

His later life makes for a fascinating subtext. He made 302 appearances for Ajax and after World War Two made repeated flights to London, to borrow kit from his old club for a poverty-stricken Ajax side.

To this day Ajax wear a kit similar to Arsenal as a result, although Keizer himself got into trouble when he returned from one of his mercy missions and was found with an illegally large amount of foreign currency on him, earning him six-months in prison.

He later reinvented himself as a greengrocer and became a director at Ajax before his death in 1980. His grandson Peter Keizer, not to be confused with the Dutch international Piet Keizer, became a distinguished artist and sculptor.

Gerrit's short-term legacy however, was a Daily Mail reader's wet dream, an English league almost entirely free of foreigners.

For Arsenal the first victim of this policy was Albert Gudmundsson, the first ever Icelandic professional, who made a handful of appearances for Arsenal in the autumn of 1946 before he was forced to leave after failing to obtain a work permit.

According to The Times, Gudmundsson was forming a highly promising partnership with George Curtis at inside forward, but faced with the British game operating a closed shop he instead went to Nancy and then Milan, before embarking on careers as a businessman and later a politician, eventually holding two cabinet positions in his home country and also becoming president of its FA.

In 2010 a lifesize (if slightly peculiar-looking) bronze statue of Gudmundsson was unveiled outside the headquarters of the Icelandic FA in Reykjavik.

A trickle of players qualified through residency. The Chilean-born but Yorkshire raised brothers George and Ted Robledo played for Newcastle in the early 1950s, while South Africa's Bill Perry scored the winner for Blackpool in the 1953 FA Cup final (the so-called Matthews final).

The most remarkable story was that of Bert Trautmann, a German prisoner-of-war and former Luftwaffe paratrooper who played for Manchester City with a broken neck in the 1956 FA Cup final.

20,000 people protested against Trautmann's signing in 1949. Within a month he had won most of them over, but given the proximity of the conflict it was unsurprising his arrival rankled.

There would have been no such resentment towards a French player, but "Keizer's law" remained on the statute books until 1978, when the FA accepted a European Community ruling that the football associations of member states would no longer be able to bar players on the grounds of nationality.

The result was hardly the opening of a sluice gate.

Arsenal's tentative move into the new era began when they signed an Australian striker called John Kosmina, though he was perhaps the kind of ineffectual player the authorities had in mind when they drew up Kaizer's law in the first place, his sole start in a goalless four-game career coming in a 1978 UEFA Cup defeat at Hadjuk Split.

There was a mini-influx of "proper" foreigners, though ironically the most successful of these, with the exceptions of Dutchmen Arnold Muhren and Franz Thijsen at Ipswich, were from politically unfriendly regimes to the UK from outside the EC - Osvaldo Ardilles and Ricky Villa at Tottenham were from an Argentina then governed by a fascist junta, while, Poland's Kazmierz Deyna at Manchester City and Southampton's Yugoslavian Ivan Golac both came from behind the Iron Curtain.

There were no barriers, other than linguistic, to French players.

After the 1982 World Cup Michel Platini was coveted by both Tottenham and Arsenal. Had the latter signed him, Platini could plausibly have reinvigorated a side that had been on the cusp of something great a couple of seasons beforehand but was now entering a period of relative decline.

It's possible Arsenal's French evolution would have happened 15 years earlier, but Platini, a player with Italian ancestry, opted for a move to Juventus, while Arsenal signed Vladimir Petrovic, an altogether softer midfield playmaker who was almost instantly found out by bruising opponents and fled to Belgium just six months later.

Instead the first French pioneer was Didier Six, a veteran centre-forward of two World Cup campaigns.

Six was a flamboyant winger from Lille, a city just 80 miles from Dover, even though the two towns are culturally about as similar as Cardiff and Lisbon.

He sported the kind of early 80s Heavy Metal hairstyle, a kind of permed demi-mullet that a decade later would become a prototype for the Argentina 94 World Cup squad.

Six had enjoyed a successful couple of seasons with Stuttgart either side of his trip to the World Cup semi-final with the national team in 1982.

However, by 1984 he was on the fringes of the national team and although he was in the squad, playing in three of France's five games in the European championships, he didn't play in the final with Spain.

Nor was he universally popular at home, having thrice been relegated, with Valenciennes, Lens and Marseilles, whose supporters barracked him when France played Portugal there in the 1984 semi-final - not that being booed by the crowd at the Stade Velodrome made him in any way unique.

If conformed to the moody latin stereotype, Six was regarded as something of a loose cannon even in his own land and was happiest in the Bundesliga.

After Euro 1984 he somehow found himself at FC Mulhouse, a French second division side who struggled to pull in crowds of 2,000.

Unsurprisingly they were unable to afford him and he was sent out on loan to Aston Villa.

Asked why he'd swapped his vast Alsatian house for rented accomodation in Birmingham, Six would simply tell reporters: "Je suis professionel."

He would later admit to being initially "pissed off" about having to move, but after just two days he was starting to warm to his team mates, who wasted no time in trying to get him to join their drinking club.

Even though he hadn't played a competitive game in four months he did well in his first game against Manchester United, setting up Peter Withe for the opening goal in a 3-0 win and getting an ovation when his legs finally gave out 15 minutes from time.

A needless booking for a foul on Jesper Olsen, however, hinted at the underlying reasons that would make his long-term impact more questionable.

"It's a special type of football here," he said. "I've already noticed that it's more physical, although I was used to that in Germany. It's also faster and because of that there are more mistakes. I think it would be very difficult for a foreign player to succeed here in midfield or at centre forward, but as a winger I think I will find it easier."

He'd also noticed other cultural differences.

"In England there is less mental pressure on players," he said. "I've been amazed how players only have to arrive for games a couple of hours before kick-off. In France they bring the team together the day before a game and watch over you so closely that they even tell you what you can and can't eat. The match is the only thing in your head and that is not always a good thing."

Here was the paradox. In the mid-1980s in France players took the game ultra-seriously, but the general public barely batted an eyelid, even after two World Cup semi-finals and a European title.

English fans took the game too seriously at times, as the Heysel disaster of 1985 would prove, but the players often prepared for the games like remnants of the amateur era.

Ron Atkinson, manager of Manchester United when Six made his debut against them, knew which of his players liked a drink and rather than slap a curfew on them he would offer them a pint as a night cap on the evening before a game.

He was not alone. Brian Clough, who enjoyed a long and not always healthy relationship with alcohol, would regularly offer his players a shot of whisky before kick-off.

In the mid-1980s players like Norman Whiteside and Bryan Robson were out-drinking their fans, but at 30 Six was too old to suddenly start competing with Olympian class boozers, either on or off the field.

"I came over a bit too late," he later reflected. "Had I been 20 to 26 I would have blown their defences but at 30 we saw things in a different light, even though I improved my headers!"

Six didn't do badly at Villa Park, but he never quite matched his early promise and at the end of the season he left for Metz, never to return.

France's next export wouldn't arrive in England for another seven years, but when he did his impact was seismic.

Eric Cantona had burned almost all his bridges in France, having fallen out with a succession of managers and officials, when he spent a week on trial with Sheffield Wednesday in January 1992.

The Owls then manager Trevor Francis, one of an embarrassingly small number of English professionals to have enjoyed a successful part of his career abroad, knew that Cantona represented a gamble.

By the age of 22 he had already been at six clubs, leaving a trail of shattered professional relationships in his wake.

At Auxerre a 17-year-old Cantona punched keeper Bruno Martini in the face and a year later he chose a tv interview as the ideal moment to call Henri Michel, then manager of the national team, a "bag of shit."

Cantona decided to abandon the game and was enjoying his retirement in Val d'Isere when he took a phone call from Jean Cacharel, the founder of the Cacharel empire and more pertinently for Cantona, the chairman of his club, FC Nimes.

The conversation ended his dreams of a quick retirement. Cantona owed Nimes serious money for breach of contract and he had no choice but to carry on playing.

When his agent, Six's equally flamboyant and hirsute former team mate Dominique Rocheteau, suggested going to England, Cantona agreed, but he was aggravated by Francis's insistence he should go on trial. When Howard Wilkinson at Leeds offered him a better deal he agreed to join them, only to leave within months.

Both Francis and Wilkinson would repent at leisure.

Cantona provided the additional impetus Leeds needed to stave off Manchester United to win the 1991-92 league title, but early the following season he left for Leeds' greatest rivals, having already exasperated Wilkinson. The Leeds manager sold him after a speculative request from Alex Ferguson - who Wilkinson had called in an attempt to buy Denis Irwin.

Leeds entered a period in the wilderness, while Manchester United won their first league title for 26 years - at the same time Sheffield Wednesday were losing League and FA Cup finals to Arsenal.

Francis might be forgiven for wondering how Wednesday might have fared in those finals had Cantona been in his side, though given his track record it seems doubtful he would have stayed on the field for long in either.

At Old Trafford he inspired an era of domination. Whether he was a better player than Paul Scholes or Ryan Giggs is debatable, but for the ability to generate headlines, good and bad, and a show-stopping sense of theatre, Cantona was unrivalled.

When Cantona fell out with people, he at least did it with a certain sense of style and part of his heroic appeal to English fans and players alike may have been that he did what they dreamed of doing but never actually dared to.

When he was disciplined for throwing a ball at a referee in his final game for Nimes he didn't do what Ian Wright habitually did and say sorry before enduring a ritual slap on the wrist, as aware as the men disciplining him were of the hypocrisy of the situation. Cantona carefully and deliberately approached each member of the committee in turn and called them an "idiot".

And when Matthew Simmons, an unreconstructed Crystal Palace fan with a history of racially aggravated violence, verbally abused him at Selhurst Park in 1994, how many players, amid the sanctimonious posturing the incident generated, could help but feeling a vicarious thrill, a feeling that Cantona had kicked Simmons for every time they had been subjected to personal abuse from a fan?

Patrick Vieira said he admired his "big mouth and explosive nature" and Emmanuel Petit was another admirer.

"I used to follow his feats on TV … The English don't give a damn whether the guy has personality or is somewhat crazy. What they are interested in is his performance on the pitch. Canto was not welcome in France anymore, so he started all over in England. I told myself, with the nature he has, the fact he was almost plague-stricken in France and that I sometimes feel people don't understand me, I might have an opportunity to flourish there."

The second French player to flourish in post-war England (we can skate over the month William Prunier spent at Old Trafford) was David Ginola at Newcastle, an attacker Cantona had once derided as a "footballing non-entity", but one who had entranced George Graham to the point that the Scotsman harboured dreams of bringing him to Highbury - until he found out that even matching his salary at PSG would have shattered the wage structure at Arsenal.

Ginola wasn't really Graham's type in any case - nor Arsenal's for that matter.

They had tried to sign Vladimir Petrovic from Red Star Belgrade in August 1982, but were initially rebuffed by the Yugoslav Football Federation, which at the time, in common with several Eastern Bloc countries, refused to allow its players to go abroad before they reached 27 or 28.

After a few months of cold-war posturing (not unlike the saga that surrounded Andre Arshavin's move from Zenit a quarter of a century later) Petrovic did join, for a reported £500,000, in January 1983, but he lasted just five months and the continental experiment was deemed a failure.

David O'Leary said that while Petrovic's team mates appreciated his quality, it was obvious he would never be able to handle the physicality of life in England and for the next decade and beyond, the only foreigners Arsenal signed were Scandinavians who habitually spoke better English than most of the natives but were unencumbered by some of their refuelling habits.

The Icelandic international Siggi Jonsson signed in 1989 but was dogged by injuries and made only nine appearances in three years.

The first European "flair" player to arrive at Highbury was Anders Limpar, a Swedish winger who signed from Cremonese in 1990. He spent the next two seasons jinking his way round lumbering full backs and collecting a championship medal, only to fall out with Graham and spend two seasons in detention before reluctantly joining Everton.

Wenger would have loved Limpar, though it's probably safe to deduce he would have been less thrilled by either of the Gunners' next Scandinavians, the Dane John Jensen or Norway's Pal Lydersen.

Jensen had at least scored in Denmark's shock victory over Germany in the Euro 92 final, although just how freakish a result that was would be proved over the next four seasons.

When a player strikes a football it can travel in 360 different directions, especially if the player in question possesses the level of shooting accuracy Jensen had.

He scored once, in a 3-1 home defeat to Queens Park Rangers on New Year's Eve in 1994, a performance that illustrated just how stale the Gunners had grown under Graham.

This was partly down to Graham's dealings in the transfer market and it was these that led indirectly to Wenger's arrival.

Talent like Michael Thomas and Anders Limpar was allowed to fester in the reserves, their market value steadily deteriorating before they were sold prematurely. A heartbroken David Rocastle was sold to Leeds, but manifestly inferior players like Jensen and Lydersen were signed after Graham accepted illegal inducements worth £425,000 from the agent Rune Hauge.

Graham claimed the money was an unsolicited gift and repaid it in full, but only after he'd been caught out, giving the club all the ammunition they needed to sack him.

The affair was mishandled by Arsenal, who stalled and allowed Graham to sign three players, the strikers John Hartson, Chris Kiwomya and the Dutch winger Glenn Helder, just days before they fired him.

That also allowed Graham to claim he had been the victim of a "kangaroo court". On the night of his sacking he was consoled by his friend Terry Venables - possibly not the first choice for a character reference in the circumstances - who held a party for him and presented him with a cake saying "George, this is an unsolicited gift."

Graham was neither the first nor last manager to take a bung, but he was one of very few to be caught doing it, something which allowed him to develop and cultivate a sense that he had somehow been the victim.

He produced an unapologetic autobiography, "The Glory and the Grief" and quickly found work at Leeds and then Tottenham, where he was largely reviled for his un-Tottenham-like behaviour, (specifically having the temerity to win a trophy, the 1999 League Cup).

For some Arsenal fans, Graham's decision to join Tottenham was a far greater crime than taking a bung, even if his personal greed made the team demonstrably weaker.

He did, however, leave the club with a parting gift: the single greatest, most cohesive and effective defensive unit ever to grace the English game remained intact.

This was Graham's creation. David Seaman in goal, Lee Dixon at right back, Nigel Winterburn on the left and Tony Adams in the middle, alongside either Steve Bould or Martin Keown.

At various stages in their careers, all six of these men were sneered at and looked down on by both domestic and continental observers.

Seaman supposedly made errors in high-profile games, Dixon and Winterburn were too limited and regularly overlooked for international duty, while Adams was derided as a donkey and Keown laughed at for having a "monkey's head."

Adams in particular was often disparaged for being "unable to play football", a conclusion derived from his perceived lack of technical quality.

This was a myth, as he later proved when his career flourished again under Wenger and he was given license to "express himself". Keown too was a far more gifted player than he was given credit for, as he proved when he spent the best part of a season in midfield under Bruce Rioch.

Much of the criticism of Keown, Bould and Adams stemmed from their physicality, both in appearance and the way they would fracture the laws of the game by intimidating strikers, with a range of subtle digs and ankle taps. The full backs were deemed to have limitations going forwards and considered inferior to the likes of Graham Le Saux, Stuart Pearce, Gary Stevens and the Neville brothers, but had both the intelligence and aptitude to thwart virtually any winger they faced.

Thus while the midfield decayed in Graham's later seasons, the defence helped Arsenal to four cup final appearances in three seasons, three of them victorious. His sacking left Arsenal with a void to fill in the summer of 1995.

The board approached the former England manager Bobby Robson, who had just won the Portuguese title with Porto and had signed a new deal with them, having made a verbal agreement with them that he would be free to leave if a "big club" came in for him.

When David Dein approached him he flew to London and had a meeting with the directors at a house in South Kensington, where he was offered the job.

He accepted, only for Porto's president to renege on their verbal arrangement and threaten to take him to UEFA to have his contract enforced.

"Arsenal would have been a fantastic job for me," he reflected in his autobiography. "To think I turned down Manchester United in 1981 and here I was about to reject Arsenal as well. I called them.

"Look, I said, the President's being very unpleasant. He won't let me go. He's not interested in compensation, so I'm going to have to stay here for another year."

Yet even had he been allowed to leave Arsenal would soon have had to make alternative plans.

Within weeks Robson, who had been complaining of a permanently blocked nose, discovered he had an aggressive form of cancer behind his eyes that came close to killing him.

Dein instead tried and failed to convince the board that they should approach the man he had first met in the South of France seven years previously, Arsene Wenger. Instead they appointed Rioch.

It was suggested in Jon Spurling's book "Highbury, the Story on Arsenal in N5" that Rioch was effectively a caretaker and there to keep the seat warm for Wenger, though as Spurling himself writes, there is little evidence for this. It also does a disservice to Rioch, who at the time was one of the most impressive emerging managerial talents in Britain, having taken Bolton Wanderers to the Premier League and masterminded a series of giant killing performances, including a 3-1 win at Highbury in the previous season's FA Cup.

It was Rioch who signed Dennis Bergkamp, the first major international star to arrive at Highbury, and Rioch who persuaded David Platt to join Arsenal ahead of several other interested clubs who at the time either rivalled or exceeded Arsenal in stature.

While it's impossible to overstate the long-term importance of Bergkamp's arrival, the immediate effect was to heap pressure on Rioch by raising ambitions.

In 1994-95 the club had finished 12th, its worst league position since 1976. At one stage after Graham's sacking there was even a distant possibility they might get relegated. At the end of the campaign the Swedish playmaker Stefan Schwarz left after just one season, having been rendered almost obsolete by the long-ball tactics and Platt wasn't going to be able to revive the midfield on his own.

Keown's reinvention helped, but for goals the team still relied on Ian Wright, whose relationship with Rioch never recovered from a dressing room flare-up when the manager compared Wright unfavourably to a journeyman striker, saying "John McGinley would have scored that" after he had missed a chance.

Arsenal did make progress under Rioch, but having been expected to challenge for the title, fifth place and a league cup semi-final represented a disappointment.

During the close season it seemed that Arsenal had turned into Tottenham. They were linked with an embarrassing number of top continental players, none of whom actually signed, despite the daily appearance of tantalising headlines on teletext that were designed to lure the deluded into ringing the premium rate telephone lines that peddled transfer news to the addicted during the pre-internet era.

And in a move that had Tottenham written all over it for its sheer classlessness and apparently cack-handed timing, on August 12 1996, five days before the start of the new season, Rioch was fired, ostensibly over a "failure to communicate" with the board. Arsenal entered a rudderless period in limbo.

3) THE ALSATIAN

It's an exaggeration to say that Arsene Wenger was a complete unknown in England at the time he was named Arsenal's manager, but only a slight one.

To the wider public he was effectively anonymous, but he had a handful of highly useful contacts and admirers, including the new England manager Glenn Hoddle and even more importantly David Dein, then the most powerful figure on the Arsenal board.

The first time he came to the attention of the English media was when the new England manager Glenn Hoddle recommended Wenger for the newly-created role of FA technical director.

He turned the FA down, but generated a few column inches and impressed a number of British journalists who were covering a Newcastle United friendly in Osaka. They were relieved to meet a manager who didn't immediately treat them with the kind of contempt they were by then used to getting from Alex Ferguson and others.

Wenger had known Dein since the 1980s and the latter was by now able to persuade the rest of the board that they needed a manager who knew the European game and not just the domestic scene.

The names supposedly in the frame included Terry Venables, Robson, (who was by now in remission but heading for Barcelona), Johan Cruyff, who Robson had replaced at the Nou Camp and even Frank Clark, who had succeeded Brian Clough at Nottingham Forest.

When Wenger's name was first circulated it sank morale among some supporters. As Nick Hornby memorably admitted to Wenger's biographer Jasper Rees: "I bet it's fucking Arsene Wenger because I haven't heard of him."

I actually had heard of Wenger having spent a year (1993-94) studying in his home city of Strasbourg, though at the time I had no idea that I was attending his old university, nor would it have meant anything to me if I had.

His was a name I read about in "Onze Mondial" magazine, which I preferred to Le Figaro and Liberation, but aside from being a fairly regular attendee at the Stade de la Meinau, the home of Racing Club de Strasbourg, I didn't follow French football, preferring to stay in touch with how Arsenal were doing at home. That, in the pre-internet era, meant using a pay phone and watching the credit vanish in a matter of seconds, trying and failing to get a decent signal on the BBC World Service or relying on day-old newspapers.

Like many of the players who would join Arsenal, I watched "L'Equipe de Dimanche" on a Sunday night, the equivalent of Match of the Day, but a programme that had a wider brief. It devoted a significant amount of airtime to other European leagues, including England's, even if its dispatches from across the channel were inevitably dominated by Manchester United, and more specifically Cantona.

Strasbourg in 1993 was a city still trying to throw off its past and reinvent itself as a modern European capital.

At the bus stop outside our student residence you could see the European Court of Human Rights being built, but you were equally aware that the pensioner standing next to you in the queue could, for all you knew, have dedicated his youth to the extermination of that cause.

It was difficult not to be curious about the elderly in Alsace. You could still look at almost anyone over the age of 70 and wonder what they'd been doing half a century beforehand.

One of the city's focal points, the Place Broglie, had been renamed Adolf Hitler Platz in 1940. The university restaurant Gallia, where an overwhelming number of students ate the cheap, mass-produced sustenance food, had once doubled as a Gestapo holding centre.

And the whiff of totalitarianism lingered in the "Biblioteque Universitaire," which was without question the least helpful public institution I ever had the misfortune to need, a building whose efficiency was in inverse proportion to its grandeur.

To borrow a book you had to fill in a form, hand it to a librarian and then wait for an hour before they would tell you whether or not it was in stock.

It's a miracle Wenger even had time to complete his degree here let alone play football.

In the university residences up to 40 students would share a corridor, all living in rabbit hutches and having to make do with one dual hob between them.

It was a recipe for malnutrition and in a city where you could eat like Louis XIV if you were wealthy, the only alternative was the "Restau-U", university subsidised canteen food almost designed for the purposes of destroying France's culinary reputation. This might explain why Wenger is so thin, though where his sense of humour came from is perhaps more of a mystery. In Strasbourg the mere act of entering a shop can be a ritual degradation, though this would at least have prepared him for dealing with the English media.

In France, and especially Paris, the retail industry's prime function is to enlarge the egos of jumped-up shop workers through the belittlement and patronising of customers, with the concept of actually selling goods a distant and secondary goal.

In Alsace the shop workers have an interesting twist on this ideal, speaking French to each other and then switching to Alsacien whenever a foreign-sounding customer asks to be served.

(Alsacien, or Elsass, is supposedly a dialect but in reality it's no further removed from German than the average Geordie is from English - and in the case of Paul Gascoigne considerably less so. Non-Alsatian French speakers mock their accent in a kind of sing-song way, the closest equivalent in English perhaps being the undulating pitch of the Welsh).

If a human is partly the product of his or her environment then Wenger's internationalism can be partly explained by the political climate he grew up in, when the pan-European ideal was considered infinitely preferable to the destructive nationalism that had reached a murderous nadir during World War Two.

He was lucky in that he was raised at a time where political leaders were finally succeeding where generations had failed. Robert Schuman, the French Foreign Minister, proposed a solution that was so obvious it only highlighted the poverty of previous leaders: to pool France and Germany's steel and coal resources as the precursor of a union that would make war "not merely unthinkable but materially impossible".

This was the start of the European dream and in Alsace more than anywhere it was a message people desperately needed.

Even today Alsace remains a profoundly confused region, in the sense that it's still not quite sure if it's French or German, but what it does know is that nationality no longer matters and that it never should have.

Arsene Wenger's philosophy, that he never looks at a player's passport, is a reflection of this and it's one that's shared by an overwhelming majority of football professionals. In this sense football is arguably a more enlightened than many other industries.

Managers who pay inflated prices for English players now invite ridicule and when the Jewish Israeli Yossi Benayoun signed for Arsenal it didn't even merit a mention that he would be sharing a dressing room with Muslim players, just as it hadn't when Benayoun had previously joined West Ham, Liverpool and Chelsea.

The Alsatians are proud of their traditions and culture, but the idea that anyone should die for a flag is dead and gone, discredited by the raw memories of recent history.

In January 2011, then-president Nicolas Sarkozy was addressing a group of farmers in the village of Truchterheim when he accidentally referred to Alsace as Allemagne, the French word for Germany.

Most people treated this Freudian gaffe as an innocent but Sarkozy was still criticised.

An angry Alsatian scolded him: "You should be ashamed, we fought for this region three times. You are ignoring the millions of people who died in three wars."

There were many reasons to upbraid Sarkozy, but this wasn't necessarily one of them. Alsatians did indeed fight for the region, but they weren't always fighting on the French side.

Alsace was part of the Holy Roman Empire for several centuries, up until 1648, when it was officially ceded to France in the treaty of Westphalia.

It remained French until the Franco-Prussian War in 1871, when it was annexed by Bismarck, meaning that when World War One broke out in 1914, Alsace was on the Kaiser's side and its soldiers were known as the "malgre-nous" (in spite of ourselves).

The official line following Germany's defeat was that Alsace had been liberated but the region remained a tinderbox where resentment lingered.

In 1922, four years after Alsace's supposedly euphoric return to the Republic, there was a programme of ethnic cleansing which saw 500 Germans, many from "good middle class families" according to the Times, forcibly evicted from their homes. They were expelled, and dumped in the miserable border town of Kehl with only their hand luggage and 10,000 marks, one of many episodes that instilled an ultimately fatal sense of injustice in the defeated Germans.

When it was France's turn to capitulate in 1940 Alsace was spared the fate of the rest of occupied France because Hitler regarded it as part of Germany and simply incorporated it into the third reich - but he never trusted the natives.

When the tide of war turned against Hitler and the Waffen SS in particular began to suffer heavy losses, the master race began forcing men from Alsace, Lorraine, the German-speaking part of Belgium and Luxembourg to enlist.

An estimated 140,000 were drafted into the Wehrmacht, including the 24-year-old Alphonse Wenger, Arsene Wenger's father.

Alphonse was called up in October 1944, five months after the Allied invasion began, and sent to the Eastern Front, where he was separated from fellow Alsatians by superior officers who feared them as potential fifth columnists.

Of these 140,000 around 30 percent were either killed outright or disappeared. Another 10,000 were crippled and 30,000 wounded.

Some deserted and tried to join the Soviets, but most of these were shot as supposed war criminals and 10,000 died in the Tambov prisoner of war camp, where temperatures dropped to minus 30.

The rations for inmates amounted to watery soup and 600 grammes of bread per day, contributing to a mortality rate of 50 percent. Even the inmates at Auschwitz were given more.

32 men from Wenger's village, Duttlenheim, died and those, like Alphonse, who returned found themselves in the unsettling position of being defeated troops who found themselves on the winning side.

Emmanuel Petit once said had that he been alive during the second world war he would have joined the resistance, but this was an easier choice to make with 60 years of hindsight than the one faced by Alphonse Wenger.

Had he refused to enlist, Alphonse would have been interned and probably executed.

The "malgre-nous" were under suspicion, resented by their newly-liberated French compatriots and accused of collaboration by apologists in the French communist party when they attempted to speak out about the conditions in Stalin's camps.

Their plight was only acknowledged in the mid-1980s when the Federal German government agreed to pay the families affected a total of 250 million marks in compensation.

Paul Frantz, the man who coached Strasbourg to the French Cup in 1966 and who was later a key figure in Arsene Wenger's developing career, was a malgre-nous who had to put up with being called a "bosche" when he played against teams from elsewhere in France.

"Alsatians of my generation are not friendly," he told Jasper Rees. "They are untrusting. Because he comes from a younger generation Arsene does not have these problems."

But in one sense at least Alphonse Wenger was lucky merely to have survived against such odds and to have been able to return home when some survivors were still in Soviet camps six years after the war.

He ran a car parts business in Strasbourg but also helped run the family restaurant, the Croix d'Or, which is still a going concern in Duttlenheim today, albeit one no longer in the Wenger family's hands.

When Arsene was born in 1949 he grew up free of the psychological baggage that affected previous generations of Alsatians, perhaps because for the first time in nearly 80 years there was political stability, but also because he was obsessed with football.

He spent much of his childhood in the Croix d'Or and Rees argues that this early exposure to the effects alcohol had on the human body convinced him that it was "a sin for alcohol to touch the lips of player."

This is a slight exaggeration and it is a myth that under Wenger Arsenal's players are teetotal.

Some, like Robert Pires, conform to the monastic stereotype, but Petit smoked and drank red wine throughout the 1998 World Cup and Gallas, another smoker, had a penchant for both champagne and whiskey and coke.

Wenger himself has a fondness for red wine, although he seldom if ever drinks to excess and growing up in a pub would at least have prepared him for the first major crisis of his time at Arsenal. When his captain Tony Adams declared himself an alcoholic in September 1996, Wenger hadn't even arrived in the UK.

At a conference in 2009 he said: "There is no better psychological education than growing up in a pub because when you are five or six years old, you meet all different people and hear how cruel they can be to each other. From an early age you get a practical, psychological education to get into the minds of people.

"It is not often that a boy of five or six is always living with adults in a little village. I learned about tactics and selection from the people talking about football in the pub – who plays on the left wing and who should be in the team."

If you didn't drink there wasn't a lot else to do in Duttlenheim other than play football. It's a pancake-flat village in the Rhine basin, stuck in a no man's land between Strasbourg and the Vosges mountains, though it's another myth that Wenger is obsessed with football to the exclusion of everything else.

As an economics graduate he is "au courant" with both British politics and current affairs, perhaps because he realises football doesn't exist in a vacuum and needs to be aware of how global fluctuations will affect his plans.

When the sub-prime scandal broke in the summer of 2008 he managed to make a joke about the then-chancellor at a post-game press conference, saying that after hearing Alastair Darling on the radio that morning he was too scared to buy anyone.

It might not have been up there with his best one liners but it did prove illuminating in a couple of ways. It revealed that Wenger listened to the radio like a normal person and that he knew who Alastair Darling was which, even during a financial crash, was something a large percentage of the population didn't.

Wenger doesn't seem to have a lot of room in his life for anything else, but perhaps he was like the venerable Australian cricket commentator Richie Benaud, who pointed out that he'd tried a great many things and found that test cricket was what he enjoyed the most. The logical conclusion for him was therefore, to play and watch of it as much as possible.

As a player Wenger was gifted enough to stand out at a local level and he enjoyed a respectable playing career, albeit one that was completely eclipsed by his coaching achievements.

When asked how good he was as a player, Wenger would quip: "I was the best … in my village," a joke that masks a typically accurate analysis.

In a village of around 2,500 inhabitants Wenger stood out, but not to the extent he was picked up by any of the bigger sides in Alsace.

Until the age of 18 he played for his village side in the D2 Departmentale, roughly the equivalent of the Kent County League, when he was finally spotted by the manager of AS Mutzig, Max Hild, during a youth team game.

Mutzig, a village a few miles to the south west of Duttlenheim, were then in the French third division, although the regionalisation of the French league system meant this was more like playing in the English fifth tier, a fact reflected in the gates they attracted (around 1,500).

Mutzig are justifiably proud of their most famous son and devote an entire page of their website to his achievements, though as Hild admitted, at first he struggled to adapt to the game at that level.

"It wasn't easy for him, there was a big difference between the rhythm of the two competitions," he said. "He was tense and nervous before his first game with Belfort, but after a month of work and matches he imposed himself in midfield.

"He was subsequently selected for the France university team and picked up by Mulhouse, where he spent two years playing in Division 2, while keeping his amateur licence."

Wenger was officially an economics student at the time, though he was far more engrossed with studying the game. Hild acted as a de facto personal tutor and ferried him to nearby Bundesliga games.

The Mulhouse coach Paul Frantz also mentored him on train journeys to the south of Alsace and Wenger's on-field contribution to a successful bid to stave off relegation was again secondary to his input as a tactical sounding board.

When, in 1974, Wenger rejoined Hild at ASP Vauban, a team from a suburb of Strasbourg, his playing career seemed to be taking a downward trajectory, but there was a curious coda to his career when, at 28, found himself playing in the top flight.

In 1978 Hild was named the director of the Racing Club de Strasbourg's training centre.

"I quickly realised we needed a stabilising player in a young midfield, so I asked Arsene to join me full time at Meinau," Hild said.

It wasn't a straightforward appointment.

"Arsene made me realise very quickly that going full time with Racing wouldn't be as easy as that," he said. "He would have to discuss it with his father because he was supposed to be taking over the family business. He didn't want football to be his job."

He nonetheless struck a deal with his father giving him a few years' grace to develop as a coach, when an injury crisis unexpectedly handed him a shot at the big time.

Up until they imploded in a way that made Leeds United look like a model of financial probity in 2011, the Racing Club de Strasbourg were one of the regional powerhouses of French football, but their history had a turbulence that mirrored the city - and the region - they represented.

They were formed in 1906 as Fussball Club Neudorf, but when the political wind changed at Versailles in 1919 they found themselves in France. They adopted what they thought was a more French sounding name, even though by aping the Racing Club de Paris they actually chose the anglicised handle by which they are still known within the city.

Outside Alsace fans refer to the club as Strasbourg - inside it they are Racing, pronounced Rass-ing, the team that became an emblem of resistance.

Racing is a club whose importance to its region and its people cannot solely be measured in the dubious currency of silverware.

In those terms alone Racing might not qualify as an elite club but generations of politicians and officials knew the city's strategic value and awarded it prestigious fixtures, the first when the Stade de la Meinau hosted a World Cup quarter-final in 1938 between Poland and Brazil.

In February 1984 Didier Six scored the only goal in a friendly for the French national team with West Germany that must have been a deeply confusing experience for many present and it also hosted two games in Euro 1984, the tournament for which it had been effectively rebuilt.

In 1988 it was handed the European Cup Winners Cup final, a game which saw a young Dennis Bergkamp come on as a first-half substitute for Ajax as the Dutch side suffered a shock 1-0 defeat to the Belgian side FC Malines.

But for most of its history the team didn't often operate at any kind of a comparable level. Racing were a community club, whose players turned up at the ground at 8am on a match day to paint the pitch and put up the goal posts, then attended dance events organised to raise funds for the club.

They didn't turn fully professional until 1933, but by then they were building their first great team around the German striker Ossi Rohr and one of the few players for whom the term legend is fully justified, Oscar Heisserer. Shortly before his death in 2004, at the age of 90, Heisserer described himself as being a player like Patrick Vieira, "but stockier and more attack-minded."

In 1936-37 they finished second in the league, missing out on the title by a point to Sochaux and losing the French Cup final 2-1 to the same opposition.

Even then they were an international team, with only five French players. In addition to the German Rohr, the manager, Josef "Pepi" Blum and one of the defenders, Karl Humenberger were Austrians. The keeper was Ferencs Mayer, a Hungarian who also took penalties and most exotically of all there was Elek Schwartz, a Transylvanian Jew who spoke Hungarian but was a Romanian national.

Schwartz survived the war and went on to manage the Dutch national team and Benfica, who he took to the 1965 European Cup Final. Four decades after the final with Sochaux he returned to Racing as manager and guided them to the French top flight in 1977 as Division 2 champions.

Heisserer was named captain of the French national team for the 1938 World Cup and scored against Italy in the second round, but before anyone had the chance to see how Racing would properly develop, politics once again intervened.

During the "phoney war" they were briefly evacuated to the South West and played in the Dordogne, but by then Heisserer was otherwise engaged.

He had joined up to fight the Germans in 1939, only to find himself stranded on the Maginot line when France collapsed.

When he returned to Strasbourg, his home city had been incorporated into the Reich and he was arrested by the SS at Meinau and taken back to their HQ.

The local commandant "invited" him to join the SS on the grounds that he was officially now a German and he gave a response that might have got him killed: "Yesterday I was the captain of France, so how can I join the SS today?"

He was interrogated for three hours and eventually released, later spurning a less sinister plea from Germany's manager Sepp Herberger to play for their national team.

The team meanwhile had been ordered to change their name again to something that sounded suitably German.

The result was the Rasensport-Club Straßburg, but in a gesture that might have signed their collective death warrant, when Rasensport played SS Straßburg - the team from the SS that had a habit of winning easily - they pointedly wore blue shirts, white shorts and red socks. It was an unsubtle gesture of defiance that sent a subversive thrill through the crowd.

Not all of SS Straßburg's players were Nazis but they were given little choice other than to play under the SS banner and they were born no animosity by the Rasensport players, most of whom they knew from before the conflict.

As the war dragged on SS, once known by the equally totalitarian name Red Star, were bolstered by a number of more ideologically driven recruits and Rasensport's players were obliged to give the Nazi salute before each game, but otherwise the Meinau fulfilled the same role for Alsatians that the Camp Nou did for Catalans during the Franco era.

"It was the one place where people could scream and shout some abuse," said Pierre Heintz, who played for Rasensport from 1941 to 1945.

"From the pitch we could clearly see SS officers on the terraces surrounding the fans, but that didn't stop anything. Everyone booed Red Star and cheered us."

Heintz said the tricolore kit wasn't a deliberate gesture. Racing's colours were light blue shirts with white shorts and yellow socks, but he claimed: "We came across those socks by chance and it was only when we saw the fervour of the fans that we realised."

Yet according to another report, Heintz's father, the club president had to lobby the authorities for the change in colours, in which case they inadvertently handed him a huge propaganda coup.

Deliberate or not, they won the game 3-0 in front of 15,000 fans and they never lost against SS. By 1942 however, with the tide of the war turning, the Reich began its enforced subscription programme and Racing's players began to flee.

Heisserer continued to live dangerously, smuggling Jews across the border to Switzerland and fleeing himself in 1943 after being ordered to join up.

Other Racing players underwent surgery to simulate injury in a bid to avoid the draft.

One player reportedly ordered his team mates to break his arm.

They complied, but only on condition he downed a significant quantity of cognac first.

The player, who stayed anonymous, spent months in hospital and escaped to join the resistance.

Heisserer meanwhile was serving in the Free French forces, although even these acts of heroism were not enough to convince everyone of Racing's patriotism.

The newly renamed Racing nearly won the double in 1947 and won the French Cup in 1951.

Yet when they repeated that feat in 1966, 21 years after France's liberation, the gaffe-prone commentator Thierry Roland commentator caused significant offence in Alsace by saying "the cup is leaving France" on live TV.

When Wenger was growing up the authorities tried again to make the region more French, though this time through more progressive measures.

Alsacien and German wasn't discouraged, but there were advertising campaigns designed to encourage young people to speak French, with the slogan: "C'est chic de parler francais."

Wenger's arrival at the club he supported as a boy coincided with the golden era in the club's history.

Under Gilbert Gress, a charismatic Alsatian who was a key member of the cup-winning side in 1966, Racing won their only French title in 1978-79, with Wenger making a handful of appearances.

Gress's ethos was that "the star is the team" and he disliked lauding individual talents. Of the team that won the league, the biggest name was probably that of Raymond Domenech, although this is due to notoriety rather than fame, given the way he presided over the disintegration of the French national side in 2008 and 2010.

Wenger's role remained primarily as a coach who could be pressed into action as a bit part player in an emergency.

Wenger did well enough against limited opposition, but Gress claimed nerves got the better of him when he played in front of a full house against Monaco and he was badly exposed in a UEFA Cup tie at Duisberg, which Racing lost 4-0.

Wenger's equivalent at Arsenal would be a player like Paolo Vernazza or Adrian Clarke, who made a handful of appearances in a top flight side before drifting down the divisions and into the non-league game.

What was unusual in Wenger's case was that his taste of the big time came so late in his career. Against Duisberg he had his Gus Caesar moment, but Caesar was only a callow 22-year-old when he had his limitations so brutally exposed in the final five minutes of the 1988 League Cup final defeat to Luton.

Wenger was 28 when he was laid bare in similar fashion by Duisberg. He was in the side purely because Strasbourg, with just 15 full time professionals, had no other options and his career was almost coming to its natural end. He made a final first team appearance in 1979 at the age of 30 and spent the next four years in the background, before moving to AS Cannes to become assistant manager to Jean-Marc Guillou.

Years later Racing fans would come to see Wenger almost as messianic figure and would pine for his return, but by then he had long outgrown the team he was never really good enough to play for. In the mid-1990s Wenger's star ascended just as Racing began a dizzying and desperately sad decline.

By 2011 the financial incompetence of the club's directors had succeeded where even the Nazis had failed.

Racing dropped from the first tier to the fifth, a descent almost unmatched in a major European league, with only Fiorentina falling from a greater height to a similar depth. While Arsenal were depicted as a crisis club at the start of the 2011-12 season, Racing were in the CFA2, playing Auxerre's third team and a group of village sides.

At Cannes Wenger's salary was described as meagre, but it was still around £24,000 per year and he was given the use of a seafront apartment in Villefranche-sur-Mer, the Rivieira town where the Rolling Stones had recorded Exile on Main Street a little over a decade earlier.

Mick Jagger later said the Stones had been completely oblivious to their surroundings during the recording and Wenger seems to have been similarly shut off from his environment.

When he wasn't working he was watching videos in his flat, but his meticulousness paid off as within a year he'd been appointed manager of AS Nancy, almost entirely on the recommendation of Hild.

This was Wenger's first shot at top flight management and he used it to apply everything he had learned on preparing players, from altitude training in pre-season through to diet, even handing the WAGS a booklet on the kinds of meals they should be preparing for their husbands.

However, at 34 he was not much older than some of his players and still young enough to take part in training sessions.

He was popular with his players partly because he kept a benevolent distance from them. That style has ensured that in nearly three decades of management he has rarely fallen out with a player, even when dealing with characters as temperamentally volatile as Adebayor, Gallas and Petit.

This distance, however, means he is less popular among fellow managers and while it's difficult to find any former player badmouth him, Wenger has become embroiled in feuds with a significant number of rivals, from Guy Roux and Bernard Tapie in France, to Alex Ferguson, Mark Hughes, Sam Allardyce, Gianluca Vialli and Phil Brown in England.

He once told Alan Pardew to "fuck off" after conceding a late winner at West Ham in 2006 and probably unwisely squared up to Martin Jol during a North London derby.

The former West Ham and Charlton manager Alan Curbishley once claimed that Wenger was disliked precisely because he kept a distance from his fellow managers, citing the fact that he declined the English tradition of the post-match drink, which was perceived as aloofness.

It is rare however, for these feuds to develop into a longstanding enmity.

Within a year of his spat with Pardew, who had since been hired by Charlton, he loaned him Alex Song and he invariably defends managers who have been fired by trigger-happy owners - even Allardyce.

In the later stages of his career, a Wenger tantrum was headline news. After a 2-1 win at Liverpool in in the 2009-2010 season, Wenger admitted he had subjected his players to a furious tirade at half-time when they trailed 1-0.

"I have never seen him like that," a shocked Cesc Fabregas admitted, though he added, "Maybe he should do it more often."

Wenger pointed out that this would dilute the impact, though he conceded: "I believe sometimes you have to respond to what the team needs. It was good to be able to surprise the players after 13 years."

At Nancy he was less circumspect according to one of his players, Jean-Luc Arribart.

"At the start of his career he reacted more and he showed emotions more," he told Jasper Rees. "He has learnt to control his reactions. He has learnt that it's no use throwing tantrums except for now and then."

Another reason Wenger is disliked by some rival managers and openly reviled by opposition supporters is his occasional churlishness in defeat.

This again was obvious from the start according to Arribart, who claimed Wenger had once had to halt the team bus after a 3-0 defeat to Lens so that he could vomit.

Although the number of great managers who are always gracious in defeat can be counted on the fingers of an amputee's hand, to some, this is arguably Wenger's greatest flaw.

This is, to some extent unfair. When defeated managers attend post-match press conferences they often make a point of giving their opponents credit, but this is deemed less newsworthy than a complaint about a refereeing decision, a reckless tackle or simple ill fortune.

Yet for someone as media-savvy as Wenger, it is surprising how often he falls into obvious traps in the immediate aftermath of a poor result.

The examples are legion. At Monaco he bemoaned a refereeing performance after a 4-1 defeat to Auxerre, allowing his opposite number, Roux, to slap him down by responding: "When you let four in you keep your trap shut."

His reputation as bad loser in England stemmed from a league cup semi-final with Chelsea in 1997-98, his first full season at Highbury.

In the first leg Arsenal were dominant, outplaying Chelsea to the point they ended Ruud Gullit's career.

The Dutchman had insisted on playing as a sweeper, but made so many errors that his players mutinied. Gullit was fired, the first in a long line of managers to fall victim to the power of the new money in the Stamford Bridge dressing room, even before the Russian takeover in 2003.

But Arsenal only won 2-1 and before the second leg kicked off Chelsea's new manager Gianluca Vialli gave his players a glass of champagne to relax them.

A liberated Chelsea won 3-1 and the scoreline flattered Arsenal. Wenger gave a sour, bitter post-match interview gifting Vialli the chance to say: "Mr Wenger had passed up the opportunity to be a gentleman."

There were times when this gracelessness has embarrassed his players.

Ashley Cole, a natural authority in the field of human dignity, winced after a 1-0 defeat at Newcastle when he saw an interview in which Wenger had bemoaned the home side's approach: "When the boss complained about Newcastle getting physical and roughing us up (Alan) Shearer responded: 'I never saw Patrick Vieira pulling out of challenges'. Add to the scoreline Shearer 1 Wenger 0."

Yet in the overwhelming majority of his dealings with the media he is polite, genial and charming.

He is far more accommodating than Ferguson, who seldom bothers to mask his contempt for journalists, but again he maintains the benevolent distance he keeps from his players and has deliberately chosen not to give exclusive interviews to British reporters.

Occasionally he can give off an air of paranoia but given his background he has more legitimate reasons than most managers to resort to conspiracy theories.

In three years at Nancy he managed to keep the club in the top flight twice, once via a relegation play-off. Although the third season ended in relegation, the job Wenger had done in helping Nancy compete on mediocre gates earned him a deal to take over Monaco at the start of the 1987-88 season.

Here Wenger would cultivate an enduring sense of paranoia. And here they really were out to get him.

4) JUST BECAUSE YOU'RE PARANOID

If Racing can be likened to a powerful club from the English regions, like Derby or Leeds, albeit one who at the time of writing have fallen on hard times, it's difficult to find an equivalent for AS Monaco.

In terms of silverware they are one of the most decorated clubs in France, having won the title seven times, the cup five times and reached a Champions League final.

In this sense they might be likened to Chelsea as their success is almost entirely down to the benefaction of the Monegasque royal family, but they play to an indifferent public, with gates of between 5-10,000 similar to those pulled by Wimbledon during their time in the English top-flight.

In the right kind of stadium a crowd of this size can be as intimidating as one ten times larger, but in the Stade Louis II they sound about as intimidating as rabbit droppings rattling around in an empty tin can.

Wenger arrived back on the Cote d'Azur in 1987, but it was known for a year beforehand that he would be in charge and while still in charge of Nancy he was instructing Monaco to buy Mark Hateley from AC Milan and Glenn Hoddle from Tottenham.

Grafting this duo onto an already gifted unit brought Monaco the title in Wenger's first season. Both would thrive in France with Hateley, a classic, aerially dominant English centre forward, liberated after three seasons struggling against stifling catenaccio defences and Hoddle relishing the time he had on the ball and the greater protection he got from referees.

Yet it was Wenger's misfortune that his era in Monaco coincided with the arrival of Bernard Tapie at Olympique de Marseilles.

It wouldn't be the last time in his career that Wenger would suddenly have to contemplate a drastically altered playing field, but while Roman Abramovich transformed Chelsea with a huge but legitimate injection of cash, Tapie operated both inside and outside the law.

At first glance Tapie looks like the kind of overweight, orange-skinned light entertainer one would find carving out a living on a cruise ship or at an all-inclusive resort, but this description does him an immense disservice.

Although he does sing, badly, this is only the beginning of his talents.

He is a thespian, in more than one sense, a one-time politician (that inherent contradiction, the socialist millionaire), businessman, impresario, television host and above all, crook.

He became a public figure in the 1980s, gaining a measure of fame, or perhaps more accurately notoriety, as the founder and owner of the "La Vie Claire" cycling team.

This immersion in the murky world of professional cycling might partially explain the methodology Tapie would later use to secure OM's supremacy in the French League.

For three seasons, from their inaugural campaign in 1984 to 1986, La Vie Claire dominated professional cycling.

Their roster included the five time Tour de France winner Bernard Hinault, triple winner Greg LeMond, the new French hope Jean-Francois Bernard and the future Tour of Italy winner Andy Hampsten.

They were also innovative, using new technology such as carbon frames and clipless pedals to gain a legitimate competitive edge over rivals who weren't always competing by the same rules.

Given that Tapie would later become infamous for an orchestrated campaign of sporting fraud, there is a paradox in that La Vie Claire were the victims of serious foul play in the professional peloton.

As their name suggests, La Vie Claire were that rarity in cycling, a clean team. LeMond and Hinault were two of the last Tour de France winners to be completely free of the suspicion of drug abuse.

In cycling however, there were other ways of manipulating results than merely using the best drugs, ranging from informal alliances between teams who agreed not to chase their rivals in return for support in later events, to the outright fixing that occurred in minor races.

Cyclists made much of their money from appearing in lucrative criterium races after the Tour de France, where there were no doping controls and where the finishing order was often pre-determined.

The logic behind this fixing was that the public wanted to see its champions win, not humiliated by some unknown upstart and this was the rationale Tapie exported to football.

Marseille was possibly the one city in France where football had a comparable grip on the population to that of a major English city.

It was a one-club town with the potential to dominate French football for years and Tapie duly invested in number of excellent players, such as Dragan Stojkovic, Abedi Pele, Enzo Francescoli and Chris Waddle.

They may not have been the world's very best, but combined with the club's native talents - Jean-Pierre Papin, Basile Boli and an emerging Didier Deschamps, they were easily good enough to win the French title.

This however, was not enough for Tapie, who craved recognition on an international stage.

His dream, one easily peddled to OM's supporters, was to win the European Cup and in the pre-Champions League era this rather quaintly required a team to win their domestic league in order to qualify.

The ease with which they did so in consecutive years between 1988 and

1992 renders these achievements suspicious.

Wenger himself believes that at least one of these titles was acquired by foul means at Monaco's expense, but quite when OM began buying off their rivals is unclear and Tapie's decision to stack the odds in his favour may also have been inspired by the time he fell victim to an act of sporting larceny.

On April 18 1990, OM were defending a 2-1 lead from the first leg of their European Cup semi-final against a Benfica side managed by Sven Goran Erikson, in front of 120,000 fans at the Stadium of Light.

With seven minutes to play, the future PSG star Valdo took a corner for Benfica that was steered into the Marseille net by the arm of the Angolan Vata Matanu Garcia.

It was every bit as blatant as Diego Maradona's hand of God (and was subsequently dubbed the hand of the devil), but the goal was awarded and OM were eliminated on the away goals rule.

It was Tapie who consoled OM's understandably livid players as they left the arena and Tapie who gave an ominous post-match declaration.

"I have reacted (in the past) to journalists who treat us like a small club. Well tonight I've realised why they treat us like a small club," he said. "Our lack of success is because the referee's decisions didn't always go in our favour in the first leg and frankly they went against us in the second."

Thus far Tapie merely sounded like any other embittered football manager (which he effectively was, overseeing a series of puppets at head coach), bemoaning a bad decision, but what was most revealing was his pay-off line.

"I learn quickly. Next season, believe me, this will not happen to us. Never again will we concede a handball goal."

Thus began Marseilles' fall and the start of a saga that had no winners.

Nobbling a referee was one way to get a result and it had been tried before, specifically in 1984 when Anderlecht overturned a 2-0 first leg deficit to beat Nottingham Forest in the semi-finals of the UEFA Cup, with the help of a referee who had been bunged £20,000 by the Belgian club's president Constant Vanden Stock.

Yet that result proved just how unreliable it was to rely on bent officials alone. Even with the referee in their pocket Anderlecht only just beat Forest, courtesy of a penalty, an 88th-minute goal and the disallowal of what would have been a last-minute winner for Forest.

This demonstrated that against 11 fully committed players a corrupt referee might not necessarily be enough to guarantee a result.

Against only eight or nine fully committed players however, a result was almost a formality and it seems Tapie's choice of coach was made with that in mind.

Raymond Goethals had been slapped with a life ban from coaching in his native Belgium for his role in bribery scandal in 1982, when his Standard Liege side offered bribes to their opponents Thor Waterschei in an attempt to ensure that - of all teams - Anderlecht would not be able to catch them on the final day of the season.

The ban was lifted and Tapie had no qualms about employing Goethals in 1991 when he needed to replace Franz Beckenbauer, after the unmalleable German lasted just four months at the Velodrome.

It was Goethals who was nominally in charge of OM when they finally won the European Cup in1993 with a 1-0 win over Milan, but by then Tapie's skulduggery was unravelling.

According to Emmanuel Petit, suspicion was already engrained.

"Tapie needed the club for his political ambitions and for that reason he would never have bothered with any other club," he wrote. "Marseilles therefore used to benefit from extremely generous refereeing. Penalties were frequently awarded in their favour. Players from opposing teams would bizarrely become unavailable and when they did play they would often find themselves substituted or appear non-existent on the field. They also benefited from a laissez-faire attitude by the federation when it came to anti-doping controls."

A week before the 1993 European Cup final the definitive proof that OM had been fixing matches arrived when a Valenciennes player, Jacques Glassmann, blew the whistle on an attempt to fix a league game.

On May 20 Glassman, another Alsatian, contacted the Valenciennes coach Boro Primorac telling him that OM's Jean-Jacques Eydelie had phoned him with an offer, authorised by the OM board.

OM would give Glassmann, Jorge Burruchaga (the Argentine scorer of the winning goal in the 1986 World Cup final) and Christophe Robert a substantial sum of money to ensure Marseilles's players were "uninjured for the final."

Robert and Burruchaga accepted but Glassmann refused and informed the referee at half-time. Police would later find F250,000 (then worth around £25,000) buried in the garden of Robert's aunt while Primorac went on to testify that Tapie had made a personal approach to him, asking him to carry the can.

Standing up to someone as manipulative as Tapie isn't the best way of enhancing your job credentials, but Wenger at least would remember Primorac's role by making him his coach when he joined Arsenal.

The short-term effect saw OM posthumously stripped of their title and booted out of the following season's Champions League by UEFA, although their victory over Milan in the 93 final remains on the record books.

Valenciennes were relegated by a single point.

PSG, who had finished second, bizarrely opted not to take OM's place in the Champions League, handing Wenger an unexpected first tilt at the competition with his third-placed Monaco. They would lose to Milan in the semi-final.

The longer term effects on French football's credibility were less easy to gauge.

Tapie spent four months in jail and two of his henchmen were fined token sums. Robert and Burruchaga were sentenced to a year in jail, but the sentences were suspended and their fines were a meagre 5,000 francs (£500) each.

Tapie, like any number of unrepentant OM apologists, merely saw this as an extension of the logic used in cycling. The public wanted to see its champions perform on the greatest stage, so why waste energy on games against inconsequential opposition?

Even the prosecutor, Eric de Montgolfier would eventually belittle the affair, saying in a 2009 interview that: "If the President of OM hadn't been Bernard Tapie, he would never have gone to prison. The facts didn't merit it."

This was a scarcely credible argument given the damage the affair did to the game in France and to Marseilles, let alone the carcinogenic affect it had on rival teams.

Buying off the opposition neatly circumnavigated the major side effect of nobbling a referee, namely instilling an "us against the world" team spirit in the victims.

Buy bribing rival players Marseilles destroyed multiple relationships as players found they could no longer trust their team mates.

It also seems to have eluded De Montgolfier that had Tapie not authorised the illegal approaches they might never have happened.

The idea that OM would have won these championships anyway was also a fallacy.

They may have had an excellent side, but PSG were emerging and Wenger had assembled a unit capable of challenging them, recruiting Weah from Liberia and grooming the future World Cup winners Youri Djorkaeff, Lilian Thuram and Emmanuel Petit.

For a man who was subsequently unable to conduct an interview at Arsenal without lauding his team's character, mental strength and "spirit", the discovery that any of his players could have committed this form of treason must have been insufferable.

He already had his doubts. With three games to go in the 1991-92 season,

Monaco and Marseilles met at the Stade Louis II for what should have been a showdown for the title.

On the previous weekend Wenger's side had moved to within a point of OM at the top of the table by winning 4-1 at Nantes, while Marseilles could only draw 0-0 at home to Montpelier.

After four consecutive wins the momentum was with Monaco, but on the Wednesday before the game they had a draining trip to Feyenoord in the semi-final of the Cup Winners Cup.

A 1-1 draw earned them a 3-3 aggregate scoreline and they qualified for the final on away goals.

This was a potentially historic moment for French football. Although it was a Frenchman, Gabriel Hanot, who invented the concept of pan-European competition, no French side had ever won a European trophy at that point.

Under the circumstances delaying the Marseilles game to allow Monaco additional time to recover wasn't an unreasonable suggestion, but the FFF turned Monaco down flat.

Marseilles duly won 3-0 without breaking sweat but it was obvious to Wenger that the loss couldn't simply be attributed to fatigue.

The club held an internal enquiry. Wenger called Emmanuel Petit into his office, shut the door and asked him to sit down. He produced a cassette of the Marseille game and showed Petit the goals twice, before slowing down the tape and asking him: "What do you think when you see these goals?"

Petit didn't immediately realise what was going on, but as the youngest and least corruptible member of the team he had been singled out as the most reliable witness by Wenger.

"I hesitated before responding," he said. "In the end I told him we had committed beginner's errors, which we didn't usually do. For the first goal we were numerically superior to them, but Bruno Germain scored with his head and he didn't have much of a leap."

For all his dislike of OM, Petit admitted Wenger's response stunned him.

"Ok, you can go, that confirms exactly what I was thinking. There are a number of us who think some of our players have been bought by Marseilles."

The final confirmation Wenger and his coaching staff came when one of the suspects walked into a trap they'd set for him at La Turbie, but perhaps mindful of the increased damage to Monaco's image that could be done by going public and, more pertinently, a lack of admissible evidence, they opted to keep the affair in house. The suspects were never outed.

If they had been, it would be interesting to see if they attracted as much derision as Glassman, who was later treated like a leper by some fans - just as the cyclists who complained about drug use in the peloton were despised by their peers. Reporting the crime seemed to be a far greater sin than committing one in the first place.

Monaco would lose all hope of the title a week later when they crashed 3-0 at Le Havre.

"When I left Arsene's office I wondered what the point of playing the next match was," Petit said. "At Monaco you're already playing without the public behind you. If, in addition to that, you have guys sinking you in your own dressing room while you're trying to win the title it's not possible."

UEFA's decision not to strip Marseilles of its 1993 European Cup win looks tenuous in hindsight given that OM arguably only qualified for the tournament in the first place by foul means.

Their route to that final has also been the subject of almost continuous speculation. In February 2011, Mark Hateley, once of Glasgow Rangers, alleged he had been offered a bribe not to play in a potentially crucial group game with OM that season via an unnamed agent, a "friend of a friend" from his days with Monaco, who phoned him offering him a "substantial sum of money".

He angrily refused, but was subsequently shown a highly dubious red card in a game with Club Bruges that saw him suspended for the game at the Velodrome.

"As soon as (the red card) came out the phone call came straight to the front of my mind again," Hateley later said. "At the time I didn't know if it was a hoax or real. I know it was real now because of the proceedings that followed. I felt 100 percent cheated, it was a once in a lifetime chance for Rangers. Marseilles should be stripped of the title. Why haven't the powers that be taken action?"

UEFA baulked at allowing OM to defend their title and the French Federation eventually stripped Marseilles of the 1992-93 domestic crown. They decided to relegate them to the second division, but even this was met with incredulity by apparently sane judges in France.

When the news of the demotion came through, in April 1994, I was staying with a friend in Poitiers who supported both Arsenal and OM. "They've just decided to kill the club," was his considered reaction.

While Wenger remains scarred by the events of the Tapie era, under his tutelage Monaco made a reasonable recovery. The rotten apples were expelled and replaced with a mixture of established European talent like Jurgen Klinsmann, Enzo Scifo (who as an 18-year-old had scored in Anderlecht's "win" over Forest) and prodigiously talented youngsters like Lilian Thuram, Thierry Henry and David Trezeuguet.

Monaco would go on to win the French title in 1997, but by then Wenger had been fired for the only time in his career, the victim of a poor start to the 1994-95 season.

In the summer of 1994 Wenger had asked to leave Monaco, having received an offer from Bayern Munich.

Monaco refused to release him, but after eight games of the new season, with the team just one place above the relegation zone, they sacked him, following a 1-0 defeat at Le Havre.

If the decision seemed harsh, it ultimately benefited both parties.

While Monaco's revival continued under Jean Tigana, a jaded Wenger rediscovered his enthusiasm for life, if not necessarily football, in Japan.

While attending a coaching conference in Abu Dhabi Wenger was offered a job by Nagoya Grampus Eight, who were acting on the recommendation of their star player Dragan Stojkovic, a key member of Tapie's OM side.

This was either a pioneering move by Wenger to establish the game in previously uncharted territory, or a self-imposed exile in a footballing backwater.

He recruited Primorac, who like Glassman had become a pariah in France despite having been a victim rather than a cause of the VA-OM affair, but the duo got off to a catastrophic start, losing seven games in a row.

Japanese players were respectful to the point of subservience and subsided so meekly that Wenger eventually had to throw one of his rare tantrums and drag to them to a mid-season training camp in France where he injected them with a hint of the streetwise skills they needed to win matches.

They shot up the table to finish fourth at the end of the season and won the Japanese equivalent of the FA Cup, but for all Wenger enjoyed living in such a vastly different culture - he wrote two books about his experiences in Japan - he was playing to even smaller crowds than in Monaco.

"When you see only 2,000 people in the stands, you wonder 'why do I do this?'" he later admitted.

Managing a side still held more attraction for Wenger than the prospect of a desk job with the FA but by the summer of 1996 he was clearly hankering for a return to a major European club. It was then that Dein approached him.

A delicate period ensued as Wenger tried to extricate himself from his contract while Arsenal tried to avoid giving offence - a national past-time in France, but a heinous crime in Japan - to his employers.

This meant that while nobody at Arsenal was prepared to go public it was an open secret that Wenger would be taking charge, because the Alsatian was already recruiting for his new team, ordering the purchases of Remi

Garde and Patrick Vieira.

By the summer of 1996 I was working as an English teacher at Dover College, teaching students from around Europe, including a significant number from France.

Lessons had a habit of mirroring the scene in the film version of Nick Hornby's book Fever Pitch, when Colin Firth's students know the easiest way to distract him is to ask him about football: "I've got a question Sir, it's about Alan Smith."

In every class of teenage Europeans there were always a handful of football fans whose knowledge of the English game at times bordered on the obsessive and I seldom needed an excuse to offer a gang of foreign teenagers a lecture on why Manchester United were inherently evil.

On this occasion I needed to pick their brains.

Garde, they told me, was an international and a good player, but the way they talked about Vieira gave me an uncharacteristic sense of optimism heading into the new season. It wasn't universally shared.

An exasperated Stewart Houston took charge for an opening day win over West Ham. He said "from what I've seen of Patrick he could be a very good box-to-box midfielder," but he didn't hang around long enough to find out. Unwilling to wait and see if he'd be wheat or chaff under the new regime he accepted an offer to join Queen's Park Rangers, leaving Pat Rice as the caretaker manager.

Vieira's class was immediately obvious however and it did a great deal to enhance Wenger's credibility, which would come under a sustained assault during his first weeks in England.

5) WINDOWS

Wenger's unveiling to Arsenal supporters took part in stages, with the first direct contact coming via a pre-recorded video message that was played on the Highbury Jumbotron prior to a Premier League game with Sheffield Wednesday on September 16 1996.

In hindsight it's possible to see this game as representing the end of an era at Highbury.

It was one of the last times fans could actually turn up and buy a ticket on the day of the game, from a portakabin along the side of the West Stand.

And perhaps symbolically, given that there was still a power vacuum at the club, the electricity failed, delaying the kick-off by half an hour.

When it was restored Wenger's message was played, but the sound quality was poor, his accent heavy and his glasses seemed to magnify the size of his eyes to unfortunate comic affect, earning him the unflattering nickname "Windows" among his players.

He seemed to mumble something of a welcome to Pat Rice but nothing else was discernible and the message was greeted with a mere ripple of polite applause.

It certainly felt like the end of an era for the team. For much of the first half Arsenal looked like a team in a steep decline as they were outplayed by a Wednesday side managed by one of Highbury's least favourite managers, the former Luton and Tottenham man David Pleat.

The defence, almost invulnerable under George Graham, looked aged and creaky without the injured Tony Adams. After 25 minutes Guy Whittingham, a prolific but limited striker who would have been easily handled by the back four in their pomp, slipped through to make it 1-0, having already squandered two good chances.

After half an hour Rice took drastic action, hauling off Ray Parlour and sending on Vieira. Where I was sitting in the North Bank people were openly wondering if that was the last we'd see of Parlour in an Arsenal shirt. To his credit, Parlour was one of many players to reinvent himself under Wenger, becoming a star in his own right, but this was an historic moment for Arsenal football club.

Vieira became the first Frenchman ever to play for the North London side and his arrival invigorated both the team and the crowd.

Wednesday also hit the bar before the break, but Arsenal equalised through David Platt just before the hour and cruised to a 4-1 win, with Ian Wright scoring a hat-trick.

Although he hadn't been directly involved for any of the goals, Wright made a point of jumping into Vieira's arms to celebrate after one strike and by the end of the game supporters were chanting his name: a straightforward, repetitive mantra of "Vieira! Vieira! Vieira!" in the days before the Volare chant had evolved.

The logic was simple. If Wenger had bought a player of this calibre, he had to know something, although even the most optimistic of Arsenal fans wouldn't have believed just how successful he would be.

The evidence of his first direct influence on the team on a match day was less encouraging.

Wenger flew over from Japan for the second leg of a UEFA cup tie with Borussia Monchengladbach on September 25, as an unofficial adviser to Rice.

Arsenal had been shocked 3-2 by the Germans in the first leg at Highbury, but a last minute goal by Ian Wright had at least given them a glimmer of hope.

Despite falling behind to an early goal from Andrej Juskowiak in the return leg, Wright equalised, meaning Arsenal trailed 4-3 on aggregate at half-time.

It was the first opportunity for Wenger to win over his English players and he blew it.

Paul Merson levelled the scores with a 25-yard drive, but at the back Arsenal unravelled, Effenburg and Juskowiak picking them off on the counterattack with two goals in the final 15 minutes.

Adams blamed the unofficial advisor for his tactical intervention at the interval and his scepticism stemmed in part from the fact he and the rest of the players still had no idea who Wenger was.

When David Dein told them the identity of the new manager at the training ground blank looks were exchanged. Dein elaborated, saying that he had been personally recommended by Gerard Houillier, technical director of the French Football Federation, but as Paul Merson pointed out, nobody had heard of him either.

As Wenger's official arrival grew closer Glenn Hoddle, now the England manager, paid him a glowing tribute and the man himself showed a glimpse of his sense of humour when he was quoted on the subject of Tottenham, just days after his arrival, saying: "I tried to watch their game with Leicester in my hotel, but I fell asleep."

But the lack of concrete information on the new manager left a vacuum that was filled by malicious allegations, spread via the internet.

The world wide web was a fraction of the size it is today, but its ability to tarnish reputations via the dissemination of unsubstantiated rumours was already eclipsing the tabloid press, which could still be gagged by the right kind of lawyer.

This story was a fabrication and Arsenal's lawyers ensured it never appeared in print, but it was still proving difficult to contain. Wenger himself appeared on the steps outside Highbury, against the advice of his own PR department, to confront journalists head on and a number of Arsenal fans had also turned up, not as a lynch mob but to act as unofficial bodyguards, forming an early bond with the new man.

"If something comes out that is not correct I will attack," Wenger said, but it was only a small victory. If the threat of legal action succeeded in taming a largely ungovernable tabloid press, the internet was like the wild west, a lawless new frontier where anyone could say absolutely anything with no fear of any kind of redress.

Damage was done. As a direct result of this early smear campaign, to this day Wenger is subjected to horrendous, personal abuse at certain away grounds, with White Hart Lane and Old Trafford by far the worst offenders.

It also generated a level of sympathy for Wenger, particularly among his fellow managers but while the rumours don't appear to have been an issue among the playing staff, he still needed to convince them of his credibility.

On his first morning in the job the squad looked at him like a class of schoolchildren assessing a new teacher, testing him for signs of weakness.

His accent was an obvious starting point. The nuances of his slightly undulating Alsatian voice were probably lost on Ray Parlour, but to an English ear he sounded very French indeed and Parlour did a Peter Sellers impression, whispering: "It's a burrm!" into Merson's ear at every opportunity.

A year later Wenger was emerging from the dressing room at Selhurst Park, not realising that the game had been abandoned because of floodlight failure when he saw Parlour walking back down the tunnel.

When he asked what was happening Parlour replied: "Zair eez a burrm!" but both men were smiling. By then Wenger's authority was unquestioned and no disrespect was intended. Parlour knew the boundaries but also knew Wenger could take a joke in a way that George Graham wouldn't.

According to Merson, whose later career as a pundit admittedly revealed a man prone to exaggeration, Wenger was accepted almost instantly: "By the time we'd finished our first training session I knew that life at Arsenal would never be the same again. The bloke was a genius."

In hindsight what Wenger did at first doesn't seem that revolutionary. His reign at Arsenal can be broken down into several distinct eras. In the first he caught Arsenal's rivals off guard, exposing how far behind English football had fallen in terms of diet, training and preparation by reviving an already strong squad.

By the time these rivals then caught up Arsenal were in a financial position to compete for the best available talent on the market, leading to the "invincible" era, but even before the start of the unbeaten season the ground had shifted again.

Both United and Chelsea were by then in a position to better any offer Arsenal made to a player, forcing Wenger to improvise and ushering in the Fabregas era, when Arsenal produced some of the most exhilarating football ever seen in England but were repeatedly thwarted on the cusp of greatness by their defensive failings.

The contrast between eras is starkly illustrated by the line-up for Wenger's first official game in charge, for what was a difficult looking trip to Ewood Park on October 12 1996.

His first ever Arsenal selection was: Seaman, Dixon, Keown, Bould, Adams, Winterburn, Platt, Vieira, Merson, Wright and Hartson, with Parlour, Paul Shaw, Andy Linighan, Matthew Rose and John Lukic on the bench.

It looks defensive, comprising a world-class goalkeeper and five equally rated defenders, but even allowing for the way the game evolved over the next 15 years, (Dixon himself said players became far more athletic and technically gifted) I and many others would have backed them to beat the team that ended the 2010-11 season:

Szczesny, Sagna, Djorou, Vermaelen, Gibbs, Nasri, Diaby, Wilshere, Ramsey, van Persie and Chamakh.

At Ewood Park Arsenal took the lead after just three minutes when Winterburn aimed a long ball at Hartson, who headed the ball across to Wright. He then produced a characteristically brilliant piece of skill to wrong foot the Blackburn defender Nicky Marker and curl a shot into the top corner.

Blackburn did threaten, with Tim Sherwood hitting the post, but six minutes after the break Vieira played a one-two with Merson, surged into the Blackburn half and split their defence with a pass that Wright dinked over Tim Flowers.

This was a team that knew how to defend two-goal leads, though according to Merson at the final whistle there was a queue for the toilets because Wenger had given them caffeine tablets before the game, which he described as the equivalent of drinking ten cups of coffee.

Merson was also fairly dubious about some of the other methods used.

When his second autobiography: "How Not To Be A Professional Footballer" came out, reporters jumped on a passage in which he described being injected by a syringe "filled with a lorry-load of yellow gunk" which Wenger, pointing to the club's impeccable record with drug testing, dismissed as a financially motivated slur.

This was the era when cycling was nearly destroyed by the use of EPO, with riders doping so heavily they had to set their alarm clocks to go in the middle of the night so they could pedal on rollers to stop their blood clotting around their heart.

But while it would be naïve to assume doping never happened in football there was a difference between getting an advantage from taking illegal drugs that could harm and in some cases kill athletes and using legal products like vitamin supplements, or creatine, which became de rigeur among footballers.

In hindsight some of the steps Wenger took, like banning alcohol and changing players' diets now seem so obvious the only surprise is that nobody else in England realised beforehand, particularly after Euro 92, when Graham Taylor mystifyingly claimed the Swedes were "of an outdoor pursuit" after the hosts left England panting and wheezing in the decisive group game.

The standard line on alcohol is that "everybody was doing it" and as Remi Garde pointed out, English clubs had won the European Cup on a diet of junk food.

But this was only going to give Arsenal a short-term advantage. The Arsenal players who used Wenger's stretching routines on England duty were initially laughed at, but word got round the circuit quickly enough. When the advantages in stamina and recovery became obvious other clubs quickly copied them.

The case of Roy Keane was instructive. The cruciate ligament injury he suffered during the 1997-98 season can't be directly attributed to alcohol consumption, but while brooding in recovery - and watching his team mates blow a 12-point lead in the Premier League - Keane became aware that drinking enhanced a player's chances of sustaining a career-ending injury.

And what really hurt, quite apart from being unable to play, was being unable to win.

Keane needed a post-binge trip to the cells, three days before the 1999 FA Cup Final, to finally absorb his lesson, but by the time of the 2002 World Cup he had become evangelical and was so irate about Ireland's amateurish preparations ("Cheese Fecking Sandwiches?") that it contributed to his decision to storm out of their squad.

Thus Wenger's first "era" was arguably over almost as soon as the double season concluded, the advantage of fitness now eradicated. The timing of that success, however, was still critical.

Arsenal qualified for the Champions League for the first time, just as the European competition was becoming a licence to print money, with the rewards even for failing sides dwarfing anything on offer domestically.

While "Bubble" clubs like Lazio and Fiorentina blew fortunes on underachieving players, Wenger kept the team in the top two, earning millions from the Champions League even when the team never went beyond the quarter-finals.

In 98-99 they came desperately close to another double. For the next two seasons United were a long way ahead, but in the summer of 2001 Arsenal were still in a position to buy the best talent on the market, like the newly available free agent Sol Campbell, while just as importantly, retain the World Class players they had like Vieira and Henry.

Yet when Wenger spoke of a "sea change" in English football after winning the league at Old Trafford in 2002 he was premature. The top talent began to slip through Wenger's fingers.

Arsenal were close to signing Cristiano Ronaldo in 2003. He trained with the first team, was handed an Arsenal shirt with his name on it as a gift and was offered a generous deal, but then he played United in a friendly and so impressed the senior players that Ferguson gazumped Wenger.

Money always talked to some extent in football, but its importance was about to be amplified.

Any idiot can take charge of a football club, run up multi-million pound debts mounting a European challenge while siphoning off a vast personal fortune and leaving somebody else to clear up the mess. This was almost a standard operating procedure in Italy and Spain, but there were plenty of examples of mismanagement in England as well.

The scale of Wenger's achievement is best measured against the English clubs other than Manchester United who qualified for the Champions League during its early years of expansion, Newcastle, Liverpool, Chelsea and Leeds.

All four experienced some degree of financial crisis within a decade of first appearing in the Champions League.

Liverpool were comparatively well run under the Moores family, but in 2007 they sold the club to the Americans George Gillett and Tom Hicks who used a "leveraged buy-out" to complete the takeover. This essentially involved buying the club with some of its own money and if that sounds like a legal con trick it's because it is.

That story at least had a happy ending because Hicks and Gillett, who were paying themselves £2 million a year just in expenses, had picked the wrong city for a heist. They ended up losing an estimated £144 million.

By then however Liverpool had fallen out of the top four and looked unlikely to return in the short term.

At Newcastle, a one-club city with the potential to become a serious European force, directors made a total of nearly £45 million out of their club between 1998 and 2005.

In 2008 Mike Ashley paid £134 million to buy Newcastle and then another £100 million just to reduce their debts, as several seasons of mediocrity culminated in relegation in 2009.

Leeds, another one-club city, were the most spectacular example of what could go wrong. Intoxicated by a run to the semi-finals of the Champions League in 2001, Leeds' directors rented goldfish for their boardroom, flew to away games in private jets and assumed qualification for the tournament would be an annual formality.

They borrowed £60 million against predicted future revenue but were beaten to the third and final Champions League qualifying place by Liverpool and went into a nosedive.

This could easily have happened to another club with delusions of grandeur, but at almost exactly the same time Arsenal lost out on Ronaldo, Roman Abramovich took control of Chelsea and at a stroke wiped out the accumulated debts of £96 million.

Chelsea were every bit as badly run as Newcastle and Leeds, but while the former clubs were forced to repent at leisure, Chelsea were effectively give a free pass, freed to run up £726 million in losses by May 2010, when they announced they were "debt free," on the grounds that Abramovich didn't want the money back (watch this space on that front …)

That largesse represented an operating loss of over £100 million per year but it gave Chelsea an incalculable advantage in terms of player recruitment.

Unaffected by any normal business considerations, despite laughable repeated protestations that they were aiming to break even, Chelsea were now free to acquire almost any player they liked, to the point they began to stockpile players they didn't need.

Wenger witheringly called this "financial doping", which given the disproportionate advantage it gave Chelsea wasn't an unreasonable description.

He described his subsequent approach to transfer dealing thus: "First try to sell him to Chelsea, then get back to me."

When Wenger was merely competing with United for the likes of Ronaldo he could at least draw comfort from the fact that as Ferguson could only field a finite number of players, he could at least go for the next best option on the market.

Now he was reduced to buying players after United had had their pick and after Chelsea had filled both their first team and their reserves.

It took a while for the affects to filter through however. In the build-up to the 2003-04 season Arsenal went almost unnoticed by pundits, barely dabbling in the transfer market, punting Jeffers back to Everton on a loan deal and selling Giovanni van Bronkhorst to Barcelona but otherwise staying very quiet.

The most significant business was tying Pires, Henry and Vieira to new deals, but the other masterstroke was reinventing Kolo Toure, who was obviously a brilliant talent but had yet to find a settled position, as a central defender.

A year earlier Wenger had been ridiculed for suggesting his side could go unbeaten during a full season, but all he'd said was that such a feat was theoretically possible and that was what Arsenal should aspire to.

As no (honest) manager ever goes into an individual match planning to lose it, this was just a logical aim, but by the time it had been through the twisted prism of the English media it had been transformed.

Wenger had "vowed" that Arsenal "would" be undefeated and fans from rival sides who believed what they wanted to believe, cited this as arrogance and revelled in him getting his comeuppance when he failed to deliver on a promise he'd never made in the first place.

This supposedly chastened side was still exceptionally strong and was still holding together.

United were in decline and Chelsea weren't yet a unit, giving Arsenal an opportunity that they took brilliantly.

The obvious regret from the 2003-04 campaign is that it was probably Arsenal's best ever shot at winning the Champions League, but to make history by becoming the Invincibles was arguably a greater achievement, measured over 38 games.

It also represented the high watermark for Arsenal. Wenger and Dein both knew Chelsea's monetary power would bring results sooner rather than later. In 2004-05 Arsenal finished with 83 points, which in many other seasons would have been enough to retain the title, but wasn't against a team now able to buy world class players and sit them in the reserves.

The strategy had to change. Struggling to retain their best players and unable to compete for the equivalent replacements, Arsenal now had to identify the best prospects before they became established stars and see how many years they could get out of them before they moved on.

Even without the demands of building the Emirates this would have been difficult, but Wenger came heroically close to pulling it off.

The post-Henry era from 2007 to 2011, brought three sustained title challenges, two finals, three semi-finals but no silverware. This fact was bandied around by the moronic as proof that he should be fired, on the grounds that this was what every other club would have done, regardless of how successful or otherwise those clubs actually were.

And who had won anything in that time? The only English clubs to win major trophies, i.e. the title, Champions League or FA Cup were Chelsea, and Manchester City, both the playthings of billionaires, Liverpool and Manchester United, both the subject of questionable takeovers and Portsmouth, who bankrupted themselves in the process.

Perhaps it was the disappointment talking but Wenger also sounded increasingly paranoid, regularly alluding to the work of the dark forces that disfigured his final years in France.

The trouble with blaming refereeing decisions is that almost every other club does the same thing. Smaller clubs claim referees favour the big sides, while big sides claim referees favour rival big sides, even when it's an act of the most breathtaking chutzpah, designed to put pressure on officials to compensate them and to deflect blame.

Sadly there is evidence that this works.

The greatest exponents of the art are Jose Mourinho, who indirectly caused Anders Frisk to retire, and "Sir" Alex Ferguson, who appeared to genuinely believe United had been robbed of the title in 2010, after a 2-1 defeat at home to Chelsea.

"When I saw the referee was Mike Dean I did worry, I must admit," Ferguson said, slurring Dean's integrity and getting away with it.

It was a view shared by millions of his acolytes and parroted in sections of the media. Even the BBC's report of the game said Didier Drogba's second goal was: "scored from a clearly offside position" in the second paragraph. Only several paragraphs down did the writer say there was a "hint" of handball about Federico Macheda's goal for United with two minutes remaining.

As an impartial observer, e.g. someone who loathed both sides equally, I felt the result was entirely fair, both on the balance of play and the key decisions.

In reality there was no "hint" about the handball. The goal wouldn't have been scored had it not hit the striker's hand. Meanwhile the Daily Record said Drogba was "yards" offside and while it's true he was fractionally ahead of the last defender, it was almost impossible to tell in real time with the naked eye.

This revisionism also conveniently ignored all the decisions that gone in United's favour earlier that season.

I felt the 2-1 win over Arsenal at Old Trafford was little more than a heist but I then was never an impartial observer when it came to the Arsenal.

During that 2010-11 campaign I started to compile a mental list of incorrect decisions that had both cost and earned Arsenal points - not knowing that the journalist Tim Long had been conducting a scientific survey into exactly the same phenomenon. Long produced a "correct" league table, which placed Arsenal second, five points behind United and well ahead of City, who according to Long were comfortably the team most favoured by referees.

It was an interesting experiment, albeit one that was clearly an inexact science.

Long looked at 731 "significant" incidents concerning penalties, offsides and goal line queries with the aim of debunking claims that technology would be unworkable in football.

As such it was only partially successful. My own calculations concluded that Arsenal had certainly taken a hit, but just how many points they'd been "robbed" of was impossible to prove.

Long claimed Arsenal had been unfairly docked four points. I thought the figure was hypothetically six to eight given, enough to knock Arsenal out of contention for the title and into a treacherous Champions League qualifier with Udinese.

The first incident was clear enough: at Sunderland Arsenal led 1-0, with the "minimum" four minutes of injury time expired, only for Darren Bent to equalise 30 seconds into a fifth minute. There had been no significant interruption in added time, and play could have been halted when Arsenal cleared their lines with exactly 94 minutes on the clock.

While some fans can see a penalty every time a player falls over, some decisions are not open to serious debate.

One at Braga arguably cost Arsenal first place in their Champions League group, sending them to Barcelona when they could have had the kind of cushy draw earned by Chelsea and Manchester United.

At Wigan the home side escaped with a handball in the area - precisely the transgression that Arsenal were penalised for at home to Tottenham - and a 2-2 draw was the result.

And perhaps the most painful incident of them all was at home to Liverpool when having taken the lead with a penalty in the eighth minute of injury time, Arsenal conceded in the 11th, when Emanuel Eboue gave Lucas Leiva an excuse to dive in the area under minimal contact and another two points disappeared.

When Arsenal visited Bolton on April 24 they conceded their ninth penalty of the season, an incorrect call for a foul on Johan Djorou against Daniel Sturridge. It took them top of the table for conceding penalties and all but mathematically wrote off the title chances the media had been prematurely calling dead for several weeks beforehand.

The resulting Bolton penalty was missed however and even had Arsenal been awarded a better ratio of decisions, there's no guarantee they would have scored from them.

And even when a decision goes in your favour, you still have to take advantage. In the League Cup Final with Birmingham Arsenal could have been 1-0 down and playing with 10 men for 89 minutes but for a generous decision in Wojciech Szczesny's favour. They still couldn't win when it mattered, fuelling the idea the team lacked that vaguely defined English term "arsehole".

A win would have stopped the specious carping about not winning anything since 2005, but it's unlikely it would have changed anything in the long term.

The summer of 2011 brought no respite, as the English media reprinted the same Fabregas and Nasri stories ad nauseam, drip-feeding a constant stream of bad news.

At the first home game of the season Wenger, drenched by an unseasonal downpour and with a shell of a side losing 2-0 to Liverpool, did indeed look haunted.

In an interview he gave with the French radio station RTL a few weeks later he effectively admitted his entire life was consumed by his job, even though he was well aware how spiritually limiting this was.

This was the extraordinary paradox of Wenger. With the possible exception of Roy Hodgson, it's difficult to think of any English manager with the intellect and breadth of experience to give an interview of this depth.

It called to mind an observation the broadcaster John Arlott once made to the England cricket captain Mike Brearley, a profound thinker who eschewed the post-retirement circus to practice as a psychiatrist: "The best thing about you Mike is that you're the only England captain who knows it doesn't really matter."

Wenger knew that what he did didn't really matter, but was powerless to break the game's hold on him.

"This summer was the most agitated I've ever known," he said. "I had half the players in the dressing room who wanted to leave … I have periods when I'm tired … I'd like to go to Tahiti for a month, but I can't. From time to time I would like to because I'm running out of time, everyone gets older. When I arrive at the gates of heaven the good lord will ask 'what did you do in your life?'

"I will respond, 'I tried to win football matches'. He will say, 'are you certain that's all?' But that's the story of my life."

A few weeks later he was interviewed by L'Equipe and said he would consider his position at the end of the season. He quickly tried to clarify that statement, but it was difficult to spin his more poignant remarks.

"What's hard is that feeling that something is coming to an end," he said. "You had a project with guys you had bought at 18 and who left at 23. That's not what you dreamed of. As well as players leaving you had injuries. It's simple, last year our midfield centred on Nasri, Diaby, Fabregas and Wilshere. Now Diaby and Wilshere are injured for the long term and Nasri and Fabregas have left for Manchester City and Barcelona."

It was over. There were times when it was difficult to bear, but what's often overlooked is just how great some of the football was.

The comedian Dara O'Briain's column in the Guardian should be compulsory reading for every social networking quarterwit: "I'm sorry; it's a pleasure to watch them. Even if we're not there, it's still a rush to be thereabouts. I did my time in the early 90s when it was John Jensen and Eddie McGoldrick and we couldn't buy a goal. And you want me to tear my hair out now, when I've got Fabregas and Arshavin in front of me and Wilshere and Vela waiting in the wings?"

That was possibly the most lucid thing I'd read about Arsenal since Fever Pitch.

Another era began. During a previous transfer window Wenger had responded to a question about a lack of signings by saying: "Give me the names of the world class players who are available."

In the 2011 summer transfer window he went on what by his standards was a spree, signing Per Mertesacker, Gervinho, Mikel Arteta, Yossi Benayoun, Andre Santos, Carl Jenkinson and Ju-Yung Park.

If Harry Redknapp had brought in the same half a dozen players nobody would have batted an eyelid, but Wenger was accused of panic buying.

Perhaps there was an element of truth to this. Jenkinson and Gervinho aside, the deals all came in the final days of the window and after the 8-2 loss at Old Trafford, with the deals for Arteta and Benayoun completed just moments before the deadline.

They were hardly marquee signings. Some would perhaps have been useful squad players a few years earlier, but would any have got into the Invincible side? Or even the 2006 Champions League line-up?

But this again ignores the circumstances Wenger was working under.

Tony Adams believed that Danny Fiszman's hefty investment in Arsenal in the mid-1990s was equally as important to the club's development as Wenger's arrival, citing his own improved contract as just one example and in 2001 only United had greater muscle among English clubs in the transfer market.

By 2011 Chelsea, City and United could all outbid them, with Tottenham and Liverpool at roughly the same level.

Had the age of the billionaire never arrived, who might Arsenal have signed? Probably not the stratospheric names like Ronaldo and Messi, but Drogba, Essien, Torres and others of a similar stature might all have ended up at the Emirates and Arsenal would almost certainly have been more successful if they had.

It's also instructive to look at who Wenger chose not to sign in that time. The Arsenal-supporting Gareth Bale might have been a mistake, but in a distorted market Wenger didn't make too many errors and certainly nothing to compare with Kenny Dalglish and Damien Commoli's at Anfield, where even the untrained eye could see that Andy Carroll's £35 million fee was missing a decimal point between the 3 and the 5.

The biggest regret has to be that Wenger failed to pick up a more reliable keeper before he found Szczesny by accident and that he didn't buy an affordable centre-half like Brede Hangeland or Gary Cahill, defenders who might have made the difference during the years of near misses.

It would also have helped if he'd recruited less fragile players.

Whether it was sheer bad luck or due to shortcomings of the medical department, from 1998 onwards, Arsenal's squad was almost constantly depleted by at least two key players.

Before a 2-1 defeat to Manchester United at the Emirates in 2012 Wenger delivered an injury update that was almost a parody.

Vermaelen (who in fact played) was a major doubt, Henry had a calf problem, there was "positive" news that Jack Wilshere was a few weeks away (he wasn't), Sagna and Gibbs were two or three weeks away, Coquelin, just when he was starting to come good, had wrenched his hamstring, Jenkinson was "running, but it will be a few weeks", while Santos was "progressing well" but two months away.

Abou Diaby didn't even merit a mention, presumably because hearing he was "a few weeks away" was more than anyone could stand, and to put the tin lid on all of it Fabianski was fit. Nine players who might have been very useful were out while the one who was anything but had recovered.

Luck like that has earned many a manager their P45 and this was another side-effect of Wenger's success.

He helped increase Arsenal's fan base to multiple millions worldwide, but this meant that every time Arsenal lost a game a few million of these would call for him to be sacked.

This is the logic of Piers Morgan, the ultimate professional controversialist, a man who realised there was money to be made by offering people someone they could despise and who brilliantly performed his role.

Morgan's reaction when Wenger brings on Andrei Arshavin vs. Manchester United is to question his position.

If only the logic been applied to Morgan's own career he would have been a hospital radio DJ well before he ever got the chance to publish fake pictures of squaddies pissing on Iraqi soldiers.

What if the board had acquiesced? The best available replacement on the market would have been Arsene Wenger.

Even describing him as a genius is to sell him short. He meets the criteria several times over: the Oxford English dictionary describes a genius an exceptionally intelligent person or one with exceptional skill in a particular area of activity.

Wenger is exceptional in multiple ways. As a teacher, linguist, artist, diplomat, mentor, economist, architect and more.

Yes, he made mistakes, and yes he has flaws but cherish this man while he's here.

When he eventually leaves, we are unlikely ever to see his like again.

6) PATRICK VIEIRA

IT'S almost impossible to overstate the impact that Patrick Vieira had, both at Arsenal and on the English game as a whole.

He was the first French player to pull on an Arsenal shirt, the player who did more than any other to restore the team's status as a major domestic force and the man who almost single-handedly defined the role of the box-to-box midfielder.

To this day Vieira is the reference point for any aspiring midfielder, although the term "the new" Vieira has become as debased a currency as it is when applied to virtually any other great of the game - precisely because Vieira's standards were almost impossible for pretenders to live up to, as we'll later see in the case of Abou Diaby.

As with almost all of Arsenal's French Legion, there's a question mark over just how French Vieira is.

He was born in Senegal in 1976 and raised by his mother Emilienne, whose surname he took. Vieira has no memory of his father, a Gabonese student who divorced his mother soon after Patrick's birth and the son later spurned his father's offers to establish contact.

"I have never particularly felt a need to know him," he wrote in his autobiography. "I grew up in a house with four uncles and a grandfather so I have always had male role models and have never felt I lacked anything in that part of my life."

What they did lack however, was material comfort. Although Vieira's mother hailed from the Cape Verde islands, by the time she had Patrick she was living in the Sicap area of Dakar, the Westernmost point of Africa and an area where the levels of poverty are such that they make the supposedly neglected Parisian banlieue look like Belgravia.

The Vieiras were considered relatively affluent because they had a television, but when Patrick was seven they emigrated to Trappes, the suburb on the far Western tip of Paris, also the home of the Anelka clan.

He spent a couple of years with the local team before the family moved around 40 kilometeres west to Dreux, a kind of French version of Wokingham, a pleasant satellite town where his race and country of origin was never an issue, except when it came to proving his date of birth.

Physically taller than most of his peers, Vieira's age was regularly questioned when he played for FC Drouais, with rival clubs reluctant to accept the date on his birth certificate because of issues with previous African players.

"The suspicion was always there and I found that tough to live with," he wrote, before adding with a prescience that foretold the kind reception he could come to expect at Old Trafford. "I had the impression that other people thought I was a cheat and I have never cheated when it comes to football."

Vieira never experienced culture shock when he left Senegal for France, but he did when he joined FC Tours as a 16-year-old because the distance from Dreux meant he was parted from his mother for the first time.

He formed lasting bonds with the other boarders at Tours, something which may explain the depth of the relationships he had with team mates later in his career, though his stay with the club itself was short-lived as it went bankrupt when he was 17.

Although Tours was three hours from the family home, he was at least able to see his mother regularly, something he couldn't do at Cannes, who he spurned Auxerre and Nantes to join.

While Vieira was no monk as a teenager, if he did go out clubbing he was always astute to enough to avoid getting caught and to continue studying accountancy.

At Cannes Vieira was fast tracked into the first team and made his debut in a 1-1 draw with a Nantes side who were becoming one of the strongest teams in the country with the likes of Claude Makele, Patrice Loko and Christian Karembeu.

Wenger first noticed him in a league cup tie with Monaco, when he came on at half-time and turned the match by stifling Claude Puel, who had previously been running the midfield.

"Suddenly Puel looked like a kid compared to him," Wenger later wrote. "I immediately told myself that this Vieira guy would one day be a great player. It had taken 45 minutes of a league cup fixture to convince me."

By the autumn of 1995 Vieira had established himself as a regular starter at Cannes, who were already planning to cash in on him. Yet Vieira had no inkling he was about to sold until he turned up for training and was told: "You're not training today, you're going to sign for AC Milan."

He later compared the deal to being kidnapped, having been flown to Milan in a private jet. He was told he shouldn't even consult his mother before signing the deal.

In hindsight it's clear that Cannes were desperate to force the deal through and that Vieira was ambushed, signing a contract in a language that he didn't understand, bewildered by the sheer number of zeros any financial transaction involving the lira involved.

Almost as soon as he'd signed the deal, Vieira knew something had gone awry and confessed to his agent that he'd "fucked up".

The agent in question, Marc Roger, had been kept out of the loop completely and understandably went ballistic, threatening to sue both clubs unless the deal was renegotiated.

Vieira was rewarded with a quadrupled salary, up to £300,000 from the £75,000 he was on at Cannes, but otherwise the move was ill-considered for all the parties directly involved.

By the time an assortment of parasites had been satisfied Cannes were left with almost nothing from the transfer fee. Coincidentally or not they went into a nosedive from which they have yet to recover, while Vieira was left to kick his heels at Milanello, stranded at the back of a queue of six foreigners, all of whom were competing for three places under the rules Serie A operated under at the time.

Milan would later repent Vieira's departure at leisure but at the time they were still an overbearingly strong side. Desailly, Weah, Savicevic and Boban were all ahead of Vieira and while the fifth foreigner, Paolo Futre, was just about ready for the glue factory, Vieira's opportunities were limited to almost zero, at a time when he desperately needed to play to further his development.

When he was picked it was for a low-priority UEFA cup tie with Bordeaux as part of a virtual shadow side. Milan won the home leg 2-0, but for the return Vieira was moved away from the centre to the right flank. The midfielder he'd shackled at the San Siro, Zinedine Zidane, announced himself as a world class player by inspiring a 3-0 turnaround.

By the end of the season Vieira was for sale, a victim of the quota policy. His account of how he came to join Arsenal backs up the theory that Rioch was merely looking after the manager's office until it became politically expedient for Dein to bring in Wenger.

"When I was at Milan I had regularly come across Arsene Wenger because I often sat in the stands at San Siro," he wrote. "We had talked on several occasions. He had told me that he was taking over at Arsenal and would I be interested?"

Vieira was first outed as an Arsenal target on July 26, when the Dutch paper De Telegraaf caught wind that his proposed move to Ajax was in trouble, well before the deal that brought Wenger to Arsenal was uncovered.

In 1996 the Arsenal team, unlike its latter incarnations, didn't lack for steel, either in defence, where the back four still formed an iron curtain, or in attack, where to a varying extent Ian Wright, Dennis Bergkamp and John Hartson all backed up a goal threat with physical presence.

What Arsenal lacked was any kind of physicality in midfield. While Paul Merson was still a class act, Ray Parlour was a work in progress and Bruce Rioch had resorted to using Martin Keown in the centre. While Keown performed this role better than expected, his selection didn't reflect well on the likes of Jensen, Morrow, Hiller, Selley, Helder and even David Platt.

Arsenal were one or two midfielders short of making a serious challenge for the title, but the feeling in the boardroom was that Rioch wouldn't be in a position to deliver the signings needed.

Having brought in Bergkamp and Platt in the summer of 1995, Rioch was damaged by his failure to repeat this coup. Arsenal were linked with the likes of the De Boer twins almost every week, but the pile of rejection letters was becoming almost Tottenhamesque and the embarrassment at board level was a key factor in persuading them to move for Wenger.

Arseweb, one of the first and best Arsenal websites on the internet, helpfully listed the players Rioch had been "linked with":

"Barton (Warren), Beresford, Ferdinand, Sherwood, Jarni, Thatcher, Lombardo, Ronaldo, Southgate, Ince, Sinclair, Sergi, Nedved, Poborsky, Dublin, McAllister, Lizarazu, Zidane, Dugarry, Stoitchkov, Thomas, Kinkladze, O'Neill, Berger, Vialli, Djorkaeff, Karembeu, Le Saux, Shearer, Klinsmann, Hazem Imam, Moore, Letchkov, De La Pena, Speed, Seedorf."

A decade and a half down the line this makes for fascinating reading for a number of reasons.

The first and most obvious is that none of these players actually joined Arsenal. The second is that players like John Beresford and Ben Thatcher were then considered hot properties and the third is that Rioch and the scouting network were well aware of the European market, knowing who the established stars were as well as which French players who were about to emerge - the list included five members of the squad that would win the 1998 World Cup.

Knowing who these players were was one thing. Persuading them to sign was quite another. At the time Arsenal's profile in Europe was far lower, despite the Cup Winners Cup success of 1994 and Rioch's refusal to sign a contract played into the club's hands. After a summer of complete inactivity in the transfer market Rioch was sacked on August 12 while at the same time Vieira was in Amsterdam, contemplating a move to Ajax.

Three days later he was an Arsenal player, his signing announced just hours after the Garde deal was completed (Wenger, writing in Vieira's book, actually gets the chronology wrong, saying the player joined in July - one of many instances of False Memory Syndrome that lurk in autobiographies).

Ajax, trying in vain to halt their own decline, had asked Vieira to take a pay cut, which he refused. He also rejected an offer from Bordeaux, joining Arsenal for £3.5 million, a first of many bargain deals, arranged by a manager who was still officially working for Grampus 8.

"I called him in Holland from Japan and told him to go and sign for Arsenal," Wenger said, in a tribute penned for Vieira's book. "I told David Dein he should not hesitate about the signing because if he wanted Vieira to come to the club he had to act quickly, otherwise he would lose him."

Once again, Vieira experienced culture shock. In 1996 Arsenal lagged a long way behind Milan in terms of pastoral care and Vieira was left to fend for himself, unable to speak English and reliant on Garde and occasionally David Platt to act as his interpreters.

With the team in limbo before Wenger's arrival, the French duo were shunted between the first team and the reserves by a distracted caretaker manager Stewart Houston and to add to the air of chaos Tony Adams confessed to being an alcoholic in an emotional speech to the dressing room, which neither French player understood.

Where Arsenal differed from Milan however, was in the players' willingness to integrate the duo. Although Vieira was close to Roberto Baggio, he otherwise lamented a culture at the Italian club in which every player was in it for himself, including Marcel Desailly, who later became his friend, but whom he initially felt cold-shouldered by.

He was further boosted by being handed the number four shirt, which he rightly believed implied he would be an immediate starter.

And even though he hadn't understood a word of it, Adams' speech had the curious effect of convincing Vieira that he'd come to the right place: "I realised that I must have come to the right place if a man - the captain - could stand up in front of his friends and tell them about something like this and moreover if these people could then help him through his problems," he wrote. "For me Arsenal was Tony Adams. He symbolised everything about the Gunners, in terms of his career, his aura, his permanent will to win, in fact in terms of everything he stood for."

Adams would, in time, pass that torch to Vieira, although their relationship was more complicated than that of a master and his apprentice. Adams thought the younger man could be arrogant and Vieira struggled to understand some of the criticisms his predecessor made after his retirement, even if the two remained friends.

In the short term however Vieira's impact was immediate.

"When I arrived I immediately picked him," Wenger said. "I never had the slightest doubt. At the time we were playing 3-5-3. In the middle I had Vieira, David Platt and Paul Merson. In order to win the ball from Patrick Vieira in 1996 it didn't take one man, it didn't take two, it took at least three men around him. And even those couldn't be sure of winning the ball. He was huge for me, immediately."

It was a significantly more brutal era and Wenger was more aware than Vieira that French players had a reputation for shying away from physical contact.

This was a myth Vieira almost instantly dispelled. "When the English saw that this guy who had just arrived and didn't look anything special with his long gangly legs was going to Wimbledon and stopping everyone in their tracks they loved that."

Cantona and Ginola had cultivated a reputation for petulance, or perhaps more specifically for failing to see the funny side in certain situations.

When Neil Ruddock played one of his side-splitting japes on the field, by pulling down Cantona's upturned collars, the United player, incredibly, didn't burst out laughing.

Ginola meanwhile had a running battle with Lee Dixon that resulted in a red card in League Cup quarter-final that reportedly had Ginola close to tears in the tunnel, wailing: "they won't let me play football."

"When all the English teams saw this giant who was crunching into everyone the whole time they couldn't believe their eyes," Wenger said. "When players had a go at him he gave as good as he got and when they had a go at him the second time he would make sure he returned the favour three times. And the English loved that immediately!"

This made him a target, in more than one sense. Opposing teams would try and take him out early in matches, while trying to unsettle him behind the scenes with almost permanent transfer speculation.

For the first time in the modern European era, when fans were able to watch televised matches from around the continent, Arsenal had a player with a strong claim to be the number one in his position in the world.

"Every year we told ourselves that we were going to feel the heat during the summer because there would be pressure on us and we would end up selling him," Wenger admitted. "We're not a club with infinite resources. So on the one hand it was a fantastic feeling to have a player like him and the other it was a bit concerning as well."

This was something fans would later have to get used to.

Vieira meanwhile was making rapid progress at learning English. With no one other than Garde to talk to this was partly out of necessity, but the fact he did so indicates he was also an intelligent man.

For the time being Arsenal were having to readjust to the stresses of a title challenge for the first time in five years. Vieira's first goal for Arsenal came in a 3-1 win over Everton, when he drilled a shot from just outside the area through a crowd of bodies and even more impressively past the salad-dodging figure of Neville Southall in the Everton goal.

Vieira's form earned him an international debut in a 2-1 win against Holland at the Parc des Princes in February 1997 after which he exchanged shirts with Bergkamp, who he still considered one of his three "idols", the others being Frank Rijkaard and Zidane.

Arsenal spent most of the season in third place, always at arm's length from Manchester United and Liverpool, but poised to gain a Champions League place under the new qualifying rules if either faltered. Liverpool duly slipped away, but the Gunners crucially lost their final home game of the season 1-0 to Newcastle, who leapfrogged them to finish second.

If Vieira's adulation for Bergkamp hinted he was still slightly overawed in his company, any last traces of that faded away the following season.

It was the greatest year of Bergkamp's career, mainly because it was his most consistent, but it was also the season that Vieira emerged as the English league's dominant central midfielder, an accolade for which he would vie with Roy Keane for the next seven seasons.

By the time the duo were scheduled to go head-to-head on November 9 however, Arsenal were spluttering and Keane was out injured.

Arsenal were leading 1-0 through Anelka when Vieira scored a second, rifling the ball past Schmeichel from the edge of the penalty area after a partially cleared corner.

In the delirium that followed Vieira performed a sliding celebration on his knees and duly injured himself. He limped around till until half-time, by which time United had drawn level, but came off for the second half, allowing David Platt to enjoy one of his rare moments in the limelight as an Arsenal player with an 82nd minute winner.

Vieira was out for a month until he returned as a substitute against Blackburn, coming on with Arsenal trailing in a game they would lose 3-1. It was the club's final league defeat of the season and after lurking as many as 15 points behind United at one stage, the momentum shifted decisively in March, when Vieira played a key role in the 1-0 win at Old Trafford alongside his now inseparable partner Emmanuel Petit.

Before that victory Arsenal's main focus was still on qualifying for the Champions League by coming second. Afterwards the title was theirs to lose.

"I was having a fantastic run of matches," Vieira wrote. "I was on good form, I was 100 percent fit, not only winning the ball but distributing it just at the right time, creating chances and even scoring some great goals myself."

None of which was greater than the goal he scored against Newcastle at Highbury, when he collected a pass from Anelka on the edge of the centre circle, took two touches and then launched an astonishing strike from 35 yards that curved into the top corner.

For a player with that kind of shooting power it was perhaps surprising he didn't score more often, but throughout his career he averaged roughly one goal every ten games almost everywhere he played.

Vieira carried his form through the title run-in and the FA Cup final win over Newcastle and into the 1998 World Cup, though here he found himself behind Petit and Didier Deschamps.

This was baffling, both to the more insular elements of the English media (whose logic was that if Vieira was the best player in the English League, he had to be worthy of a place in the French team) but also to many in the French press.

Deschamps, famously dismissed as a "water carrier" by Eric Cantona was never much to look at, but his value to the teams he played for was incalculable, even if, like Gilberto Silva, his contribution was only obvious to the layman when he wasn't actually playing. He helped turn a previously disorganised team from a rabble into a cohesive unit, while Vieira, at the age of 21, was happy just to be involved in the squad. He had no complaints about acting as Deschamps' back-up, though he later regretted this lack of ambition.

One of the reasons he was selected was because Aime Jacquet knew that unlike the long-discarded Cantona and Ginola, and perhaps Anelka who was one of the final six players who failed to make the cut, Vieira wouldn't cause unrest behind the scenes, even if he spent a month on the sidelines.

Paradoxically, this relaxed attitude cost him his place in the side. Jacquet told him he had been disappointed by the level of commitment he showed during the pre-tournament training camp, while his team mate Petit had by contrast thrown himself into every tackle and seized the place alongside Deschamps.

"When it came to that World Cup I arrived on tiptoes and I lacked ambition," he reflected.

He played in the third group game against Denmark, though only as part of what was effectively a reserve team.

Jacquet's shrewd handling of the squad meant that after qualification had been achieved with two straightforward wins over South Africa and Saudi Arabia, the fringe players could be involved against the Danes, in what was still a competitive game with the leadership of the group at stake, but one that could also double as an audition for the knock-out stages.

Keeper Bernard Lama, still furious about being overlooked for Barthez, refused to play but Petit, having been dropped for the second game, again seized his chance with a goal.

Vieira, while competent against Denmark, wouldn't have played again in the tournament had Desailly not been sent off in the final against Brazil.

Jacquet had been planning to bring on Thierry Henry to run at a faltering Brazilian defence, when Desailly lunged into a challenge during a French counterattack and was shown a second yellow card.

Petit was forced to drop back into central defence, meaning Vieira would have to fill his role in midfield.

"I hadn't expected to go on," he later admitted. "I was on the bench, quietly watching game, enjoying it from the sidelines… I came on without truly being aware of what was happening, with the intention of not going further up than midfield. The aim was to defend, at whatever cost."

But the Brazilians were a busted flush. Although Denilson clipped the crossbar with an angled shot in the final minute, the French were still 2-0 ahead in injury time when they decided the best form of defence was to counter attack.

Denilson's corner fell to Christophe Dugarry, who languidly strolled out of the penalty area and took the ball to the centre circle. Knowing the chances of Brazil now scoring twice were somewhere in the thousands-to-one, Vieira broke down the right while Petit hared towards the area.

Vieira played Dugarry's pass first time into Petit's path and he rolled the ball into the far corner, leaving Kevin Keegan, commentating for ITV, to say: "That goal had Arsenal written all over it. How many times are we going to see that next season?"

Piers Morgan, the infamous, Arsenal-supporting editor of the Daily Mirror, went further commissioning a special front page in North London saying: "Arsenal Win The World Cup," replete with a picture of the two midfielders embracing.

Morgan's exuberance was understandable, but Keegan's voice also contained an element of pride at seeing two English-based players succeed on the highest stage.

It had been a long time since any World Cup winners had plied their trade in England and the presence of two at Highbury reflected the growing strength of the English competition, at the expense of a waning Serie A.

In the tournaments to follow France 98, there was always a heavy Arsenal presence, with too many players to list playing for too many nations for there to be any continuing novelty value. In 2002 a Highbury-bound Gilberto Silva won the trophy with Brazil, while four years later the French team that lost on penalties to Italy contained past, present and future Gunners in Vieira, Henry, Wiltord and Gallas.

In 2010 Cesc Fabregas and Robin van Persie were on opposite side as Spain beat Holland, but back in 1998 having two winners was a big deal for Arsenal, whose only previous link to the Jules Rimet Trophy was George Eastham's role as a squad player in 1966.

If reflected glory was one emotion, resentment was another. A few miles away at Stamford Bridge Frank Leboeuf spent the next season reminding everyone "he'd" won the World Cup, an interesting spin on his participation in the event, which saw him mark an attack containing a striker who'd suffered a fit before kick-off and then only because Laurent Blanc had been suspended in one of football's worst ever miscarriages of justice, sent off in the semi-final because of Slaven Bilic's play-acting.

If a player like Leboeuf was getting delusions of grandeur, it was no surprise the likes of Vieira and Petit were becoming increasingly attractive targets for the English league's "reducers."

In October 1999 Arsenal lost 2-1 to West Ham at Upton Park in a game that was overshadowed by a red card for Vieira and an "incident" with Neil Ruddock that followed.

Ruddock was a player who represented almost everything I despised about the game in England, going all the way back to the school playground.

Everyone has a moment when they realise that football isn't merely a wonderful game you can play in your parents' garden but also a platform for the thugs of tomorrow to take their first steps in intimidation and bullying. It's often the moment when you meet someone like Ruddock for the first time.

He reminded me of the kind of kid who would wade into the middle of a game being played by students from the year below and hoof their ball into the stinging nettles.

His merits as a player were open to debate. He won an England cap, but then so did Andy Sinton, while his wikipedia entry describes him as a "tough and uncompromising" defender, which is certainly one way of looking at it.

Another would be to describe him as a severely limited plodder with the pace of a backfiring Trabant, who compensated for a lack of talent by performing reductive challenges on more gifted players.

He inspired a level of devotion among fans at some of the clubs he played for, with the Liverpool History website describing him as both a "colossus" and "Mount Everest" though critics would counter he was about as mobile as the latter. At Swindon it was reported he had to have custom-built shorts made because his arse was too big to fit into any of the 86 pairs the club already had.

After retirement he embarked on a career as an after-dinner speaker, a self-congratulatory environment where former footballers trot out anecdotes to easily pleased businessmen for £50 or more a time and an environment he had little trouble blending in with.

Part of his routine involved talking about his spats with Cantona.

"Every time we went out on that pitch he destroyed me so I had to put him off," he said at one such event. "I turned his collar down and he swang for me. By the end of it all he wanted to do was fight me. I got into his head, he was easier to play against after that."

Cantona retaliated on one occasion by gesturing that Ruddock was so overweight he might be pregnant and while this just about falls into the "banter" category - the agency which hires Ruddock out quotes him as saying: "Trust me to pick the only Frenchman around who wanted a tear-up."

Ruddock thus had "form" with French players. Then again, Ruddock had form with everyone.

In a reserve game with United he broke Andy Cole's leg in two places and said afterwards: "Basically I loved kicking Andrew Cole and I know it's not big and it's not clever but in one tackle I did break both his legs because he annoyed me. I didn't mean to break both his legs if I'm honest, I only meant to break one."

Ruddock was of course joking, which it's worth pointing out both for legal reasons and because this joke comes so brilliantly disguised as a piece of unrepentant thuggery.

Peter Beardsley ended up with a broken jaw after a clash with Ruddock in a testimonial and he later punched his own team mate Robbie Fowler in the face at an airport.

At Upton Park, Arsenal's frustration had been mounting ever since Trevor Sinclair got away with handling in the build-up to Paolo di Canio's first goal.

When the Italian then added a brilliant individual second Arsenal found themselves in the then-rare position of being 2-0 down with 18 minutes to go.

Davor Suker's volley gave them a lifeline, but with six minutes left Vieira, already on a yellow card, left his foot in on Di Canio and was sent off.

Even though he was barely 20 yards from the tunnel, that was time enough for Ruddock to wade in for a spot of gloating and Vieira's reaction was to spit on his chest.

What happened next was the kind of tabloid posturing that followed Cantona's assault on a Crystal Palace fan in 1995.

It was as impossible to defend Vieira's response as it was to defend Cantona, but neither man had acted with malice of forethought.

An already seething Cantona had snapped after being subjected to a xenophobic tirade from Simmons, a Thornton Heath thug who years later convicted for assaulting the coach of his son's junior team.

His kung-fu kick on Simmons divided opinion. While it was roundly condemned by all the usual moral high-ground occupiers, the Brighton & Hove Albion fanzine "Gull's Eye" published a cartoon on its front page saying "CANTONA ATTACKS PALACE FAN - VIVE LA FRANCE!"

Yet there was almost universal revulsion at Vieira's behaviour. It was rumoured that even Wenger was planning to make a statement condemning his behaviour and a draft copy was leaked to the media, though it never saw the light of day.

By devoting a chapter of his autobiography devoted to referees and red cards, Vieira went some way to addressing the reputation he acquired during his nine years in England, though he rarely showed any contrition.

He admits being ashamed of the Ruddock saga and concedes: "even the boss couldn't support me on that one," though at the subsequent tribunal the club presented evidence of what it called "extreme provocation."

In a post-match interview Ruddock had smirkingly claimed: "he missed me but it was close enough to smell the garlic on his breath", a remark that amused Daily Star reading simpletons and managed to be offensive on a number of levels without going quite far enough to earn him an FA charge for racism.

Vieira claimed Ruddock had said much worse to him in the build-up, though when the tribunal came, "French prat" was the only remark reported, which, given Ruddock's rich repertoire for incitement, seemed fairly innocuous.

"We have to ensure that the provocateurs are judged in the same light as the people they provoke," Wenger said, a trying to fight a battle that has been doomed to defeat ever since the game's birth. "For me what Ruddock said after the game was more shocking even than what he did on the field."

He later rowed back from that slightly, saying: "What he said in the interview was only minor. I am a Frenchman and I don't like garlic. You can call me a French so and so and I don't think it is racial."

Football could be greatly improved if it adopted the policy used by the Australian Rugby League a few years ago, when the authorities decided they would only take action against a player who provokes an incident - any retribution was considered fair game. Overnight this would transform standards of respect and courtesy on the field, while simultaneously ending a number of careers, but it will never happen. Had the FA's disciplinary body been in charge when the second world war broke out they would probably have found a way to punish Poland for retaliation.

When the punishment came, Vieira was saddled with a meaningless £45,000 fine and a rather more meaningful six-game ban. To put this into context it was two games more than the suspensions awarded to Martin Taylor and Ryan Shawcross, after their tackles broke the legs of Eduardo and Aaron Ramsey respectively.

Ruddock was let off.

The English never quite forgave Vieira for spitting, but he never received the same level of opprobrium for any of the 12 other red cards he picked up as an Arsenal player, or his 118 bookings.

For all his explanations of innocence and plausible claims of victimisation, it's impossible to pick up that kind of a disciplinary record without having been guilty of some regularly reckless behaviour, though curiously this affected the team less than it might have.

Wenger overused the word "spirit" in his later years in charge when the likes of Adebayor and Gallas were spreading sweetness and light in the dressing room, but in the Vieira era the team produced some of its most obdurate performances when reduced to ten men.

For the player himself frustration began to kick in as it became clear that it wouldn't be as easy to win trophies every year as it was in 1998.

He was unlucky not to repeat the double the following season, but by 1999-2000 the performance levels of some of his team mates were beginning to dip. The team lost so many games in the first half of the season that by the end of January they were well adrift in the title race and out of all cup competitions bar the UEFA cup, which they were dropped into having finished third behind Barcelona and Fiorentina in their Champions League group.

In hindsight Arsenal deserve credit for emerging from the pack to claim second spot but the way they lost the UEFA Cup final to Galatasaray still sticks in the craw.

Arsenal were beaten by a team who clearly wanted to win more than they did, though for once there were mitigating circumstances.

Galatasary's supporters' fanaticism had spilled over before their semi-final with Leeds, resulting in the fatal stabbings of two travelling fans in Istanbul.

What happened in Copenhagen in the build-up to the final went well beyond football, where it seemed as if the past multitude of sins of all English supporters abroad were suddenly being revisited on Arsenal.

Reports claimed that English fans from clubs who usually detested Arsenal had flown to Copenhagen specifically to exact revenge, the media did its best to inflame the situation and the police did nothing to contain it.

Eyewitness accounts from Arsenal fans claim thousands of Turks, including some of the 30,000 members of the diaspora living in Copenhagen, were actively trying to murder them. One, Paul Dineen, was stabbed in the back.

Their accounts, still available on the arseweb.com archive site, make it clear that the only real result achieved that night was the fact that nobody died as it could easily have turned into a repeat of Heysel.

In the stadium Arsenal's fans, most of whom were shell-shocked by what they had experienced, were drowned out.

"The Turkish End behind the goal was a frightening site," wrote Greg Thomas, in one of the eyewitness accounts. "Packed to the gills with six huge kettle drums hanging over the tunnel. The whole atmosphere from that end was like some ancient army marching to war. The Arsenal fans were as insipid as they have been since Highbury went all seater."

So were some of the players. Although the Turks contained a number of the players who would reach the semi-finals of the World Cup two years later, they were clear underdogs and could have been comfortably defeated had Arsenal taken a series of chances in extra-time.

That was despite the fact that Petit and Bergkamp effectively went AWOL, leaving Vieira swamped in midfield.

When the shoot-out came Arsenal were already three-one down when Vieira smacked his kick against the underside of the bar, leaving Gica Popescu to convert the winner, but in hindsight this was perhaps one game worth losing, given how horrendous the reaction might have been had Gala lost.

Vieira at least wasn't the type to sulk and channelled whatever anger he felt into helping France win Euro 2000, this time as a fully involved member of the squad as opposed to a bit part player given a cameo in the final.

For the next five years Arsenal's fortunes would rise while France's would fall, culminating in a shocking defence of their World Cup in 2002, when Vieira arrived in the far east dead on his feet and the French were eliminated at the first round stage.

But in 2000, after a summer of relatively cool transfer speculation, during which he turned down the chance to join Juventus, Vieira was back in the headlines for the wrong reasons as soon as the 2000-01 season kicked off, getting sent off in the first two games.

On opening day at Sunderland he was dismissed in injury time by Steve Dunn after his forearm collided with Darren Williams.

Wenger's defence was now wearily familiar, one of provocation and simulation. Williams said he'd been stamped on two minutes beforehand

and that Vieira had already been warned for that incident, though he added the caveat: "He's not a dirty player, he's just so big and strong and I think it doesn't go for him with some referees."

Within two days he was off again, in a home game with Liverpool on Monday night.

This time the referee was Graham Poll, an official with an unerring knack of being able to place himself at the centre of any storm and who did so on this occasion by sending three players off.

The BBC's match report contains the line: "Ironically it was not a dirty game …" which was an interesting way of putting it. On 37 minutes Poll sent Gary McAllister off for an over the top tackle on Vieira.

Vieira picked up a second yellow card for a two-footed tackle on 72 minutes and Dietmar Hamann followed suit six minutes later, overshadowing a 2-0 win for Arsenal that ended a 14-game losing streak against Liverpool.

Poll was showered with criticism from all sides but despite delivering a robust defence of his decisions and agreeing to revoke Hamann's second yellow, he had his knuckles rapped by the FA's advisory panel.

McAllister, apparently convinced Vieira was about to "do" him, successfully appealed against a ban, only for the FA to refuse to accept the panel's verdict, pompously declaring it to be an irrevocable law.

In the immediate aftermath Vieira was rumoured to be on the brink of quitting, though once the initial storm had abated he declared he would "never" leave Arsenal and alleged he was being victimised.

"I hear stuff after the game, I know that some players in the other team are told their job during the game is to wind me up. I feel sorry for managers who feel they have to do that."

From then on however, Vieira was constantly linked with moves away from Highbury. In the summer of 2001 one tabloid plastered the headline: "VIEIRA: I'M OFF!" all over its back page and while this particular exclusive was, like many others, subsequently proved to be bullshit, the sheer number of stories that were churned out had to be coming from somewhere.

In some cases they were from rival clubs and in others agents, but it was the nature of the potential destinations that caused angst. While fans might have forgiven him for moving to Real Madrid or Juventus, going to Manchester United, as was persistently rumoured, or even Tottenham at the end of his career as Harry Redknapp claimed he'd wanted to, would have forever tarnished his legacy at Highbury.

As it is Vieira's flirtations with unpalatable rivals still serve as a reminder that he wasn't always the man who would die for the Arsenal that he's sometimes remembered as.

In his book he describes having to reject an approach from United because to move would have been "the ultimate betrayal" and dismisses an interview he gave at the time, in which he was quoted as saying he wanted to go there, as a "web of lies".

But even if Vieira admitted to having his head turned, his commitment when he was on the field, and particularly against United, was unquestionable.

It needed to be, because for all manner of dark reasons, you were rarely just playing 11 players at Old Trafford, where 70,000 fans bayed like ancient romans demanding a gladiator be put to death every time an opposing player dared to put in a challenge and where every refusal of a penalty claim, no matter how ludicrous, was cited as evidence of a refereeing conspiracy against them.

George Graham was no naif as a manager, but after one of his first away games at Old Trafford he realised Arsenal had been mugged and resolved never to allow one of his sides to be intimidated there again.

The short term result was the brawl early in the 1990-91 when Arsenal won 1-0, but had two points deducted for a brawl that started after a late tackle from Nigel Winterburn, who was subsequently kicked several times as he lay prone on the ground. The tabloids foamed at the mouth as they effortlessly applied double standards to convict Arsenal for the kind of squabble seen a dozen times a season in less high profile matches - no side has been punished for any comparable offence since.

It was seven years before Arsenal won again at Old Trafford in March 1998, by which time Vieira was there to make sure nobody tried to take any liberties.

During Vieira's nine years in England, Arsenal's record there, in league games, was played nine, won two, drew three, lost four.

That isn't conspicuously successful, though he also played in an FA Cup win there in 2003, but the statistics only hint at some of the things that happened during the defining rivalry of the era.

Much, perhaps too much, was made of his individual battles with Roy Keane, a player who Vieira sussed out fairly quickly.

"He tries to get a psychological edge over his opponent," Vieira said. "He wants to put pressure on him and place him in a situation where he gets all steamed up. The fiercer the midfield battle is, the more at ease he becomes. I soon cottoned on to his game and after that it didn't bother me. On the contrary, I loved it."

The relationship between the two, while antagonistic, was also based on mutual respect and while Keane wasn't the type to publicly reciprocate Vieira's occasional admissions of admiration, when he was manager of Sunderland he attempted to buy him, an act that said plenty about a man whose actions were usually better considered and more significant than his words. It was Keane after all who tried to pacify Vieira after the Van Nistlerooy incident in 2003, saying "appeal Patrick" and trying to restrain him - genuinely - as he tried to exact immediate retribution.

Vieira rated the 1-0 win at Old Trafford in May 2002 as his proudest moment in an Arsenal shirt, but it was his final two appearances there for the Gunners that still get him most agitated and also reveal just how in tune he was with the way Arsenal fans felt.

The second "Battle of Old Trafford" in September 2003 marked yet another low point in the already dismal history of football punditry, as the bandwagon of condemnation collapsed under the strain of knee-jerk morons jumping aboard.

The game itself had been largely devoid of action, with Arsenal adopting an almost unheard of defensive strategy in a bid to get a draw.

With 13 minutes to play Vieira was booked for a foul on Quinton Fortune. Three minutes later he was jumped on by Van Nistlerooy and took the bait, flicking a foot in retaliation and getting a second yellow card from Steve Bennett.

A lengthy delay followed while Vieira was restrained, by Keane and others, from seeking instant retribution.

In the final minute of added time United were then awarded a classic Old Trafford penalty, when Diego Forlan "fell under the challenge of Martin Keown" as it was euphemistically described at the time. Another stitch-up seemed complete until Van Nistlerooy blew it by hitting the bar with the spot-kick.

In the aftermath Keown screamed in the Dutchman's face and Ray Parlour and Lauren followed his lead.

Seen in isolation it didn't look clever, but even taken out of context it was difficult to see how this justified the near universal condemnation of commentators, with the debased terms like "disgrace" and "shame" thrown around as if a minor war crime had occurred.

"As professional players, given our status, there are some things we shouldn't allow ourselves to do," Vieira admitted. "But people must also forget that we are also human and that we each have our own way of reacting to situations, depending on our feelings and emotions at the time. It was the injustice that made us behave as we did and that's a feeling that we have experienced all too often when we have played against Manchester United."

Vieira remained bitter about the affair for years to come, though his ire was almost exclusively directed at Van Nistlerooy, who he devotes a tirade to in his book, describing him variously as a cheat, coward, whinger, thief, nasty piece of work and most memorably: "a son of a bitch".

Having been kept apart from Van Nistlerooy on the field, he nearly atoned in the tunnel when Van Nistlerooy allegedly accused him of having no class.

"Watch it because I'm going to land one on you," he replied. There can't be many Arsenal fans who are glad that he didn't, especially given what happened 13 months later when United pulled off a brutally executed heist.

In the build-up to that league game Ferguson used one of his oldest tricks: indignantly accusing a rival team of precisely the same offences his own players were regularly committing and had every intention of continuing to commit. The genuflecting media labelled this "mind games" which quickly became a cliché, though interestingly, if you replace the words "mind games" with the word "hypocrisy" these articles make even more sense.

Eg: "Alex's Ferguson's hypocrisy doesn't worry Andre Villas-Boas," or perhaps "Arsene Wenger has no interest in being drawn into Sir Alex Ferguson's hypocrisy ahead of tonight's trip to Anfield…" etc, etc.

On this occasion Ferguson whipped up an entirely artificial sense of outrage as he accused Arsenal of getting away with murder the previous season, only to send his team out with instructions to do a lot more than just pushing and shoving.

Their gameplan for the 2004 rematch was obvious from the start.

"In almost 20 years at United the manager never asked me to kick anyone, but did he tell us to get tight, put a foot in and let Arsenal know they were in for a battle? Of course he did," said Gary Neville in his account of the pre-match team talk, making the reader wonder how he would have reacted if Vito Corleone had told him to "take care" of someone.

Jose Antonio Reyes, who United correctly suspected was mentally fragile, was deliberately targeted, while Rio Ferdinand got away with a professional foul on Freddie Ljungberg.

Van Nistlerooy produced a shocking challenge on Ashley Cole that later got him suspended for three games but at the time went unpunished and that meant he was on the field to convert the deadlock-ending penalty given by Mike Riley - when Wayne Rooney dived over Sol Campbell's leg.

Arsenal lost 2-0, though this time United, who incredibly (or perhaps not) kept 11 men on the field, did at least meet with some media derision, This, however, was overshadowed by a story that an unnamed Arsenal player, later revealed to be Cesc Fabregas, had thrown a slice of pizza at Ferguson, hitting him on the jacket as he stood gloating in the tunnel.

Vieira says Arsenal were "well and truly robbed" and effectively accuses Riley of complicity in this result, though without any apparent bitterness he points out that as he'd played in Italy he was used to it.

Much was also written about the rematch, won 4-2 by United at Highbury the following February, when Arsenal were said to have lost the game "in the tunnel" when Keane faced down Vieira after the Frenchman had wagged a finger in Gary Neville's face and according to Graham Poll, who had somehow been awarded the fixture, threatened to break his legs.

If true - and it sounds plausible given the posturing players indulge in - this was undignified and disappointing, but to say that Keane's John Wayne act had anything to with Arsenal's subsequent defeat is absolute bollocks. The defeat had nothing to do with either man's posturing and everything to do with Poll's decision to allow Rooney to stay on the field after he subjected him to a verbal tirade that probably set behavioural standards back by decades.

Poll later laughably claimed not sending him off stopped the game from exploding and doing the image of the English game "irreparable damage."

It clearly hadn't occurred to Poll that allowing Rooney to swear at him 27 times in full view of the television cameras was already dragging English football's image through the sewers and he later made the fatuous claim that this was successful man management.

Poll also denied Arsenal a clear penalty for a foul on Pires when the Gunners were 2-1 ahead and it was this, admittedly combined with Manuel Almunia showing all the positional awareness of an incontinent spaniel on a croquet lawn, that was chiefly responsible for the 4-2 defeat.

Yet revenge came, finally, in that year's FA Cup final in Cardiff, when having been outplayed for most of 120 minutes, Arsenal beat United 5-4 on penalties.

If his miss in Copenhagen was playing on his mind when Vieira took the decisive spot-kick it didn't show, as he found the top corner with Germanic precision before sprinting over to Lehman and being mobbed by the rest of his team mates, in the final act of his Arsenal career.

The end had been a long time coming. In 2004 Vieira had been on the point of joining Real Madrid when he got cold feet at the prospect of having to live under the scrutiny of the Spanish sporting press, whose standards made the English tabloid rotters look like clerks on parish magazines.

A fee had been agreed and Wenger had even signed Mathieu Flamini as a long-term replacement when Vieira backed out of the deal, unwilling to give up on his life in north London, where he could hang out in a Hampstead café with Pires and Henry, unmolested by passers-by.

This may have been a missed opportunity for both Vieira and Arsenal, with the former missing a once-in-a lifetime chance to reform his midfield partnership with Zidane at club level and the latter losing a substantial amount of money.

By the time Vieira was sold, a year later, Madrid were no longer interested and as a 29-year-old his value had depreciated significantly. Arsenal got an extra year out of him and an FA Cup win, but the fear of Vieira leaving had become a permanent, stifling cloud over the club and by the summer of 2005 the relationship had shifted in a way that clearly hurt the player.

The centime dropped for Vieira during a phone call with David Dein, when he realised he was no longer wanted.

When Dein told him the club were "neutral" about accepting an offer from Juventus, Vieira began to get agitated before realising he now had to leave.

On Bastille Day 2005 he joined Juventus for 20,000,000 euros. In the short term it looked as though Arsenal had got the better of the deal, particularly when Vieira returned to Highbury with Juventus for a Champions League quarter-final in the spring of 2006.

For once Vieira let the occasion get to him and he was embarrassed in midfield by Fabregas, who ran rings around him to inspire Arsenal to a 2-0 win.

Vieira was booked and suspended for the goalless second leg, but in his absence Arsenal were fading in the league and only just finished fourth.

Vieira meanwhile was winning the Serie A title with Juventus, only to lose his medal when the calciopoli match-fixing scandal broke and Juve were stripped of their title for match-fixing.

Vieira, his team mates and manager Fabio Capello were painted as innocent victims in this and in the sense that they played 38 games (losing only once) not knowing that an unfair wind was blowing behind them this was true.

The fact that the title was duly handed to Inter, who five years later were accused of committing similar offences having escaped at the time, deepened the sense of injustice, but looking back at the results of Italian sides at the time it's a bit like rewatching an old edition of the Tour de France, when almost the entire peloton was taking drugs, some without bothering to ask their doctors what they were putting in their IV drips.

Cycling results for the best part of two decades from 1990 onwards are little more than a list of the riders who didn't get caught and the 2006 Serie A table is pretty much the same.

Juve fans believe Inter committed the perfect crime in escaping detection while they, Milan, Lazio and Fiorentina, to list just the biggest clubs involved, were left to face the rap for a practice that had become endemic in the Italian game.

Nobody was quite stupid enough to put anything in writing, but a number of clubs sought to influence referees by finding new boundaries to the term hospitality and seeking to get favoured referees appointed in key matches.

Juventus were the leading Italian club of the era, so it was no surprise they led the way in this particular field. What was surprising was that after years of claims of dubious officiating and reports of an orchestrated doping programme, they were actually caught. Even more surprising was the reaction of the Italian Football Federation, a previously supine body which imposed the unheard of sanction of relegating Juve to Serie B.

Crippled by the decision, Juve were forced to sell Vieira for a derisory £6.5 million, then 9.5 million euros and less than half the figure they'd paid Arsenal just 12 months beforehand.

Vieira spent the next three and a half seasons at Inter, winning a Serie A medal on every occasion.

By then, however, he was becoming a more peripheral figure, someone useful to have in your squad, but not an automatic first choice.

After an emergency stint in defence during the 2002 FA Cup semi-final win over Middlesbrough, Martin Keown had suggested Vieira might later drop back into central defence to prolong his career, as Keown himself had, but he never did and for a player whose game relied heavily on being able to sprint between penalty areas dozens of times per game, he was never likely to play into his late thirties without becoming a shadow of his former self.

This is arguably what he'd become by the time he'd joined Manchester City in January 2010, but even a shadow might have been worth having around. In the summer of 2009 Arsenal were seriously considering buying Vieira for a second time, at the age of 33.

Wenger initially refused to rule out a deal, but then backed off, trusting in the nine much younger midfielders in his squad to deliver.

For the next two seasons Arsenal challenged for the title without every really convincing anyone they would actually win it, partly because of a dire lack of defensive know how, organisation and mental resilience, all qualities even an ageing Vieira might have given them.

In the 2010-11 campaign in particular an infuriating number of points were thrown away by defenders who needed someone to scream at them and midfielders too busy bombing forwards to realise they were needed at the back as well.

Against teams at the height of their powers Vieira was now getting by-passed, but against sides like Bolton, Blackburn and Sunderland his presence might have made the difference.

Instead it made the difference for Manchester City, steering them to third place on the final day of the 2010-11 season and an FA Cup final win over Stoke.

City didn't win that final convincingly or with any kind of flair, but they weren't hit by the kind of last-minute horror show that robbed Arsenal in that season's League Cup final with Birmingham.

You can argue his contribution to all this was marginal and that his Italian medals were almost a gift, given that almost all of Inter's competitors, bar Roma, had been hobbled by the fall-out from Calciopoli.

But the statistics can't be that misleading. If you take 1996 as the start of his career proper, he won honours in almost every season. One Champions League medal, three English titles, five FA Cups, four Serie A titles (not counting Milan in 96), one Italian Cup plus the small matter of a European Nations Cup and a World Cup. Discounting supercups and charity shields, that's 16 trophies in 14 seasons, the mark of a serial winner.

In this context, Vieira's departure in 2005 was certainly the end of an era and for all the brilliance of the football that followed, the lack of any tangible reward made his absence all the more acute.

When he retired in 2011, Arsenal again considered giving Vieira a coaching role, but he instead agreed to stay at City as a Football Development Executive.

It sounded like a spurious title, but one of his first jobs was to help convince Samir Nasri to make the switch from the Emirates.

Just how much convincing a man offered a weekly wage of £175,000 actually needs isn't entirely obvious, but Nasri's comments after the deal were another blow:

"When a player like this, who has played for Arsenal, Inter Milan and Juventus tells you City is the place to be because they're the club of the future you have to listen."

If City were the club of the future, the subtext was that Arsenal were the club of Nasri's - and Vieira's - past.

7) REMI GARDE

THE first ever Frenchman to sign for Arsenal and the first to captain the club, Remi Garde is probably better known for these landmarks and for his influence off the field than his sporadic appearances in the first team over three seasons.

Garde was born in l'Arbresle in the Rhone in April 1966, an attractive but unremarkable village, like Garde himself perhaps, 20 miles north west of Lyon, where he first played football for the local team.

Small for his age, he was technically gifted and noted for a powerful shot.

He inevitably gravitated towards Olympique Lyonnais and made a natural progression through its youth teams.

In time OL would become France's dominant club with Garde at its helm as head coach, but while he was working his way up the ranks as a player he was no galactico and OL were a long way from becoming a European force.

Despite being France's third most populous city, Lyon had a very limited football pedigree.

An amateur side called FC Lyon reached the French Cup final in 1918, but the competition was being held for the first time ever and at the height of the first world war, with many clubs either unwilling or unable to take part. FCL lost 3-0 to Olympique de Pantin in front of just a couple of thousand spectators.

A series of attempts to form one unifying professional side failed until the city belatedly got its act together in 1950, forming Olympique Lyonnais and installing the war hero Oscar Heisserer as its first ever coach.

Heisserer's brief was to take the new club into the French top flight, which he did, although the impact his side made on the city's population was marginal. 3,000 watched the first game with CA Paris, 5,000 the 3-2 win over Monaco that clinched the title.

They were immediately relegated and although they returned for the top flight a couple of seasons later and stayed there for over a quarter of a century, winning a few French Cups, they lived in the permanent shade of their neighbours St Etienne, who won ten league titles while Lyon fed off scraps and were forced to sell star players, like Raymond Domenech, to their rivals.

"When it comes to football, Lyon is a suburb of St. Etienne," one former president of the latter club once observed witheringly.

By the 1980s Lyon had been relegated for the first time in a generation, but in a country where football is demonstrably taken less seriously by the general population than in the UK, France's politicians have generally been far more attuned to the opportunities for mass manipulation offered by the sport that their British counterparts.

Publicly subsidised stadia are standard and in Lyon relegation was regarded as a civic affront.

The mayor, Francisque Collomb promised to help the club to become "worthy of its name," and the arrival of Jean-Michel Aulas in 1987 kick-started Lyon's ascent, just as Garde was breaking into the first team, after overcoming a series of injuries.

Aulas was a former Division One Handball player from the same village as Garde who had made his fortune in computer technology. He transformed OL.

The usual reaction on hearing a director has unveiled a five-year-plan for a club is to fear for its future, but Aulas's vision, "OL-Europe", actually worked, and in four years rather than the usual, Stalinist five.

Vision might perhaps be the wrong word. Aulas was no dreamer, filling supporters heads with unsustainable promises. Most club owners are or have been successful businessmen, but Aulas was one of the few who managed to retain the sense of detachment needed to succeed professionally when he went into football.

He and his scouting team, headed by sporting director Bernard Lacombe, invested in players who were about to become stars, then sold them as soon as they had (something that would sound depressingly familiar for Arsenal fans by 2011).

There was no sentimentality about it. Aulas would repeatedly say that the latest galactico on the production line was "not for sale at any price" but this was an age old negotiating tactic to prise more money out of the purchasing club and it invariably worked, particularly when he sold Michael Essien to Chelsea.

Garde was a key player in the early implementation of this master plan, despite having three vitals years of his career blighted by injury. He made his full debut during the 1984-85 season in the second division, but at the age of 18 he tore one cruciate ligament and he then tore the other, meaning that by the time he'd reached his 21st birthday he'd played just three months of senior football.

When he finally recovered he impressed during a pre-season training camp in Germany and was drafted back into the first team set up, on a wage of around £600 per month.

"He was a leader," Lacombe said. "Even if he'd just come from the amateur ranks he was a leader, with regards to his every day attitude, in the dressing room on the field and in training sessions."

Expectations of Garde were not high. In an interview with Four For Two

Lacombe later admitted: "At the first training sessions we said to Raymond (Domenech, the coach) if he doesn't break anything, that's something."

Domenech, known as "the Gerland Butcher" during his playing career, thought that this slight midfielder, cast in a polar opposite to his own image, could run his midfield and in 1988-89 Lyon waltzed to the second division title, with Garde pulling the strings as a defensive midfielder given licence to bomb forwards.

Promotion was sealed with a 0-0 draw against Ales, during which Garde confessed: "Sometimes I stopped playing so I could watch the people in the stand."

On their return to the top flight Garde, now the captain, scored a brilliant goal in a symbolic derby win over St Etienne, who were by then in serious decline.

He also scored their first goal when they achieved Aulas's greater ambition of returning to European competition in the 91-92 season, but it was during that campaign a blunder by Domenech, not the last in his managerial career, had serious repercussions for both the player and his team.

With OL in the middle of a crisis in central defence, Domenech moved Garde back into the middle of the back line, but this did nothing to strengthen the rear and it weakened the midfield.

Despite this setback at club level, Garde enjoyed a run of games with the national team, earning himself a place in the squad for Euro 92.

But he didn't play at all in Sweden and although he finished as OL's top scorer the following year with nine goals, Garde left to join Racing Club de Strasbourg, where he was guaranteed a midfield role.

Aulas was moving on to the next phase of his grand scheme, bringing in former Marseilles stars like Pascal Olmeta and Abedi Pele, while Garde made what was a sideways move.

His first year in Strasbourg coincided with my year in Alsace as a student, but I'd be lying if I said he'd made any impression on me during my infrequent visits to the Meinau, when the players who did catch the eye, for contrasting reasons, were an emerging Franck Leboeuf and the Australian striker Frank Farina, who had to be one of the least effective forward players I'd ever seen.

The following year, playing alongside Franck Sauzee, Garde improved significantly and played in the final of the French Cup, which Racing lost 1-0 to PSG.

After a third season in Alsace he was on the brink of ending what he himself described as an "average" career when Wenger rang him.

The Alsatian had contemplated bringing Garde to Monaco in 1993, but considered him "a bit too fragile" something borne out by the amount of time he spent on the sidelines during his career.

At 30 Garde's fragility would only have increased in the intervening three years, but he was available for free and occupied a position where Arsenal were light in numbers.

On August 15 Garde became the first ever French player to join Arsenal, at least according to the BBC, which announced the deal on Radio 5, a few hours before the same radio station reported Vieira's move.

Garde himself recalled meeting the younger man at Highbury and the pair of them being warned they'd need to put on ties before meeting the chairman to sign their deals, a detail that impressed rather than intimidated him.

Tradition aside however, the culture shock was obvious. In Wenger's continuing absence training sessions under Stewart Houston were shambolic compared to the regimented approach Garde was used to and the refuelling habits were also drastically different.

A contemporary of Garde's at Racing, the Northern Irishman Michael Hughes, once told a story of how, after a particularly impressive away win, the coach rewarded his players by saying: "That was great! You can all have one beer."

Within days of their arrival at Arsenal Tony Adams had confessed to being alcoholic, while Paul Merson already was one and Garde had to get his head round the idea that the players' diet could include jelly babies and chocolate bars at half-time.

The perception among the existing squad was that Garde was there as an unofficial coach and he didn't actually play until October 26, when he came on as a sub for Ian Wright when Arsenal were already 3-0 up against Leeds.

A second cameo followed at Wimbledon a week later but he didn't play again until December, when he made his first start against Nottingham Forest, who were rock bottom and had just fired Frank Clark.

With Vieira suspended this was his first real chance to impress and he grabbed it, his subtle prompting contrasting with Vieira's all-action style.

This, however, was a bad time to play a Forest side who had been galvanised by the appointment of Stuart Pearce as Clark's replacement.

Wright put Arsenal in front midway through the second half after a Mark Crossley blunder, but Alf Inge Haaland equalised almost immediately, Wright was sent off and with a fading Garde subbed, the ten men conceded a late winner to Haaland.

Garde started the next three games, but in the third of these, an otherwise easy win over Middlesbrough, he was crumpled by a tackle from a 40-year-old with sciatica, Boro's player-manager Bryan Robson.

He didn't play again for another seven weeks and when he did it was in central defence against Wimbledon, probably the last team in Europe against whom you'd opt to play a 5"9 defender.

Vinnie Jones, of all players, headed the winner from a corner Garde had conceded and while it was a performance of collective poverty, he made only four further appearances that season.

If Garde is looked on purely as a player he was even more peripheral in the double-winning season, making just 11 appearances, but by then his role was evolving into a de facto au pair for the growing French contingent.

Although Wenger was often cited as a father figure by his players, this was a role he couldn't afford to play too overtly with his compatriots at a time when he was still trying to win over a largely inherited squad.

He was so anxious to avoid being seen as showing favouritism to his French players that he later admitted he would come down harder on them for any transgressions than he would have done on an English player.

As an attempt to prevent a divide from forming it was only partially successful. A bigger problem was the language barrier. Garde spoke some English, but even the most advanced of non-native speakers will struggle to understand a conversation taking place at over a hundred words per minute in a foreign language, particularly if there are accents and slang words to contend with.

Ian Wright's south London patter must have been particularly difficult to decipher and yet the French contingent all credit Wright, an ostentatiously proud Englishman, with helping to bring the squad together.

Fringe players like Jason Crowe and Graham Stack occasionally expressed frustration at being denied first-team opportunities, but there's no evidence of animosity between the English and French first team players at any stage, from any witnesses.

The dressing room at Highbury was probably far more united in the early months of Wenger's tenure than it had been at several points in the club's past, but a linguistic barrier inevitably stopped Garde and Vieira from getting as fully involved as they would like.

This changed when Wright took matters into his own hands, bursting into a formal dining setting and yelling at both the English and French players, asking why they didn't like each other.

Stories of Wright's lack of tact are legion. Perry Groves, a man who can tell a story better than most, remembers when the striker managed to fire up almost the entire main stand at the Racecourse Ground by calling them "taffs", shortly before Arsenal's worst FA Cup result of the 90s, a 2-1 defeat at

Wrexham.

But Wright also knew the dangers of a divided dressing room, dating back to his days at a young professional at Crystal Palace, where his talent was resented by senior professionals, one of whom threatened to break his legs after he humiliated him on the training ground.

And the screaming fit in the dining room proved an improbable diplomatic triumph for Wright.

Garde cited the dining room incident as a turning point in Anglo-French relations, though the obvious quality of the players Wenger had brought in probably helped just as much.

Garde was nicknamed "Uncle Remi" by Vieira, Anelka, Petit and Grimandi and if it's difficult to think of any obvious individual contribution he made during that season, by assisting the others' integration he played a key backroom role, one that would indicate the path his future career would take.

"I have rarely seen a player who has such little confidence in himself transmit so much confidence in others," Wenger observed.

Garde was persuaded to stay for another season, during which he played more and earned the honour of becoming Arsenal's first-ever non-British captain, though the occasion was more noteworthy for being the first time Wenger used the league cup to experiment with fringe players.

The result was a 2-1 win at Derby, but that preceded a 5-0 home defeat to Chelsea in the next round that, an embarrassing exposure of the limitations of Arsenal's squad, during which Garde was forced off at half-time.

His contributions remained infrequent. He set up Anelka for a last-minute equaliser with a craftily lofted ball against Middlesbrough on an otherwise desperate afternoon at Highbury, but he was mainly used as a sub and when he started he seldom lasted 90 minutes.

The final match of his professional career came on February 28, 1999 at St James Park.

After three minutes he was clattered into the advertising hoardings by Nolberto Solano and taken off on a stretcher, never to return.

If that was a sad way for his playing days to end, Garde was too rounded to let it haunt his retirement. Having already contemplated packing the game in three years beforehand, Garde's front row seat during Wenger's first seasons with Arsenal made a much more attractive proposition to broadcasters than he would have been had he simply retired after his spell at Strasbourg and he quickly carved out a niche as a pundit, commentating on the French versions of the Pro Evolution and Fifa video games.

He even appeared on Sky, when he politely agreed with a suggestion that he could be described as a "French Andy Gray" although he favoured insight over bombast.

In 2003 he took up the first of several roles with OL, by now a very different club, culminating in his appointment as head coach in 2011.

It wasn't a role he'd always coveted. "I spent four years working alongside Paul (Le Guen) and then Gerard (Houillier) and it's true that there are moments when you think about it," he'd said, when asked if ever wanted to become a number one in his own right. "But it's not an obsession, it's just a possibility. There are people who know from the start that they want to do that. I started by taking my diplomas because the idea of being a manager without a diploma didn't seem decent. But I can't say I have the idea (of becoming manager) as a goal, it's something that interests me because if I don't do it I won't be in that environment anymore, but it's not something I'm calculated about."

When he did take the job Lacombe said: "He's our Guardiola," which might have been overstating the case slightly, but when the British press spoke about the job being an audition for Wenger's successor, the comparison didn't seem quite as condescending as usual.

8) NICOLAS ANELKA

The following conversation allegedly took place in a restaurant, after a chance encounter between an Arsenal fan and a player who was at the time a member of the first team squad:

"So what was Nicolas Anelka really like?"

"What ... Really?"

The player is unsure if he should say anything, but clearly wants to. Sizing up the fan in question, he realises he doesn't look like a tabloid journalist. He doesn't appear to have any recording equipment on him and seems to be genuinely curious. Or perhaps the player just doesn't care.

The player leans in, allows himself a small grin and whispers: "A wanker."

IT'S possible that in his late teens, Nicolas Anelka was a bit of an idiot.

If this is true, it means that the boy who would grow up to be a serial misfit according to the newspapers, had something in common with almost every other teenage boy that has ever lived.

Thrust into the public eye at a time when most of his peers were still emerging from adolescence, Anelka was painted as a whining petulant prima donna by men who judged him by the standards of fully matured adults - when in many cases his judges would have struggled to meet those criteria themselves well into middle age.

It's not that unusual for an 18-year-old to be handed a starting role in a top flight football team, though it is rare for someone of that age to become an established first choice striker, which is what Anelka was by the end of Arsenal's double-winning season.

Unlike the equally prodigious Cesc Fabregas, who seemed to have been born with a diplomat's brain, Anelka occasionally said things he shouldn't have when he didn't know any better and his remarks were then twisted by men who clearly should have known better, for the purposes of making him look like an imbecile.

His body language didn't always help, but one of Anelka's main flaws was that he wouldn't conform to the stereotype of a footballer, in an era when the English Premier League was still full of "characters" like Dennis Wise and Neil Ruddock, with their side-splittingly amusing practical jokes and faux-cockney banter. Nor would he "play the game" by kissing the badge and pretending he loved whichever club he happened to be with. Anelka was in it for himself and at least he never bothered to hide it.

For most of his career Anelka was defined as awkward and in a social sense this was perhaps true.

It's certainly true that at times it appeared he'd been badly advised, apparently by his older brother Claude, who acted as his agent and who almost merits a chapter in his own right, as the kind of relative who would haunt his career in the manner of a Billy Carter or a Roger Clinton.

Enriched by his brother's transfer dealings, Claude would invest £300,000 in the Scottish First Division Raith Rovers in May 2004, effectively buying himself both a seat on the board and the manager's job.

Investors in Scottish football invariably fall into the trap of claiming they can make their chosen club a "third power" in a land where Rangers and Celtic have operated a duopoly for decades and Claude read from precisely that script, apparently oblivious to the financial demands that breaking that hegemony would make on his wallet.

The money Claude had "earned" was supposedly keeping Raith afloat, but in his five months in charge the team - supported by the former British Prime Minister Gordon Brown - drew one game and lost seven.

The former Arsenal midfielder John Hollins was hired to assist him, but quickly resigned, fearing his reputation would be irreparably damaged as Claude filled the squad with players he'd found in a Parisian 7-a-side league.

When he was finally shown the door, Claude struggled to understand the contempt in which he was held by the Raith fans.

"It has been very hard to listen to the abuse and jeering that the fans showered upon me week in and week out. What I wanted was complete control of all football matters. I believed in my thoughts and philosophy 100 percent. The truth is that I have over-stretched my limits. I quickly realised there was more to the game in Scotland than I thought."

If that sounded like a candidate for understatement of the century, there was at least something refreshing about Claude's candour.

He'd failed and Raith would go on to be relegated by a 30-point margin but at least his motives weren't obviously nefarious, something that marked him out from the asset-strippers who found football clubs so easy to fleece.

Nor did he try to extract any of his money, leaving it as a gift to Raith's youth academy.

Six years on from that debacle an even more peculiar episode followed when Claude was named manager of AC St Louis in the USA's second division.

In his first game in charge in Carolina, Claude somehow managed to send out a team with just 10 players after an administrative error meant he couldn't start with his best player, Manuel Kante.

Instead of substituting Kante and playing with 11, Claude sent Kante back to his hotel to collect some paperwork and brought him on after 30 minutes, by which time his ten team mates were already 2-0 down, the game's final score.

He somehow lasted for several months before getting fired, but if the people running St. Louis had even the most basic level of competence they would have checked Claude's credentials before employing him. The fact that they went bust 12 months later suggests they would have struggled to organise a drinking session at a rugby club.

When Claude took over Raith his mission was to do things properly, having seen a multitude of "crazy things" in football.

A kind way to look at his career would be to suggest he was a naïve optimist who was ill-equipped to deal with the sharks that infest football's waters, and where the bad guys usually win.

His role offers an easy explanation as to how Nicolas blundered from one PR disaster to the next in the early stages of his career, earning a perception for being awkward that he never really shook off.

Yet perhaps Claude was underestimated. If you look at Nicolas's career with an economist's eyes, it was a success.

He accumulated a vast personal fortune in wages, signing on fees and through endorsing everything from fast food to razors, dressing in a Robinson Crusoe costume that made him look like Snoop Doggy Dogg and then acting out a male fantasy for Puma, when he was kidnapped by a model with legs like skyscrapers and lashed to a chair.

Whether Anelka actively sought to invite ridicule is difficult to tell, but he certainly attracted it. As a footballer however, he was valuable asset to almost every club he played for and he played for a few.

Claude was a small boy when his parents emigrated from Martinique to Trappes, on the far Southwestern tip of the Parisian banlieue.

11 years his junior, Nicolas was spared this culture shock as he was raised in the nondescript surroundings of the Ile-de-France following his birth in Chesnay in 1979, although he considers himself Martiniquais and as a child spent all his summer holidays there.

Anelka is the product of a stable, loving family unit, who takes great pleasure in making his parents happy. His father was a civil servant while his mother, the cousin of the Paris St Germain defender Franck Tanasi, worked at a local school. Both have long since been able to retire and they now spend half the year in the house Nicolas bought for them in Case-Pilote on Martinique.

As a junior he played for the local team, Trappes-St Quentin, but by the age of 12 he had left home for Clairefontaine, for what he says in his autobiography were three of the happiest years of his life.

While there he signed a deal with PSG, the team he grew up supporting, but though he claims they are "the club of my heart" their relationship was strained almost from the start.

He was only 16 when Luis Fernandez handed him his debut, against Monaco in February 1996, but even though he played just twice that season he already felt he was a better player than the strikers ahead of him, the French international Patrice Loko and the Panamanian Dely Valdes.

Early the following season Fernandez's successor, Ricardo, brought Anelka on as a substitute against Lens, in a game PSG were leading 2-0. With ten minutes to go he intercepted a stray pass and scored his first ever top flight goal, before setting up Leonardo three minutes later.

For any other 17-year-old this would have been a dream start, but Anelka had already concluded his future lay elsewhere, his resentment at being sidelined for Loko and Valdes compounded when the club's sporting director Jean-Michel Moutier offered him a six-year contract and effectively told him to sign it and be grateful.

"I like group life and I've never had a problem with blending in, but I hate it when people decide things for me," he wrote. "(Moutier) thought I would wisely obey him. It didn't work like that with me. I'm a Parisian and proud of it, but I had something to say. I want to decide what I do with my life so I decided to leave for Arsenal."

Calling Anelka headstrong therefore seems a grave understatement.

Having played just 10 games for PSG, the deal was signed on February 22 1997, 12 months after his debut, for a compensation fee of just £500,000 that was immediately branded derisory by the FFF.

It was an entirely legal move, but it wouldn't be the last time Wenger's transfer ethics were questioned by a club who felt they'd been robbed of a player they'd invested years in (a feeling Wenger would later experience with Nasri and Fabregas).

For Anelka, having left home at 12, this wasn't quite the step it would have been for other teenagers, but Anelka was leaving the country. This would have been daunting even if he'd had a smattering of English, which he didn't.

What he did have going for him, other than his talent, were new contacts in Wenger, Vieira and Garde and the protection of Claude, who moved to London with him.

Just how good a player he'd be was still impossible to guess. PSG's fury and the fact that Wenger simultaneously shunted the lumbering but effective John Hartson to West Ham suggested he had to have something going for him, but the initial signs weren't overly encouraging.

A five-minute cameo as a sub in a 3-0 win at Chelsea was inconclusive, as were two subsequent substitute appearances and though he showed glimpses of talent in the season-ending 3-1 win at Derby, the following season didn't begin well.

The form of Bergkamp and Wright kept him on the sidelines and in his first start, a 1-0 UEFA cup defeat away to PAOK Thessaloniki that the former refused to fly to, he was anonymous.

His moment would come however. Wright was still in exceptional form, but at 34 his increasing vulnerability to injury meant he was likely to be sidelined sooner rather than later and with Bergkamp picking up a suspension Anelka was handed a start against Manchester United on November 9, a seminal match in Arsenal's history.

With seven minutes gone a shot from Marc Overmars rebounded to Anelka on the edge of the area.

With his route to goal barred, Anelka drifted away from goal, but then doubled back on himself, created just enough room to shoot and with minimal backlift lashed a shot that beat Peter Schmeichel at his near post.

Several million people, quite probably including some of his team mates, must have had the same thought at once: "So that's why Wenger bought him."

That electrifying 3-2 victory was followed by two lean months for Anelka, who didn't score again until he poached a goal in a 2-2 draw at Coventry, but by this stage Wright had, as expected, been ruled out through a long-term injury and the club's then record goal scorer would never regain his first-choice status.

Anelka's integration into the first XI was helped by some collectively outstanding displays. Wright aside, the squad remained largely injury-free and the stability of the back four, plus Seaman and their auxiliary shield, Petit and Vieira, gave Overmars, Bergkamp and the revelatory Ray Parlour a platform to overwhelm a succession of opponents.

The core of the team was so strong that for a (brief) while even Christopher Wreh looked like a top-flight striker, so while Anelka's nine goals certainly contributed to Arsenal's double, he wasn't yet the crucial figure he would become the following season.

The moment this diffident, awkward and gangly looking teenager (who only turned 18 on the day Arsenal won 1-0 at Old Trafford) turned from a promising striker into a World Class talent arguably came in the 1998 FA Cup final with Newcastle.

With Arsenal 1-0 ahead and 21 minutes to play, Parlour found Anelka a yard away from his marker, by the centre circle.

His first touch, with his shoulder, controlled the ball and his second bought him a yard of space.

With his speed that was all Anelka needed to drill a shot with his right foot under Shay Given's arm to make it 2-0. For a man who'd previously looked a little uncertain as to how he should celebrate goals, Anelka ran to the advertising hoardings, realised he was faced with thousands of Newcastle fans, raised his arms and then looked directly into the television camera to mouth something in French.

What he actually said was irrelevant. Anelka's time as a junior member of the squad was over and he knew it.

Wenger knew it too. He felt confident enough to release Wright to West Ham and was vindicated when Anelka became the top scorer in the 1998-99 season, with 19 goals.

If the team had carried him at times during the double campaign, this time around he would carry them, forming a clinical partnership with Bergkamp, who he admired, studied and tried to emulate.

"Overmars, Bergkamp and Petit used to hit me with long balls of diabolical precision," he later wrote. "(They were) absolutely incomparable, I never again found such a quality of passing," he added, though he was quick to add he didn't feel any regrets.

Perhaps he should have. Arsenal came within the smallest of margins of repeating their double in 98-99.

The consensus was that when Arsenal had their strongest XI on the field they were better than Manchester United, as successive 3-0 wins in the charity shield and then the league at Highbury early in the season testified, but that United's squad was stronger.

Although the striking department was operating at an optimum level, behind Anelka and Bergkamp the defence in particular was starting to creak and the firewall offered by Petit and Vieira wasn't always available.

Anelka quelled a rebellious Highbury with a last-minute equaliser against Middlesbrough at Highbury, scored from a Kanu rebound in a 1-1 draw at Old Trafford and hit a hat-trick against Leicester in a 5-0 win, but replacements like Stephen Hughes and Nelson Vivas didn't quite live up their billing. Although the signing of Kanu provided some impetus, it was more often than not left to Anelka and Bergkamp to keep Arsenal in contention.

Had the latter not seen his stoppage time penalty saved in the FA Cup semi-final replay at Villa Park Arsenal would probably have won at least one trophy, but in truth they were second best for most of the tie, only really dominating when Keane was sent off in the second game.

Anelka's response was to score four goals in the next three league games, including one in a 3-1 win at White Hart Lane, but a sickening defeat at Leeds in the penultimate fixture - made even harder to swallow by David

O'Leary's nauseating jig along the touchline at the end - cost Arsenal the title.

And Anelka was by now hankering for a move to a club he felt befitted his stature.

During this second full season at Highbury stories repeatedly surfaced about Anelka's temperament. He was nicknamed "the Incredible Sulk" by the British tabloids, supposedly because his team mates wouldn't let him play his French rap music on the team bus.

He also reportedly called Overmars selfish and although there was no indication that this had any effect on their working relationship, it was clear that where his predecessor Wright - a native Londoner - saw Arsenal as the pinnacle of his club career, for Anelka it was a mere staging post.

His market value was dramatically increased when he scored both goals as France won 2-0 at Wembley, a performance that moved Didier Deschamps to say the French had discovered their Ronaldo.

France's success in 1998 had come, like Arsenal's, as result of its core strength and an outstanding number 10, (for Bergkamp read Zidane) rather than any outstanding centre forward, with due respect to Henry and Dugarry and perhaps less for Guivarc'h.

Although the Wembley game was only a friendly, it's easy to forget the impact the win had on the French psyche, especially given how far both teams would fall from grace in the subsequent decade, during which time friendlies became debased to the point of worthlessness.

In 1999, despite being World Champions, the French had never won at Wembley. They also had a very poor overall record against the English, who could argue they had been unlucky to exit the World Cup at the second round stage and who had some exceptionally talented players in Beckham, Scholes, Owen and Shearer.

In their previous meeting, in a 1997 World Cup prequel called Le Tournoi, Shearer's late goal gave England a 1-0 win, but even so England were a team there for the taking. Glenn Hoddle had just been forced to resign and Howard Wilkinson, in caretaker charge, was handed the brief of winning the game (obviously enough) to "boost morale".

Logically enough that meant picking the strongest possible side and eschewing any temptation to experiment. As a consequence, Wilkinson picked the entire Arsenal back four, minus Nigel Winterburn.

The actual level of expectation was revealed when Lee Dixon, as surprised as anyone to receive the call up, drily told Petit: "I'll see you back here next week after we've given you a good hiding."

"I don't care, I've won the World Cup" was the reply.

On paper England's team looked good: Seaman, Dixon, Keown, Adams, Le Saux, Beckham, Ince, Redknapp, Anderton, Owen and Shearer, with a bench that included Rio Ferdinand and Scholes.

The French team sheet from that night, however, reads like a list of all-time greats: Barthez, Thuram, Blanc, Desailly, Lizarazu, Pires, Deschamps, Zidane, Petit, Anelka and Djorkaeff, with Vieira and Wiltord on the bench.

This was arguably as strong a team as has ever played the game and yet Anelka was the star, racing on to a pass from Zidane to score with a first-time volley midway through the second half and then steering in a cross from Dugarry a few minutes later, having already had a first half effort ruled out when the ball appeared to have crossed the line.

A neutral could have concluded that England played respectably and did well to avoid a humbling defeat.

The surprising thing about the French reaction was that they seemed surprised. L'Equipe carried a cartoon of a deliriously happy fan looking out of his window at the miserable weather outside, but saying: "Il est toujours le 14 juillet" (it's always Bastille Day).

11 years later England lost 2-1 to France at the rebuilt Wembley, to a universal indifference that was easily understandable after a glance at the team sheets.

England's line-up now read Foster, Jagielka, Lescott, Ferdinand, Gibbs, Henderson, Barry, Walcott, Milner, Gerrard and Carroll, a mixture of modest potential, serial underachievement, general poverty and in Carroll's case the almost laughably overrated.

The French line-up was barely any more inspiring: Lloris, Sagna, Rami, Mexes, Abidal, M'Villa, Gourcuff, Nasri, Valbuena, Malouda and Benzema.

France won and nobody batted an eyelid.

Yet speaking only a year after the event, Wenger described the 1999 result as a "symbolic shift" and felt the result had come as a shock to the English.

The biggest psychological impact was on Anelka, who may have been flattered by Deschamps' comparison to Ronaldo but certainly didn't want to downplay it.

If the hypothetical effects of Anelka's decision to leave Arsenal on his club career are unknowable, this was certainly his high watermark as an international.

Anelka had been intimidated when he'd first made the French squad less than 12 months previously, but he wasn't a man who stayed overawed for long.

One of the most extraordinary passages in his autobiography concerns his reaction to being left out of the squad for France 98.

Having made his debut in April against Sweden, Anelka was absolutely stunned when Jacquet excluded him.

"I'd just done the double with Arsenal and I still don't understand his reasons for leaving me out," he said. "He just said, 'You, I'm not taking you. It's normal'. Nothing else. Those words will stay with me for the rest of my life."

It was obviously a difficult blow to take, but his reaction was interesting. While Ian Wright, excluded by injury from Hoddle's squad, overcame his disappointment by acting as the team's main cheerleader, Anelka didn't even watch the final.

"I was on the Eurostar," he said. "I wanted to get back to London as late as possible because I was resuming training the following morning. I managed to get the last train. It was the conductor who told me about this surprise win over the team of my idol Ronaldo. So much the better because I had a lot of mates in the French team."

It's not clear if he wanted to catch the last train because he wanted to watch the match, or because he wanted to delay his arrival in London for as long as possible, but it sounds like a remarkably underwhelmed reaction to the biggest explosion of joy in France since the liberation, suggesting Anelka's focus was always individual rather than collective.

In some ways it was similar to Jimmy Greaves' exclusion from the 1966 World Cup final: "I was pleased we'd won, but inside I just felt numb."

But Greaves did at least watch the game and he was an established, top-class goalscorer who had been at his peak for a number of seasons and who had just been deprived of a once-in-a-lifetime opportunity.

Anelka was a 19-year-old with several tournaments ahead of him and he might have benefited from being around the squad even if he hadn't been able to play.

By 1999 Anelka clearly felt he was a world-class talent and so began the first of the Wenger transfer sagas. In terms of unrelenting tedium it matched its predecessors, though it differed from the Henry, Vieira and Fabregas affairs for the obvious reason that a clear majority of Arsenal fans (1) wanted to see the back of him, (2) couldn't believe how much money the club were being offered and (3) were desperate to flog him before Real or whomever came to their senses.

Whomever meant Lazio, who'd baulked at the £22 million demanded, and Juventus, who were tantalisingly offering a swap deal with Thierry Henry, then regarded as the lesser prospect.

Just how eager Anelka was to leave could be measured by his decision, in mid-July, to hire Jean Louis Dupont, a Belgian lawyer who changed the course of football history with the Jean-Marc Bosman case.

Dupont, who later specialised in helping high profile cyclists escape drug charges and incredibly managed to get Jose Mourniho off a UEFA charge when he was guiltier than OJ Simpson, claimed: "I will free Anelka for £900,000."

This remark was profoundly offensive on a number of levels, from the use of the word "free," which somehow implied Anelka was being enslaved, the absurd sum of money being quoted and the smugness of the delivery.

By now Arsenal were exasperated enough to release a statement that violated their usual policy of not commenting on transfer deals.

"It has always been (our) intention to retain the services of Nicolas Anelka. He is an exceptional young talent and it remains our primary concern that he respects his contract with the club.

"It was apparent that Nicolas was determined to leave Arsenal for his own reasons.

Consequently, transfer negotiations were held separately with Juventus and Lazio and it was believed that an agreement could have been reached. However, it would appear that personal terms were not concluded and therefore a transfer to either club was unable to proceed.

"With the season less than two weeks away, it is the Manager's priority to have the team fully settled and prepared for the forthcoming campaign. In the absence of a firm agreement for the transfer of Nicolas Anelka, the club has withdrawn the possibility of the player departing, and expect him to resume full training with Arsenal this week."

If that smacked of David Dein or Danny Fiszman trying to extract the last possible drop of blood out of the deal, Wenger it seems, was genuinely desperate to keep the player.

In one of his most memorable quotes he said: "I hope Nicolas remembers that no matter how much money you have, you still only eat three times a day and sleep in one bed. But you can miss a career."

That was possibly something Anelka reflected on when he ended up at Bolton and although he didn't exactly "miss" his career, it took him to places he clearly wouldn't have expected to go to when he was a 19-year-old. Arsenal unquestionably got the better of the deal, using the £22.3 million they screwed out of Real to build a state of the art training ground and prise

Henry from Juventus.

And even in the short term Anelka realised fairly early on that Madrid was no panacea. A club as political as Real was no place for a naif.

As at Arsenal, Anelka had a group of players who helped him settle in, particularly Christian Karembeu, but unlike at Highbury, where the native players openly welcomed anyone who was likely to help them win a trophy, at Real there were distinct and destructive cliques operating.

When he arrived in the dressing room for the first time he was spoken to curtly, then given a cold-shoulder initiation by players who guarded their own places like dogs who'd urinated on lamp posts.

A sympathetic team mate marked his card on day one. A delegation had gone to the club's president Lorenzo Sanz, telling him they had no need of Anelka because they already had Fernando Morientes.

Sanz hardly diffused the situation when he described Anelka as his "marvellous folly" and it was around this time that a genuinely bizarre short story about Anelka appeared in a compilation of essays called "Le Foot - Legends of French Football", written by an author known only as Q.

Apparently based on genuine conversations between Q and Didier Anelka, the story is called "Anelka: the Unknown Soldier," though it appears to be an exercise in self-mythology by his brothers, who compared themselves to "black knights in shining armour" fighting in Toussaint l'Ouverture's slave revolt against Napoleon.

Fiction is blurred with reality to a bewildering extent, but at one point Didier says: "Nicolas is the star, the one we have all come to see. In a Hollywood film the star is the one who carries the film."

It certainly sounds like the kind of thing the Anelka brothers might say, but even so it shows an extraordinarily exaggerated sense of Nicolas's importance given how seldom he played and that he only scored four goals in the entire season.

Two of those came in either leg of Real's Champions League semi-final with Bayern Munich, so he did make a contribution and he did play for 80 minutes of the final, but it was still a slender return for the money Real had invested in him and hardly enough to justify calling him "the King of Madrid" in Q's story.

The contrast between Anelka and the level his entourage believed he belonged at was only highlighted by Thierry Henry's form at Arsenal, where he was becoming the player Anelka already believed himself to be.

The world was never usually more than 24 hours away from a story about Anelka being unsettled breaking and throughout his time at Real the question appeared to be when rather than if he would leave.

His eventual destination was, however, a surprise. After a Euro 2000 campaign in which he became more peripheral as the tournament went on, Anelka announced he was going back to PSG.

If his career had stalled at Madrid, back in Paris it entered a nosedive. The move was a disaster on every level.

In theory it should have worked. According to the vision of the club's president Laurent Perpere, Anelka was supposed to be the returning star at the head of a team based around a core of players from Paris and the banlieue, including Sylvain Distin and Laurent Robert, with Jay Jay Okocha and a young Ronaldinho as its jokers.

As the only top-flight team in one of the world's great cities, PSG's potential has been obvious for years, but successive presidents have failed to unlock it and Perpere, despite being bankrolled by the tv station Canal Plus, was no exception.

Anelka's fee in itself, an estimated £20 million, was a permanent reminder of the club's previous incompetence, given that it was 40 times what they'd been forced to sell him for and it was indicative of a laissez-faire attitude to money that would swiftly destabilise the team.

When Anelka was presented to the Parisian crowd before a friendly with Sao Paolo, he looked like he'd come from a different planet. He wore a faintly homoerotic woollen vest, knee length trousers, which can never look anything other than absurd even in Paris and had sunglasses perched on the top of his now bald head, even though it was an evening game.

After a third of the season PSG were top of the league having won nine games on the trot, but their position was an illusory.

As with Madrid the dressing room was riven by jealous cliques squabbling over status and bonuses, but the players only had a fraction of the talent at Real, even though they still acted like superstars.

At first the coach, Philippe Bergeroo, backed his men when reports of them visiting night clubs and bringing girls to their rooms the night before matches began to surface, because he thought they were untrue.

When he realised, to his horror, that his trust had been betrayed he tried to get rid of the chief culprit, only to receive a delegation of players asking him to reconsider because they were worried that without "X" they would lose their next match.

After a 5-1 defeat at Sedan, a team for whom the word "lowly" tells only a fraction of the story, Bergeroo was fired.

Anelka, injured at the time, was rumoured to have been part of a cabal who were out to get the coach, but he denied this vehemently and as he'd previously got on well with Bergeroo this seemed to be a smear.

Even if Anelka was in on the plot it backfired when Luis Fernandez was named as Bergeroo's replacement, beginning the start of an enduring contempt between a man who had been part of a great French side, and a man who seemed to think his mere presence in a side guaranteed greatness.

Fernandez was one of the worst enemies Anelka could have picked. As a player he'd won Euro 1984 with France, won the title with PSG in 1986 and then scored the winning penalty after a thrilling quarter-final with Brazil at the Mexico World Cup.

As a manager he won the cup double with PSG in 1995, took his team to the semi-finals of the Champions League the same year (still their best ever performance in that competition) and won the Cup Winners Cup in 1996, still the only untainted French victory in a European competition, before risibly getting the sack for failing to win the league.

In a fight for the fans' affections Anelka didn't have a prayer. He later wrote that he was "disappointed" with the attitude of the Parisian public towards him, saying he could feel hatred in their looks and that they expected too much of him.

But if he was as good as he believed he was they had every right to expect more than the goal that he was delivering every four and a half games.

The reality was that Anelka was no longer fit to be mentioned in the same breath as Ronaldo and Henry, or even Andy Cole and Kevin Phillips. His scoring ratio was on a par with Kevin Davies and Emile Heskey, both of whom were famed for their selfless work rate and devotion to the cause, qualities Anelka wasn't conspicuously noted for.

In December 2001, with his homecoming having turned irreversibly sour, Anelka was offered a way out by Gerard Houllier, who took him to Anfield on loan as a replacement for Robbie Fowler.

When the loan deal expired Anelka was at a loss when Houillier chose not to offer him a permanent deal, but again he shouldn't have been overly surprised.

His goals-per-game ratio had improved slightly, but it was still markedly inferior to Fowler's and for all his talent he was being outperformed by dozens of apparently inferior strikers around the European leagues.

He was further humbled when Roger Lemerre left him out of the 2002 WorldCup squad, preferring Djibril Cisse, though given the humiliation that followed in the far east he may have dodged a bullet there and he did at least appear to be maturing.

In mitigation he was still only 22 and at Liverpool the reports of him being a disruptive influence in the dressing room dried up, with Steven Gerrard later saying he couldn't understand Houillier's decision to let him go.

Instead PSG sold him to Manchester City, for a loss of £7million.

He got on well with his new manager, Kevin Keegan and did well enough in two and a half seasons with City, but when he equalised against Arsenal at Highbury, early in the 2002-03 season, there was something heart-hearted about the "shush" gesture he made to those of us sitting in the Clock End - and in the response he received in return.

He may have got the odd v-sign but so does almost every player who scores in front of opposition fans and this was hardly the same as Sol Campbell going back to the Lane. Wiltord had already put Arsenal ahead, Henry would soon restore the lead and when the game was over hardly anyone at Highbury left the ground wishing Anelka was still an Arsenal player.

In January 2005 he was sold to Fenerbahce for less than a third of the price PSG had paid for him four and half years earlier, an indication that the market's view of his talents was at least starting to correspond to reality.

This was a move that had the potential to go seriously wrong given how frequently the passion of Turkish fans spills over into aggression, but at 26 he was now a far wiser man and as a practising Muslim of ten years he had something in common with the fans that other Turkish imports lacked.

It's easy to mock those who find religion and sport is littered with examples, like the drug-taking cyclist Luc Leblanc and the match-fixing cricketer Hansie Cronje, whose public displays of faith only served to invite ridicule. For Anelka however, his conversion to Islam seems to have had a genuinely stabilising affect.

He was not a zealot who lectured his peers in the manner of the sanctimonious South African fast bowler Fanie DeVilliers, he simply saw his faith as a natural product of growing up with a number of muslim friends in the banlieue.

"I worship at home and it suits me well," he wrote. "I'm a homebody. Maybe if I was less well known I would frequent mosques more, but for me it's a private thing and I obviously didn't sign for an Istanbul club because of its mosques or because it was a muslim country! Being (a muslim) seems something natural to me."

This time his integration was helped by a Belgian-born defender, Onder Turaci and he won the Turkish title at the first attempt.

Yet despite professing his love for the city and his admiration for the country, within 18 months he was on the move again, this time to Bolton.

There aren't many supporters at home or abroad who would regard Bolton as a "big club" and while a dwindling number of supporters can remember their FA Cup win in 1958, for much of their history they have been a provincial side who floated around the divisions before their initial return to the top flight in 1995 under Bruce Rioch, since when they have acted as a serial irritant to Arsenal.

Their subsequent supremo, the gum-chewing Black Country boy Sam Allardyce, is one of the most despised figures among Arsenal fans, though most would grudgingly admit his skill as a manager.

Under Allardyce, Bolton reached new heights and qualified for Europe for the first time by investing heavily in talent like Anelka and El Hadji Djouf once they'd established themselves in the top flight.

Part of Allardyce's genius was his ability to get the best out of both journeymen professionals and perceived underachievers like Anelka and Diouf.

Against Arsenal early in the 06-07 campaign Anelka scored his first Bolton goal, a brilliant solo effort that dipped over Jens Lehmann to make it 2-0. He followed it with a classy finish late on to lift a siege after Gilberto had pulled a goal back.

It said something about the poverty of Arsenal's league campaign, their first at the Emirates, that for much of that season Bolton were considered their main rivals for the fourth Champions League spot and their challenge was only really killed off in April, when Arsenal fought back to win 2-1 at home, after Anelka had scored a poacher's goal.

It was nearly enough to convince Wenger to re-sign him a couple of months later, a move that would have had a certain symmetry, given that he would have replaced Henry, the man who took his place eight years beforehand.

Manchester United were also supposed to be interested, but for whatever reason (personal terms would seem a reasonable bet) nothing materialised. Anelka stayed with Bolton until the January transfer window, when his form for a side struggling since Allardyce's departure finally earned him a move back to a major European club - or at least one whose pretensions matched his own in Chelsea.

Shortly before the £15 million deal was signed Wenger admitted he'd been tempted.

"We bought him in 1997 and he has since acknowledged he made a mistake in leaving us," he said. "When he left here he was a regular in the national team, just ahead of Euro 2000. He left, Thierry Henry came here and played in the European Championship. He was never accepted at Real Madrid, went back to Paris St Germain and it was always up and down for him after that. He had so much class and is now back to the top level, but he wanted to come back here. I considered it because he wanted to put it right."

Had Eduardo been injured a month earlier, during the transfer window,

Wenger might have reconsidered, especially with Van Persie a semi-permanent fixture on the sidelines, but timing conspired against him.

Chelsea's riches meant they were able to sign Anelka as a luxury item, as cover for Drogba while he was at the Africa Cup of Nations and a deluxe substitute thereafter.

Wenger bought Eduardo instead, a decision that looked shrewd, right up until the moment Martin Taylor splintered the Croatian's leg, three weeks before a showdown at Chelsea.

With Arsenal leading that game 1-0 the Stamford Bridge crowd showed its football knowledge by jeering their manager Avram Grant when Anelka was brought on for Michael Ballack.

Within two minutes Chelsea were level and ten minutes from time Anelka set up Drogba for the winner, to the delight of a crowd who'd been singing: "You don't know what you're doing," to Grant minutes beforehand.

In fairness, Anelka hadn't done a lot in the previous two months to suggest he was worth a place in the side. He'd scored 11 goals for Bolton in 22 games before the move, including a winner against Manchester United, but added just two more in 24 appearances afterwards.

He wouldn't have been the first player to coast after securing a lucrative move, but more damaging for Anelka was the idea that he wasn't capable of playing with Drogba.

Anelka claimed Grant lacked confidence in him: "(He) looked down on me a bit, as if I should have been proud and ask nothing of him, because he was the one who signed me from Bolton."

Grant was no Mourinho, but he deserved better than the response he got in that season's Champions League final with Manchester United, when Anelka treated him in a way he would never have got away with under Wenger, let alone Allardyce.

With 10 minutes of extra-time remaining and a shoot-out looming, Anelka was brought on, presumably with penalties in mind, in place of Joe Cole.

For almost every professional footballer this would have been a once in a lifetime chance to make history. Footballers at every level are desperate to get on the field and play, yet Anelka claimed he hadn't expected to go on and used this as his excuse for missing his penalty.

More damning still was his reaction to being asked to take a kick. In the ten minutes that Anelka had spent on the field, Drogba had managed to get himself a red card for slapping Vidic (unwise but understandable), leaving him and his fellow sub Kalou as the only established attackers Chelsea had on the pitch.

Under the circumstances Grant had every right to expect that both would take penalties, but when he asked Anelka if he'd be one of the five names he had to give the officials, the reply beggared belief.

"That's out of the question," Anelka reportedly said. "I have come on basically as a right back and you want me to take a penalty?"

On first reading this sounds almost defamatory and yet Anelka confirmed its veracity in his own book.

"I went on very late, without having warmed up because I didn't think I'd be on the pitch," he wrote. "The coach gave me the nod, without giving me any warning … it was a bit symbolic of my half-season with Chelsea. It's sad to say, but I knew I was going to miss my penalty."

About the only thing that can be said of this account is that at least he was being frank and that unlike Carlos Tevez with Manchester City a few seasons later he didn't actually refuse to go on.

But it's a professional player's job to be ready to go onto the pitch at any moment, whether it's for an injury in the first minute or a tactical substitution in the last.

The idea that any player, let alone one who believed he was "the King of Madrid" among other things, should feel affronted by being asked to take a penalty is ruinous to his reputation.

Juliano Belletti scored, even though he'd only played a minute of extra time, as did Ballack, Lampard and Ashley Cole.

When Terry slipped and missed it was a major psychological blow to Chelsea, but Kalou still managed to equalise when Anderson had restored United's lead.

Giggs then scored, meaning if Anelka missed, Chelsea would lose. With the Moscow rain now hammering down, Anelka shuffled towards the spot, wiping his mouth and cheek and wearing the expression of a man who'd just trodden in a cowpat.

Much was made afterwards of Van der Saar pointing to a spot and daring Anelka to shoot there, but the striker didn't need any help when it came to psyching himself out.

Football is a largely spontaneous game, with only penalties and set plays requiring more than a split second's thought once the game is underway.

In a shoot-out a penalty taker will know for minutes in advance he'll have to take a kick and for the mentally fragile that's ample time to forget that all you have to do is hit the target at speed and you've got a better than 50-50 chance of scoring.

It was a technically poor penalty, placed midway between the middle of the goal and the post at waist height, but it was identical to Michael Carrick's successful kick for United and to the effort from Ronaldo that Petr Cech saved. The only difference between success and failure was that Van der Saar guessed where Anelka would shoot.

In that sense Anelka was unlucky, but his reaction said it all. Of the players who missed, Ronaldo wept with relief when he realised his mistake hadn't cost United the trophy. Terry, stricken with grief, cried his eyes out, while Anelka simply shuffled back towards the centre circle like a teenager who'd just crashed a car and was trying to look as though it wasn't his fault.

It's become a cliché of the penalty shoot-out that in the aftermath the television cameras cut to a shot of the player who's missed being consoled by his team mates. When they cut to Anelka in Moscow he was walking alone.

A few weeks later I was at a press conference with the man who happened to be managing the West London club that week, Luiz Felipe Scolari.

Most of the questions were about Robinho, who Chelsea were so confident of signing they'd allocated him a squad number and were selling shirts with his name on via their website.

I'd never met Grant personally but I was told by colleagues that he was the kind of man who could spent an hour at a party held in his honour without anyone realising he was there.

Scolari was almost the exact opposite, a garrulous, charismatic man who had the politician's knack of making everyone he spoke to feel important, including the kind of journalists many managers would gleefully take a cricket bat to.

"Anelka is different that's all," he said, when he was asked how he would handle him. "Sometimes you have to say Anelka, you are very brilliant, but he's ok."

As a motivator he was certainly in a different class to Grant. At the same conference he claimed as many as eight teams could win the league, including Tottenham and Portsmouth, (his broken English emphasising the second syllable to comic affect) and it didn't sound too outlandish.

But once the charm had worn off the question was how would Scolari react if Anelka tried to repeat his Moscow stunt?

The answer came in January when the two had what the red tops called an "astonishing bust-up" after Scolari asked Anelka to play on the left at Old Trafford. With Chelsea having lost an unbeaten home record that dated back four years and destined to finished third, quotes about Scolari's management style attributed to "insiders" began to appear and he was soon fired.

Anelka won his only Premier League golden boot award that season, though most of his 19 goals came for Scolari and he was far more prolific under the Brazilian than he was under Guus Hiddink, who took Chelsea to a token FA Cup win.

The following year Chelsea won the double with Anelka chipping in 15 goals, but the nadir of his career was just weeks away.

It's difficult to imagine how any player could eclipse Anelka's performance in Moscow for self-defeating stupidity, but the French World Cup campaign of 2010 was an unprecedented implosion.

Anelka deserved credit for his rehabilitation after Moscow and his efforts for Chelsea earned an international recall, but his time with France had been chequered at best, from the moment Jacquet left him out of the 98 squad.

The equation was always the same. Did his superior talent merit inclusion ahead of players whose experience or application were greater?

Jacquet thought not, opting for Guivarc'h and while Lemerre initially played him alongside Henry, by 2002 he left him out of the squad altogether in favour of Djibril Cisse, a player who carried an altogether different kind of baggage.

When Lemerre said: "I've played my life with Anelka," the meaning wasn't clear either before or after translation and Anelka was baffled, but he accepted the decision with at least some grace, which was more than he would do when Jacques Santini took over.

In his glossily produced and otherwise conciliatory autobiography, a slender picture-driven volume that seems to go out of its way to avoid opening old wounds, Anelka is really only scathing about this one individual (though it should be noted this was written before the 2010 World Cup).

He accuses Santini of prejudging him from the start and of lying to him and then belittles his professional reputation: "What has he ever won? One French title with Lyon, and with that team any coach from the division d'honneur could have won it."

Any man of sound mind who agrees to manage Tottenham Hotspur as Santini subsequently did has to have some kind of a question mark next to his reputation and Santini didn't enhance his credibility when he added Daniel Moreira of Lens to the lengthening list of lesser talents preferred by French managers to Anelka during the Euro 2004 qualifying campaign.

When Paris Match asked Anelka if he was still available for selection following this snub he responded with possibly his first recorded joke: "He'd have to get down on his knees before me, say sorry first of all and then I'll think about it."

Unsurprisingly the humour was lost on Santini, who then left Anelka out of the squad for the finals, despite finding room for five attackers: Henry, Trezeguet, Louis Saha, Sidney Govou, and even Steve Marlet, possibly one of the few strikers in history so bad that one of his clubs, Fulham, actually resorted to legal action to get their money back.

When that attacking sextet failed to make a breakthrough against Greece in the quarter-finals Santini entered career oblivion at the Lane, and a chastened French side began six tumultuous years with Raymond Domenech in charge.

Where Santini lacked charisma and disguised his talents too well, Domenech was like a cross between Mick McCarthy and Glenn Hoddle, a hard, disciplinarian who invited ridicule by publicising his ludicrous beliefs in astrology.

Domenech left Anelka out of the 2006 squad, preferring Govou when Cisse was injured, but he did take him for the Euro 2008 finals, during which he was neither better nor worse than the rest of his humbled squad.

In qualifying for South Africa 2010 it was Anelka who scored what proved to be a crucial away goal in the 1-0 win in the first leg of the play-offs in Ireland but a perfect storm was brewing with Domenech.

Almost everyone who witnessed France reach the 2006 final felt they had done so in spite of Domenech rather than because of him, but the Federation would have found it politically difficult to sack him after he surpassed his brief of getting to the last four.

Even so, there were grounds for believing he was insane. Excluding Pires because he was a Scorpio was one of them; proposing to his girlfriend during the live television interview that followed the Euro 2008 defeat to Italy was another.

Asked what he had to say to those expecting him to resign, he replied: "Nothing. I've just one thing to say today, I have only one project and that's to marry Estelle."

The proposal went about as well as everything else he'd tried during the tournament, but he kept his job and stumbled through to South Africa, which led Anelka to pay him a glowing tribute in his book.

"Of all four national team coaches that I've worked with, I have the best relationship with him," he wrote. "He realised that I wasn't a shit stirrer. I can talk with him calmly, about everything and nothing. He's different to his predecessors, he gives clear explanations to the team. Until then dialogue had been non-existent. I know he gets on the nerves of a lot of French people and I can understand that if you judge him by his press conferences when he likes to provoke people, but if the journalists play him at that game he'll take them on. While he's doing that he shields us from our critics, even if (in private) he doesn't spare us."

He went on. "I know he's unpopular, but I can assure you he's a fun guy ... I'm not one of his (closest) mates, but he knows he can count on me."

The value of that promise was demonstrated at half-time during France's second group game with Mexico.

Their opening 0-0 draw with Uruguay was considered disappointing and although given the Uruguayans' subsequent performances this wasn't a bad result in hindsight, Anelka had had a poor game, doing nothing to justify his selection ahead of Henry.

Reports of players revolting resurfaced but whether or not a delegation demanded Henry's inclusion for the Mexico game, Domenech stuck to his guns and Anelka started again.

Under the circumstances he might have been expected to run through the proverbial brick wall for his manager, but instead he had so miserable a 45 minutes that he ended up losing a substantial sum of money in legal fees after unsuccessfully suing L'Equipe for its description of what happened during the break.

Anelka, who hadn't managed a shot on target in 429 minutes for France up to and including the finals, was accused of failing to follow instructions and of leaving his post, forcing Sidney Govou to cover for him and destabilising the team as a result.

It was reported that when Domenech threatened to take him off, he replied: "Go fuck yourself, you dirty son of a whore."

L'Equipe chose to report this incident by putting those exact words all over its front page in an unprecedented display of profanity by a mainstream publication. As someone who thoroughly enjoys a decent swear I wasn't offended by their actions, but I was stunned they'd had the brass neck to do it.

Anyone who's been to a football ground, let alone sat in a dressing room, would have known exchanges like this happen all the time and while it was unusual for it to leak, what was more damaging to Anelka was what followed.

In the heat of the moment players aren't expected to act like the bishop of Durham, but Domenech's alleged response was to say "right, you're off," to which Anelka replied "Ouai, c'est ca."

This was a bit like Catherine Tate saying "bovvered," and the report concluded by saying that Anelka had been smiling after the match, plainly unconcerned by the 2-0 defeat.

It's dangerous to read too much into a smile or to pin all the blame on Anelka. While Domenech had little choice other than to sub him, his choice of replacement, Gignac instead of Henry, was perverse and much was made of the way the remaining subs spent the second half shivering under a blanket.

Anelka was handed a way out when the Federation asked him to apologise but he refused.

That gave the FFF no choice other than to expel him and when his team mates then went on strike, ostensibly because his comments had been leaked, any sympathy they had with the public evaporated.

Given that they still had a slender chance of qualification the decision not to train was both self-defeating and idiotic, but though Domenech had the sense to urge them not to strike, he then squandered the moral high ground by refusing to shake Carlos Alberto Pereira's hand after the final defeat to South Africa.

Anelka was slapped with an 18-month international ban and was forced to drop his libel case, when a Parisian court ruled the two journalists concerned, Damien Degorre and Raphael Raymond, had merely been doing their jobs.

He'd claimed 150,000 euros in damages and received sworn witness statements from Henry, Evra and Eric Abidal, but Degorre and Raymond were able to produce four sources contradicting them and were backed by the former FFF president Jean-Pierre Escalettes.

"I was personally convinced that very serious words had been uttered," Escalettes said. "The proof: Patrice Evra insisted throughout the press conference that there was a traitor. If there was a traitor it was because there was something to betray. Ribery was furious because L'Equipe had reproduced the words in full and for him they should have dotted the insulting word."

In an affair from which nobody emerged with any credit, it was Anelka's reputation that had suffered most of all.

As he faded as a force at Chelsea there was a curious postscript to his career when he agreed to join the Chinese Super League side, Shanghai Shenua on a two-year deal, a move that could be interpreted as an admirably bold and adventurous move into an expanding market, or as one desperate last attempt to secure a huge pay day, at a reported £200,000 per week.

To people who believe the latter option he'll always be a villain, "le Sulk," a man who let his team mates and fans down, but it's also possible to look on Anelka as someone who did well out of football and whose crime was to take it less seriously than others.

It's also worth remembering that Anelka was almost always a very fair player, who, unlike Henry, was hardly ever accused of cheating. He seldom "went to ground easily" and didn't go around kicking or elbowing people like Wayne Rooney.

When he scored a goal he celebrated with an understated butterfly gesture and at least he never kissed a badge.

If he didn't care about the game as much as others claimed to it's not necessarily a character flaw to realise there's life beyond the game.

Anelka didn't have the career he might have expected, but he'll almost certainly have a long and happy retirement.

9) EMMANUEL PETIT

THERE was a point, during the latter part of the summer of 1998, when to the untrained eye Emmanuel Petit looked like one of the luckiest men on the face of the earth.

A double-winner with Arsenal, Petit had just scored the final goal in France's 3-0 win over Brazil in the World Cup final when he put a 10-franc coin into a slot machine in a Monte Carlo and won a £17,000 jackpot.

Petit was doing a job half the population in the world dreamt of doing and the other half, with probably a fair amount of overlap, wanted to have sex with him.

This, however, was an isolated period of sunshine in a life that was pockmarked with tragedy from an early age.

His life story could and may yet make for an excellent work of literature, but the first attempt, his autobiography, "A Fleur de Peau," is, in common with most examples of the genre, something of a wasted opportunity.

The title has multiple entendres, none of them easily translatable, though "highly strung" seems fairly apt.

On the front cover Petit can be seen with his hands behind his head, hair tied into the trademark pony-tail, bedecked in a white shirt with a plunging neckline that reveals a drab-looking but presumably ludicrously expensive medallion.

It looks like he could be advertising skin cream and given that the book's title is also name of a French blog dedicated to cosmetics that isn't entirely far-fetched, but the picture also seems to be trying to suggest a man who is at ease with himself, which certainly isn't the impression you get from the text.

In his foreword Arsene Wenger reveals his early nickname for Petit was "l'emmerdeur", again a term that doesn't translate easily, and one which doesn't sound entirely flattering, albeit perhaps not quite as unflattering as its most direct translation, "the shitter," implies.

Petit was perhaps Arsenal's first French diva, fitting the classic, brooding, moody but magnificent mould.

While he may have been tetchy, highly-strung and volatile, his magnificence was beyond doubt, absolving him for his occasional tantrums, in contrast to a player like Nicklas Bendtner, who would habitually fling the toys from his pram in the manner of a player whose ego was way out of proportion to his actual talent and achievements.

Petit's reasons for being moody were also far more deep-seated than an inability to command a place in the starting line-up or an inflated contract.

It's fairly well known that his elder brother, Olivier, died of an aneurysm while playing football for Arques in 1988, when Manu was 17.

It's less well known that the family had already suffered a horrendous tragedy years earlier, that his father narrowly escaped with his life in France's worst ever road crash and that before his teens were out he would lose a close friend to suicide and his favourite teacher to an avalanche.

The first of these incidents came when his father and grandfather were driving home from a market in Dieppe and saw the police and an ambulance crew trying to haul a car out of the dock.

Inside the car were Petit's grandmother, his aunt and his uncle.

For reasons unexplained the vehicle had plunged into the water and all three drowned.

Manu was only told about that incident much later on, though as a 12-year-old he was present when his mother received a phone call from his father, who was calling to say he had just emerged, unscathed, from the deadliest road accident in French history, an horrific crash on the A6 near Beaune that killed 53 people, including 44 children who were trapped in a coach that caught fire.

The first woman he ever fantasised over was a science teacher called Madame Lefevre, but in keeping with the theme of tragedy that runs throughout his life, she was killed in an avalanche. Shortly after he left for Monaco, one of his closest friends hanged himself.

"In Normandy people don't open up easily," he wrote, lamenting the lack of emotional support he received at the time of his brother's death. "An aspiring young footballer is completely left to his own devices. You are asked to behave like an adult, without being given the tools. In case of a major trauma, young people can pay a very high price for this (emotional deprivation). A family, one's own family can have a calming influence. Not mine. In our family we don't show our pain. You could call it modesty. Maybe it's a lack of human warmth. But that's how it is."

Petit was born in Dieppe on the Normand coast, but grew up in a village called St. Nicholas d'Aliermont about five miles to the south-east.

His father was from Douvrend and his mother from Le Havre, making him a pure Normand. As such he was also one of the few members of that team to boast the kind of ancestry that Front National leader Jean Marie Le Pen would have approved of, though quite what Le Pen would have made of Petit's long hair is less easy to guess.

The picture he paints of his childhood is not one that suggests emotional deprivation. His parents were not well off, but it seems to have been a conventional, loving family background in an unspectacular but pleasant village.

He was close to his elder brothers, David and Olivier, to the point that when he and David broke Olivier's arm with an iron bar the latter refused to tell his parents what had happened because he didn't want them to be punished.

He used to cry when his mother left him at the school gates and understandably hated his junior school nickname, "Carrot Hair", but while he was hardly academic nor was he stupid.

Petit regularly got into fights and although these were organised affairs that observed strict rules, by his own admission he could have "gone bad."

His favourite playground was the Arques Forest, but when he and his friends took a girl there and started to undress her against her will, their victim began to scream.

They at least had the intelligence to realise that what had started out as a prank had quickly turned into something altogether more sinister.

That intelligence also saved him when, having moved on to petty theft, he and his friends decided to break into the office of a local businessman and steal the wages of his employees.

This time the police were called, and Petit, engulfed by shame, kept out of trouble from then on. He concentrated on playing for ES Arques, where his father and brothers also played and it was here that he cultivated the hatred of losing so necessary in the top players.

He first attracted serious attention when he played for a Normandy youth team against Alsace before the Denmark v Spain semi-final in Euro 1984 at Lyon.

Although his side lost 4-1 Petit scored their consolation goal and a number of clubs, decided to keep an eye on him.

He joined one of them, AS Monaco, at the age of 14 in the summer of 1985, a move that provoked a vindictive act from Moustapha Oumechouk, a Seine-Maritime official. He was so irate that Petit had spurned offers from the local clubs Rouen and Le Havre that he sent a letter to Pierre Tournier, Petit's new supervisor, which amounted to a posthumous attempt to blackball him.

Within a year he'd lost his virginity to a Eurasian girl called Sophie in the garden of a restaurant, but this - and a series of petty disciplinary issues - hardly vindicated Oumechouk's decision to try to ruin a 14-year-old boy's career.

What did nearly finish him was the death of his brother.

On April 10 1988, Petit's parents were spending a weekend with him at his residence in Beausoleil, near Monaco, when the phone rang.

His friend picked up the receiver and told his father there was someone from AS Arques on the line.

From the tone of his voice it was obvious to Manu that something terrible had happened. His father began to head butt the walls before telling them what had happened.

Olivier had died on the pitch while playing for Arques, in full view of his brother David. The effect on Manu was one of devastation.

Deaths on the football field are exceptionally rare, but not unprecedented.

Two Arsenal players have died as a direct result of injuries they sustained in the line of duty.

The first was William Bellamy, a promising player from Chelmsford who was kicked in the testicle in 1910 and suffered an agonising death over the next two days.

The second and more widely known incident concerned Bob Benson, who collapsed on the field during a wartime game in 1916 and died in the changing rooms at Highbury having burst a blood vessel.

In Olivier's case it seems he was just as freakishly unlucky.

The news would have shattered anyone and for an 18-year old, from a family already battered by multiple tragedies, the instinctive reaction was to want to give up the game that had caused the death.

Monaco's dignified and respectful way of handling the situation persuaded him to change his mind.

Sending a wreath to the funeral was a small but significant gesture and Tournier's intervention proved decisive.

Petit hadn't always got on well with his coach, a far older man and a strict disciplinarian he likened to Rocky Balboa's fictional trainer Micky, but Tournier convinced him that making the most of his talent was the only way to honour both his family and his brother.

Within a year he made his first team breakthrough against Sochaux, the pre-game tension evaporating almost as soon as he began to play.

Wenger's advice was to treat the match like a third division game and it worked.

"In an instant I realised these guys didn't run faster than me, didn't jump higher than me and were no more skilful with the ball at their feet," Petit wrote.

He felt completely at ease in the company of big name players like Hoddle, Genghini and Battiston and by the end of the season was playing in the French cup final.

Although Monaco lost, 4-3 to Marseilles, Petit was now convinced his future lay in the game.

On the field his progress was prodigious.

He was awarded a then-lucrative contract worth around £40,000 per year and his boyhood hero Platini, gave him his international debut against

Poland in August 1990.

For a 19-year-old it was an impressively rapid ascent, but the psychological issues caused by Olivier's death were anything but dormant.

Wenger, worried Petit was becoming too introverted because he never saw him without his headphones on, actively encouraged him to develop a social life, but he was still almost permanently on edge.

In this context, the international call-up aggravated his issues.

Platini had been named manager of a French side that had reached the past two World Cup semi-finals and won Euro 84, but failed to qualify for either Euro 88 or Italia 90.

One of the most talented French sides ever had broken up, to be replaced by a clique of Marseillaises whose egos were artificially inflated by ill-gotten domestic success and who were quickly found out in the international arena, where there was no Bernard Tapie to nobble the opposition.

What should have been the fulfilment of a dream almost instantly turned sour. Giddy at the prospect of playing for France, Petit made an off-the-cuff remark to the press that he wasn't sure he deserved the call-up, earning him a bollocking from Platini as soon as he arrived at Clairefontaine.

Platini's first words to him were: "By saying you don't deserve your place you're making me look like a cunt. You shouldn't doubt yourself to others. Everyone is responsible for their own career so it's up to you to prove that I wasn't wrong."

Platini's parting shot, "be careful what you say," was delivered with a friendly laugh, but Petit knew he'd been warned.

As a result his relationship with Platini was good, but his new team mates gave him an icy reception. The Marseilles players effectively told him that as the only Monaco player there he was lucky to even be in their company, that he was merely being "tolerated" in their team and that he should "shut the fuck up".

The warfare was not just psychological. In the first training session Petit alleges that only the intervention of Laurent Blanc, who shouted a warning, saved him from a serious injury at the hands of OM keeper Pascal Olmeta, who, he claims, aimed a flying kick at him.

Later he saw Platini playing boules with the Marseilles players and realised reporting the issue would have been futile.

The scars multiplied when he realised what OM were being allowed to get away with at the time, though he only knew for certain that he wasn't being paranoid when Wenger called him into his office, two days after the pivotal 3-0 defeat in the 91-92 title run-in.

Not for the first time, Petit wondered if he should give up.

"At Monaco you're already playing without the public behind you," he wrote. "If there are guys scuttling you in your own dressing room it's no longer possible."

Things would get worse before the season was out. By now Petit was harbouring so much resentment towards the team mates who'd taken Tapie's 30 pieces of silver he likened them to Vichy collaborateurs and then, on the day before Monaco were due to play Werder Bremen in the Cup Winners Cup final, yet another tragedy derailed his delicate mental balance.

Again it was OM who would overshadow Monaco's big moment, though this time they were blameless. Chasing a domestic double, OM were in Corsica and due to play a French cup semi-final with Bastia when the north stand in the Furiani stadium collapsed.

Thousands of fans fell from a height of 15 metres onto ground strewn with debris that proved lethal.

18 people were killed and another 2,357 injured.

Monaco were persuaded to play against their will and better judgement just 24 hours later, at Benfica's Stadium of Light.

It was a venue that could house over 120,000 fans, but only 15,000 turned up, the majority from Bremen.

Claude Puel described the atmosphere as being more like that of a non-league game than a European Cup final and Monaco, who in other circumstances should have been used to playing in front of disappointing crowds, went through the motions, losing 2-0.

Petit was out-jumped in the build-up to the first goal five minutes before half-time, when Klaus Allofs managed to steal in to score after three Monegasque defenders failed to make a routine clearance.

He was culpable again for the second, losing possession near the centre circle after a poor first touch and lunging into an opponent as he tried to recover.

The referee played the advantage rule and the veteran New Zealander Wynton Rufer skipped round Ettori to score the second.

As someone who raged against the slightest injustice, the cumulative effect of experiencing so many serious miscarriages of justice and disillusionments was profound and almost certainly contributed to the depression he slid into in his early 20s.

From the depths of emotional trauma, Petit had emerged to fulfil a dream only to realise the lifestyle he aspired to was a sham.

His prodigious development was also stalling. He made the squad for France's Euro 92 campaign, but didn't play a single minute and was hit in the face by a bottle kicked by Platini after Demark scored the decisive second goal to beat France 2-1 in the final group game.

If that exit was embarrassing it was nothing compared to the humiliation that followed in November 1993, when France were knocked out of the World Cup in the dying seconds of their final qualifying game with Bulgaria.

It was a match that scarred a generation of French fans and players alike, a failure on an almost epic scale and one unmatched by any major footballing nation, before or since.

A French side containing many of the players that would win the World Cup in 1998, plus David Ginola and Eric Cantona needed a single point from its last two qualifying games, both of them at the Parc des Princes, the first against Israel, the second the Bulgarians.

Watching the footage again, 18 years after the events, it still defies credibility that France could have lost either match, though the manner in which they threw away a 2-1 lead in the first at least explains the nervousness that swept through the Parc in the second.

Petit, who played in both games, later admitted that complacency cost them against the Israelis.

Having beaten them 4-0 away the French assumed the job was done, which, with five minutes to go, it very nearly was.

Having recovered from an early set back to lead 2-1 the French were dominant and the otherwise respectable magazine Le Sport decided to take a flier. It went to press before the game had finished, with the headline "Qualified!" and a smiling picture of Jean-Pierre Papin raising his arms on the front.

That wasn't so much tempting fate as begging it to intervene and it did so in the unlikely form of Ronnie Rosenthal, who, with seven minutes to go surged through the French midfield to set up a bizarre equaliser for Eyal Berkovic, whose shot had just enough momentum to roll over a prostrate Desailly on the line.

At that point a draw would probably have satisfied both teams. It would have seen France safely through, albeit a little sheepishly, while representing arguably the greatest result in Israel's history.

Instead, two minutes into injury time, Rosenthal surged down the left wing and crossed for Reuven Atar, who lashed in a winner that left the Israeli commentary team in a state of disbelieving rapture, their voices wobbling like adolescents as they screamed in delight, while the cameras panned to an incredulous French manager Gerard Houillier on the touchline.

It was embarrassing, but no disaster. The French still only needed to draw at home to the Bulgarians a month later to go through, although in hindsight this was a far trickier proposition than simply holding Israel.

The Bulgarians had beaten the French 2-0 in Sofia and boasted one of their strongest ever teams, including Barcelona's Hristo Stoichkov.

After half an hour Cantona volleyed France in front, but Emil Kostadinov equalised within five minutes, leaving qualification on a knife-edge.

(In another subplot it emerged, in 2011, that Kostadinov and Luboslav Penev had entered the country illegally. Neither man had the paperwork needed and so they were effectively smuggled into France over a border crossing in Alsace by Georgi Georgiev who was then playing for Mulhouse. Their choice of crossing point was deliberate. By 1993 border controls between France and Germany were almost non-existent. From my room in Robertsau you could walk to Kehl in Germany in 45 minutes. In an entire year neither I nor any of my friends was ever asked to show a passport despite crossing the Rhine on dozens of occasions).

For nearly an hour the Parc was tortured by the prospect the Bulgarians might score a winner, but with just 20 seconds of normal time remaining that threat seemed to have receded when the French were awarded a free-kick near the Bulgarian corner flag.

Yet in an act that Houillier later described as a "crime" Ginola overhit a cross intended for Cantona.

What happened next was similar to Michael Thomas's winning goal at Anfield 89 (Where Kenny Dalglish, unlike Houillier, never blamed John Barnes for losing the ball near the corner flag).

Kremenliev gathered the ball roughly where Dixon had picked up Lukic's pass and laid the ball off to Penev.

His floated pass landed as perfectly for Kostadinov as Smith's lay off did for Thomas, but with the angle against him the danger still seemed slight, until Kostadinov let rip with a stunning shot that crashed in off the underside of the crossbar, at the exact second 90 minutes expired.

French television producers were so stunned they initially put up a caption that read France 2 Bulgaria 1.

As a student living in France at the time I'm not too proud to say that I laughed at this point, when I should have realised this was the worst feeling any sports fan could experience within the parameters of the game.

Deschamps exited the field in tears. Papin produced an outburst that was within days being pitilessly satirised by the French equivalent of Spitting Image, his puppet's catchphrase "affreux, affreux, affreux, affreux!" becoming especially popular among teenagers, students and Belgians.

Cantona blamed the Parisian public, claiming it was not and never would be a "football town," while Houllier launched an astonishingly ill-considered character assassination.

"David Ginola has sent an exocet through the heart of French Football," he said, in the kind of personal attack on an individual almost never perpetrated by a supposedly top manager. "He has committed a crime against the team. I repeat a crime against the team."

Years later the wound was still open and gaping, unhealed by two World Cup finals and a European Championship. Houillier called Ginola a bastard and the latter unsuccessfully sued.

Even for someone with Petit's background it was a devastating blow and he was not spared the lash in the nightmare of recrimination that followed.

Making the mistake of walking into the newsagent-cum-bookshop where his partner worked, Petit started to read the newspapers.

The consensus was that as Petit was the left back - and that as Kostadinov had scored from the position, he was to blame.

Ginola's "crime" had caught him off guard, although that could be said of the entire team. Caught between two minds he initially tried to pressure Penev, but by then the ball was already flying over his head and that of Laurent Blanc, the covering defender.

It didn't look good, but when he was left out of the squad for France's next match, a friendly with Italy, Petit felt he was being scapegoated, even though by his own admission he was becoming more and more mediocre.

Having previously dedicated himself to football as a means of dealing with his grief, this was a dangerous time for Petit.

Deep in depression he started to smoke marijuana and cheated on his wife, before choosing a supposedly romantic holiday in the Seychelles to tell her he was leaving her.

After "three years of debauchery" he somewhat improbably turned his career round when he read James Radfield's book, the Celestine Prophecy, a novel varyingly described as a revelatory and uplifting life-affirming read, or a platitudinous self-help manual for the terminally simple-minded.

For all that Wenger is revered by his players, his sacking in 1994 directly benefited Petit's career. Ettori replaced him and immediately moved him into midfield, a switch Petit claimed was like letting a genie out of a bottle.

Wenger, in his foreword for Petit's book, confessed he had been "foolish" not to see what was staring him in the face, but even after the move Petit's qualities were still ignored by Aime Jacquet, Houllier's replacement as coach of the national team.

Left out of the squad for Euro 96, he responded by having his best season for Monaco, captaining them to the title and to a UEFA cup semi-final with Inter Milan, one he this time tenuously claimed they would have won but for the refereeing.

And though he was by now attracting the attention of scouts around Europe, Jacquet again left him out of the France squad for the 1997 World Cup prequel, Le Tournoi, a competition remarkable for the fact that it was one of an exclusive number of trophies actually won by England, the country where his future lay.

Using timing nearly as tactless as when he'd told his wife he was leaving her, Petit announced his planned departure when he was sat next to Monaco's president Jean-Louis Campora during a television programme, broadcast two days after Monaco had been crowned champions.

Handed the microphone, he decided this was the best moment to break the news, killing the atmosphere stone dead.

Valencia were in advanced discussions to sign Petit but managed the easy feat of offending him by asking him to leave the room at a key moment in the negotiations and then - he alleges - offering him a bung.

Rangers, Liverpool, Fulham and Sheffield Wednesday all expressed an interest, but the strongest feelers came from Tottenham and Arsenal.

What happened next guaranteed Petit's popularity with Arsenal fans before he'd even kicked a ball.

There are few things in life more satisfying than finding out a rumour that sounds too good to be true actually is, but that was what happened when Petit flew into London to meet Tottenham's eminences grises.

Making it very clear they wanted him to join them, Spurs offered him in net the £28,000 gross he was getting per month. That's a sum that doesn't sound too exorbitant now that Nicklas Bendtner feels he deserves £50,000 per week but at the time it was enough to make him very interested.

Telling them he'd think about it, Petit shook hands and asked if Tottenham would call him a taxi, which he duly took to the Totteridge house of Arsene Wenger.

There he found his old manager and the amiable, French-speaking David Dein, who immediately offered him nearly double the sum Tottenham were prepared to pay, making the deal a formality.

He was unveiled, wearing a startling, pale blue suit alongside Marc Overmars at Highbury, reflecting his billing as Arsenal's second biggest signing of the summer behind the Dutchman, even though, to the English public, he was a complete unknown.

Despite Wenger's warning that the game would be far more physical than he was used to, he still wasn't prepared for what awaited him on his debut at the Dell, where the lumbering figure of Carlton Palmer, still a name that can send a shudder down the spine of any England fan who recalls his aggressive mediocrity in their country's name, lay in wait. Palmer almost immediately cracked him on the knee with a challenge that would have merited a straight red card in France but that was waved away.

Petit however got on well with his new team mates, despite, or perhaps because, he spoke so little English: understanding what his team mates were saying never proved a barrier to falling out with them later in his career.

Nor was a grasp of the English language much use in deciphering what Ian Wright was saying, although that again wasn't really necessary when "Wrighty" was pulling a pair of the jogging bottoms over the coach driver's head while the team were being driven to training.

When the driver slammed on the brakes, plastering Wright against the windscreen, the entire coach erupted in laughter, Petit included.

You could dismiss this incident as dangerously puerile and there is a whiff of the Dennis Wise about it, but it did help to create the kind of bond it's difficult to imagine William Gallas having with Samir Nasri.

Petit knew that Wenger had taken a risk in bringing in French players and despite an excellent start to the 97-98 season, that risk looked like backfiring in the autumn until a players' meeting transformed the season. Precisely when this took place is open to conjecture. Some reports claim it was after a 3-1 home defeat to Blackburn, though Tony Adams' autobiography says it was before the previous home game, a 1-0 defeat to Liverpool.

What is agreed is that Adams said the defence needed more help from the midfield and that the response saw Arsenal romp to the double.

It seems a slightly facile explanation. Almost every time a football team loses its players conduct an inquest into what went wrong and Adams was hardly a master of psychology. Barking: "You've been here two years, isn't it time you won something," at Dennis Bergkamp is hardly subtle, but it's possible it jarred him into a reaction. What isn't disputed is the role Petit and Vieira played for the rest of the season, completely locking down the midfield, perhaps because they didn't want a lecture from their captain.

Another, unconfirmed, story from that season concerns a foreign player who, having warmed up at White Hart Lane prior to the North London derby, returned to the dressing room to inform Wenger he couldn't see how he could possibly be expected to play in front of a crowd like that.

Wenger's alleged response was just to say: "Tony."

The captain allegedly pinned the miscreant against the wall and let him know that if he let his team mates down he would face a lot worse from him than he would ever get from the wags in the Tottenham crowd.

The player in question was never named, though looking at the team sheet, of the foreign players who did appear, Petit and Vieira seem to the least likely candidates. Overmars and Bergkamp would presumably have seen it all before, leaving the finger of suspicion to fall on Grimandi and Anelka.

Having grown sick of playing to the indifference of the Monegasques, Petit loved playing in big stadiums like Anfield and Old Trafford, likening himself to a gladiator.

It's also easy to see why Petit would have loved playing with Adams. He hated cowardice and Adams personified someone who would never put his own interests before the team's.

For three seasons Petit and Vieira proved to be one of the most effective midfield partnerships ever, according to the former, but his autobiography contains an instructive passage on their relationship.

"On the field he knows he can count on me, that I am the first to defend him in physical combat and that I think exactly the same of him," he wrote. "Sometimes on the field we could find each other with our eyes shut. Once we were separated, after 2000, I don't think either of us ever found the same level."

So far pretty standard. But then this: "In private Patrick is a quiet guy. He knows as well as I do, that there are no real friends in this job. We all have an ego problem, linked to competition. Some times our interests are the same as our friends. We can equally find ourselves in competition for club or country."

This is either slightly disenchanting, or refreshingly honest and perhaps both, but his relationship with the fans was almost always one of unquestioning love.

Petit loved the fact the Arsenal fans had a song for him, even if he didn't fully understand it, (he thought the last line was "his name is Porno slick" instead of "his name's a porno flick").

They recognised that here was a player who had transformed a midfield that had been by-passed for much of the mid-90s, when the centre was packed with game but limited players like Jensen, Morrow and Hillier.

The fans' warmth was demonstrated in sometimes unconventional ways. When Petit was caught on the CCTV cameras of the Sopwell House hotel having sex in the snooker room, the manager, a fan, handed him the cassette instead of selling it to the newspapers for what would have been a significant sum of money.

From the time of the Adams' meeting, through the World Cup of 1998, Petit was in a state of grace.

Perhaps the moment he became, to use the much-debased term, a legend, was when Arsenal won 1-0 at Old Trafford, the result that definitively tilted the title race in their favour.

In the post-match analysis Match of the Day's Alan Hansen, then one of the few pundits to have both gravitas and an ability to elevate punditry above parroted platitudes, demonstrated for the uninitiated how Petit and Vieira had worked as a human shield in the centre, dubbing them, "the absolute dream ticket."

Petit continued to excel, scoring his first goal in a 5-0 win over Wimbledon, then, more importantly the only goal in a 1-0 win over Derby when Highbury, now realising a title was in sight, was beset by nerves.

In the FA Cup final he set up Marc Overmars' opener with a perfectly weighted chip over Alessandro Pistone and his form was rewarded with a place in France's World Cup squad.

If that was expected, Jacquet later revealed that when he told Petit he would be starting the opening game with South Africa the player himself was visibly taken by surprise.

While Petit lamented the lack of respect he felt he was receiving in the French media, Jacquet had been watching him in England and having seen how devoted he was to the collective, knew that he represented a safer, if less exciting choice than other left-sided midfielders like David Ginola, one who wouldn't complain while being subjected to the pre-tournament boot camp that helped turn the French team into a unit - by contrast to the England team, where card schools drove a wedge between team mates.

Having picked up a booking in the opening win over South Africa, Petit bridled when Jacquet told him he was resting him for the second game with Saudi Arabia because he was unwilling to risk him being suspended for the "English" style opposition Denmark represented in the third group match.

The Danish game in Lyon started as a nightmare for Petit when he gifted possession to Michael Laudrup, allowing Denmark to equalise an early Youri Djorkaeff goal, but he redeemed himself by scoring the winner early in the second half.

When he was substituted on 65 minutes Petit was cheered for the first time by a French crowd, the public having finally forgiven him for his role in the Bulgarian debacle.

More significantly he was vindicating Jacquet's instructions of a few months beforehand, that he should overcome his shot-shy tendency and look to score more, advice that would provide him with the most glorious moment of his career - and that of almost any footballer - in the final.

World Cup finals are often staid, stilted affairs, with the sense of occasion suffocating otherwise fluent teams. The two showpieces that preceded France vs. Brazil were stultifying, miserable finals, West Germany's bitter 1-0 win over an Argentina side intent on desecrating the game's image in 1990 and a turgid, goalless affair between Italy and Brazil four years later that saw Brazil win on penalties.

Brazil's pragmatic success in the USA was tolerated by fans starved of success for 14 years, but by France 98 they were under renewed pressure to win in style, something they were only partially successful in doing on their march to the final.

Against a side as well-drilled as the French that was never going to be easy, even before the farce of Ronaldo's selection when he was patently unfit to play.

Petit set up the first goal with a corner. Knowing France's tallest players would be covered by Brazil's best markers, he aimed for Zidane, who arced his run and headed the opener past Taffarel.

When Zidane then repeated the trick from a Djoarkaeff corner from the other flank, just before half-time, the trophy was France's to lose and they closed out the second half in what was then a very Arsenal like manner, even after Desailly was sent off.

Petit admitted his mind had drifted to the Bulgaria match during Jacquet's half-time team talk, but as he pointedly observed: "these were not the same players".

Initially forced to cover for Desailly, when three minutes of added time were signalled he allowed himself to break up field.

Knowing exactly where Vieira would put the ball, Petit sprinted past Cafu, hit an angled shot past Taffarel and became one of a select few players in history to score the decisive goal in a World Cup Final.

From there the only way was down. The euphoria was momentary but Petit was hit by the same conflicting emotions Paolo Rossi experienced in 1982, when his euphoria was tempered by the knowledge that this extraordinary life-changing experience was now over.

He was never quite as effective again, either for France or Arsenal, where injuries prevented him from achieving the consistency of the double-winning season.

Petit also seemed to be even less inclined to suffer idiots than he was beforehand. A red card at Goodison Park in 1998-99 prompted him to declare he was finished with English Football and though he stayed for another season he was by now a target for opposition fans and players. The following season he earned a £5,000 fine for showing his middle finger to the home fans at Villa Park.

An anonymous display in the UEFA Cup final defeat to Galatasaray was followed by a truncated Euro 2000 campaign which saw him miss the final with chronic fatigue. Days before the start of the 2000-01 season he was sold to Barcelona in a joint deal with Marc Overmars worth £32 million - of which Petit was apparently only worth £7 million. Thus they joined in a long line of players who, as Wenger acidly observed, joined Barcelona and failed to win the European Cup.

It didn't take long for Petit to realise he'd made a serious mistake.

"If I have one regret it's leaving Arsenal for Barcelona," he later wrote. "I saw this separation as a break-up, like the end of a love story when you know it's all over but despite everything wish the other party would make the effort to stay with you."

Honeymooning on an island in the Bahamas, Petit felt flattered by the interest and irked that Wenger hadn't put up more of a fight to keep him.

Things went wrong from the moment he was stood up by Barcelona's president Joan Gaspart at the club's offices.

Enraged by the arrogance of the Catalan club's officials (whose behaviour in subsequent years would test the patience of the most Zen-like Arsenal fans), Petit walked out when they tried to renegotiate terms, telling them if they didn't honour Gaspart's commitment he would go back to Arsenal, leaving 50 journalists waiting outside.

When Gaspart's flunkies backed down the transfer was finally agreed, with Petit flown off to a training camp in Holland.

He walked into the dressing room to say hello to his new colleagues, but was blanked by a team riven by cliques.

If that was bad worse was to follow when he was introduced to his new manager Lorenzo Serra Ferrer. Reserve keeper Richard Dutruel acted as interpreter and his first words were: "Don't laugh, but he wants to know what position you play."

Petit assumed this was a joke, then when it dawned on him Serra was serious he asked if the coach owned a television set.

What's striking about Petit's account of his time with Barcelona and the "arseholes" he dealt with is just how badly this club, which claims to be the biggest in the world, was run.

The pastoral care it offered its employees was so poor it produced a series of incidents that convinced Petit he was the victim of a deliberate psychological campaign to break him. True or not, the tipping point came when the Catalans were beaten 3-0 at Beskitas and he agreed with a journalist's suggestion on the plane home that the team had "lacked character". By the time this appeared on the front of a sports daily the headline was "Petit: Barcelona have no balls," earning him a lecture from Ferrer and the senior players Pep Guardiola and Luis Enrique.

Given the number of journalists who had hotlines straight to the Barcelona dressing room, Petit was unimpressed by what he saw as rank hypocrisy but even that episode paled by comparison to the club's refusal to allow him to attend his grandfather's funeral, saying he was needed for a game at Atletico Madrid.

When he was subsequently left on the bench Petit knew it was time for a divorce, the truth having dawned on him that he was nothing more than a pawn in Gaspart's election campaign. Gaspart himself tried to smooth things over by inviting him for dinner but the gesture backfired when one his unctuous children started to lecture him on his performances.

During the winter break Alex Ferguson contacted Petit personally to say he'd be interested in signing him at the end of the season and Wenger also expressed a tentative interest in resigning him, but instead he chose Chelsea, his pride still smarting from Arsenal's refusal to beg him to stay the year before.

Ferguson rang him again, but only after Chelsea had sealed the deal, to their mutual regret.

Petit confessed to feeling a "death in the soul" after telling Ferguson he'd already signed the deal, while the Scot told him: "It's players like you I need, ones who keep their word."

Once again Petit realised he'd made the wrong move. In the pre-Abramovich era Chelsea were spending money they didn't have on players and running up vast debts, while running a Mickey Mouse operation off the field.

The Harlington training ground was a joke, with paint peeling off the walls and training pitches so hard Petit believed they directly contributed to a number of injuries to world class players.

But unlike at Barcelona, things improved, perhaps because expectations were lower, perhaps because Claudio Ranieri was a more genial character than Ferrer and perhaps because the team were making tangible progress on the field.

Although Petit felt the team was divided they still reached the FA Cup final, where his body language suggested he wished he was still playing for Arsenal.

"Psychologically I was starting to feel tired," he wrote, referring to the moment a season later when Abramovich arrived. "I had the feeling that I was an ex-Gunner at the Blues. I felt it in my relationship with the fans and with certain players like John Terry and Frank Lampard, who were dreaming of one thing: reaching the summits I had reached. Was it ambition or jealousy? I don't really know, but in any case I never really felt at home at Chelsea."

Nor did he feel comfortable with Abramovich's wealth, or more specifically where it came from.

"When he came to visit us at our training camp I had the impression he was like a mafia boss surrounded by his bodyguards," he wrote. "His attitude disturbed me. I couldn't help thinking that by investing in Chelsea he was buying his respectability and impunity. I don't think for one moment that his motivation was anything to do with a love of the sport."

To Petit the distortion of the market was obvious. Players like Essien and Drogba would, in other circumstances have gravitated either to United or Arsenal, but instead went to Chelsea because they were offered double the wages.

But aside from the few months he spent collecting medals in 1998 was he ever really at ease? At the same time his situation was improving at Chelsea, his relationship with new French manager Jacques Santini broke down completely, to the point he felt obliged to retire from international football.

Vieira and Pires told him not to, feeling with some justification that he would be needed for the Euro 2004 finals, but by then injury intervened.

He recovered from a bout of malaria but tore his meniscus during a game with Villa. Going against Chelsea's advice he sought a second medical opinion from a surgeon who told him if he carried on playing he would need a highly risky operation that involved breaking the bones in his leg and resetting them.

His final match ever was on February 1 2004 when he set up a Lampard goal in a 3-2 win at Blackburn. Ten minutes from the end, tortured by his knee, he was substituted and the following month he underwent an operation.

During a long and painful convalescence, he received one phone call from Ranieri and nothing at all from the FFF.

His contract expired with Chelsea and he turned down an offer to join Bolton, telling Sam Allardyce he couldn't accept his money knowing he'd just be sitting at home.

Instead he accepted an offer from Wenger to rehabilitate at London Colney, with the carrot of a possible deal. Given that Wenger later resigned Jens Lehman, Sol Campbell and Thierry Henry after similar spells on the sidelines this was not an empty promise. Petit dreamed of being fit enough to beat Chelsea, but both men probably knew it was over - and perhaps Wenger knew this was where a great player should bow out - at the club where he was loved and where he touched the heights he never managed elsewhere.

Retirement was no easier for Petit than it was for the vast majority of players. Within a year he was divorced for a second time and he became known as fractious pundit in the French media.

His relations with his former team mates were difficult. He adopted a churlish attitude to the France 98 reunion team and refused to play in testimonials, making exceptions only for Seaman, Bergkamp and George Weah.

The doomed channel Setanta briefly took him on as a pundit, offering him a staggering 20,000 Euros per month before pulling out of the deal on the grounds that his English wasn't fluent enough.

Instead he forged a career in the French media, but even here he was in danger of becoming remembered more for his tetchiness than for the genuinely great things he did on the field.

"He's always moaning, and saying things were better in my day" a French fan told me once at The Emirates. Wenger would surely have smiled at that.

10) GILLES GRIMANDI

OF all the ways a footballer can earn hero status among a set of supporters, Gilles Grimandi's was probably the least orthodox.

His time with Arsenal represents a beacon of hope for any player who initially looked out of his depth, because he ultimately managed to win over the crowd to the extent that he became a cult hero.

Just how he did it is probably a source of some embarrassment to the man himself, who away from the field is one of the game's more placid and deep-thinking characters, but from the moment he gave Diego Someone a forearm smash during a Champions League game with Lazio in 2000, Grimandi became one of my favourite ever Arsenal players - and I was not alone.

Condemning him for "raising his hands" as the terminology would have it would, for me at least, be an act of hypocrisy, though clearly some context is needed.

Off the field Simeone was an apparently intelligent man who went on to become a successful analyst and manager, but as player he epitomised a style of play in which every form of provocation was accepted and even admired, provided the perpetrator got away with it.

In Argentina this was known as viveza or picadia criolla, the inherently contradictory concept of legitimate rule-bending, though it's worth adding that it would be a myth to think it doesn't happen in England, where every league has a park thug who'll elbow you during the game and then act affronted if you fail to shake his hand afterwards.

To an Englishman vainly trying to cling to the notion that the game ought to be about honour and respect however, viveza was a recipe for the kind of serious miscarriage of justice that Simeone perpetrated at the 1998 World Cup.

During Argentina's second round game with England, Simeone barged into David Beckham's back, knee first, making sure he hurt him on both the way down and the way up, provoking the young Englishman into the retaliatory kick.

In no other walk of life would the victim of an assault be punished more severely than the man who started the fight, but Beckham was shown a red card by the moronic Danish referee Kim Milton Nielsen - who applied FIFA's warped rulebook to the letter by awarding Simeone only a yellow.

The memories of this stain on football's integrity were still raw when Arsenal met Lazio in the Champions League in Rome in 2000.

At Lazio Simeone was the ringleader in a team who had a card-carrying fascist in midfield in the shape of Sinisa Mihailovic and several thousand more of them in their stands, creating a poisonous atmosphere.

While Lazio tried to defend a 1-0 lead following an early own goal by Sylvinho, Mihailovic was busy trying to get Vieira sent off by calling him a: "fucking black monkey."

And in a turbulent closing period to the game, during which Robert Pires grabbed a superb equaliser on the break, Grimandi managed to hit Simeone just above the eye, so hard that he allegedly needed six stitches.

Pictures of the incident show Simeone, perhaps choking on the taste of his own medicine, showing the cut to the referee, while Grimandi gives the most brilliant of Gallic shrugs.

If this had been an unprovoked incident on a street corner it would have worthy of a jail term, but it was difficult to suppress a vicarious thrill at seeing this act of payback, the karma only enhanced when the referee failed to see the incident and an outraged Simeone flew into a rage at having been force fed his own medicine.

"At the start of the game, when we shook hands, the Lazio players were spitting in our faces and making racist remarks to Patrick Vieira," Grimandi claimed afterwards, adding, perhaps somewhat disingenuously, that he hadn't meant to injure Simeone. "It was disgusting behaviour. I thought we handled ourselves very well."

If that sounded slightly defensive, it was perhaps because he knew a three-match ban was coming and perhaps because he was anticipating a backlash.

Instead Grimandi was suddenly a hero among England fans still traumatised by the World Cup and the incident cemented his growing popularity with the Arsenal support, after a difficult start with the club.

A website, sadly now defunct, had already been created in his honour, starting the cult of "The Grimster".

A sample headline was: "France Win Euro 2000 Without The Grimster" but it also contained a link to send messages to the man himself, who would often respond.

In the pre-twitter era this had quite a novelty and I once emailed him out of curiosity, asking if he'd found it as difficult adjusting to life in England as I had France.

I was pleasantly surprised when he sent me a reply, admitting he'd found it difficult at first but that he was now really enjoying himself and having some great experiences.

That may not sound especially profound, but it was a way of connecting with a player and a friend of mine was equally delighted when Grimandi emailed him back with advice on the stock market.

My brother once saw him on the Gatwick Express, did a double take and after politely receiving an affirmative to the question: "Excusez moi, etes-vous Gilles Grimandi?", simply said: "Je suis un grand admirateur," provoking a surprised smile from the man himself.

A few months after Gilles Grimandi joined Arsenal, a fanzine carried an article which claimed: "We will never win the league with players like Grimandi in the side and that is an undeniable fact."

Yet at the end of that season, Grimandi had won the league with Arsenal and picked up an FA Cup winners medal, a trick he would repeat in 2002.

None of this was expected. Grimandi did not have a tough childhood in the banlieue, was not spotted by scouts at an early age and did not dream about football as an escape from poverty, because he came from a comfortable family in Gap.

His paternal grandparents moved there from Italy, hence his Le Pen-riling Italian name, but otherwise Gilles was of pure Gap stock and he might never have left.

Its location means Gap is dominated by the winter sports industry, but Grimandi's destiny was partly decided by where his parents lived, just opposite the local stadium.

From his bedroom window he could see the pitch and from an early age he joined in with the junior teams.

He was good enough to be selected for the regional youth team, but at this level he was coming up against peers like Emmanuel Petit, who by his own admission had far more obvious talents.

Lyon and Monaco invited him for trials, but he flunked both, later claiming that he did so because he wasn't ready to leave his friends and family behind, and instead played for Gap's senior side in the Division d'honneur.

Istres and Bastia both offered him deals, but he was more interested in becoming a coach.

"I was very flattered by their offers and negotiations were going well, but at the last moment I decided to give it all up," he said. "At the moment I wasn't sure about becoming a professional footballer and earning my living that way. I didn't know if that was a good way of doing it and my parents wanted me to get my baccalaureat … to be honest (football) wasn't my main preoccupation, I was just happy with my easy life. I had to force myself to study for my precious bac."

A recurring theme in Grimandi's infrequent interviews over the years is that he is happy with what he has out of life and sees anything else as a bonus.

He was 19 when his performances for Gap earned him an offer from Monaco, but where a majority of players of that age would have seized the chance, Grimandi agonised both before and after accepting it.

Accept he did however, and it was here that the work ethic that would prove crucial throughout his career turned him into a first-team player.

After a productive year in the reserves he was given his debut against Nancy by the man he would continue to call "Monsieur Wenger" in November 1991, just after his 21st birthday.

Military service restricted him to eight appearances the following season, but by 93-94 he was back in the frame, helping Monaco reach the semi-finals of the Champions League.

He was a squad player for most of his time there, averaging just 11 games per season, but when Monaco won the title under Jean Tigana in 1996-97 Grimandi was more heavily involved, playing 24 times.

Something still wasn't right however.

"Despite our good results the atmosphere at the heart of the group wasn't very good," he said. "Relationships between players were complicated (but) to be honest I never thought of leaving Monaco at that time and I was in that frame of mind when Arsenal approached me."

Grimandi tried to get advice from Eric Cantona, who had a house in a village near Gap, but when he couldn't find him he decided to sign anyway, saying his only reservation was about the climate.

There was now a growing French enclave at Highbury and his compatriots called him "bouclette" because of the curly hair that made him look a slightly unlikely footballer.

Curly hair in itself didn't preclude Graham Rix or Ray Parlour from a career in the game, but combined with a slightly startled looking facial expression and some shaky early performances, it did make Grimandi look as though he'd just wandered out of a university refectory and into the Arsenal dressing room by mistake.

It didn't help that he was deployed as cover for Adams, Bould and Keown in central defence, where his every mistake would be highlighted, but he had a look in his eyes that resembled fear.

Grimandi said he was fascinated by the idea of playing in front of 40,000 fans every week, but performing under that weight of expectation was something he struggled to get used to.

With Monaco he seldom played in front of more than a few thousand and on the rare occasions he did, e.g. the 1997 UEFA cup semi-final with Inter, the hostility of the crowd was expected because he was playing for the opposition.

At Highbury however he seemed to radiate nervousness, which was exacerbated by the reaction of the crowd. Derision is far harder to deal with when it comes from your own fans and although it never reached the levels later suffered by Emmanuel Eboue, there were times when a perceived error would provoke audible abuse.

As the team's performances improved however, the atmosphere became more forgiving and Grimandi, who'd be playing at every position across the back four, started to turn the tide when he scored the only goal in a 1-0 win over Crystal Palace, when injuries forced Wenger to pick what was effectively a reserve side.

Hovering to the left of the goal just outside the six-yard box, Grimandi, covering for Nigel Winterburn at left back, volleyed in a partially cleared corner from a difficult angle and looked as surprised as anyone to see it fly in.

His delight was obvious, as was that of his team mates, and although it was his only goal of the season it clearly lifted both his self-esteem and the esteem of the crowd.

Yet while his versatility was now being seen as an asset, Grimandi was never going to be a first-choice in a team of that calibre and he described the following season as "a form of torture" as he competed with Nelson Vivas for the role of chief domestique.

1999-2000 was better and although he was sent off twice, the second dismissal came in a 2-1 win against Tottenham and a red card against Spurs rarely lowered an Arsenal player in the eyes of the fans.

Petit's departure in the summer of 2000 opened up an opportunity in his preferred central midfield role, but it was while covering for Adams in the Champions League at Lazio that he lamped Simeone and cemented his status as an unlikely Arsenal legend.

"Two or three seconds later I thought why did you react like that," he told the Guardian shortly afterwards, apparently oblivious to the clamour for an honorary knighthood that was now gathering. "I react too quickly. Off the pitch I don't like fights, I'm not aggressive, but it's my personality in football. I got two or three red cards at Monaco as well. Sometimes opposing players are not fair but I have to learn not to react. I'm 29 and I think I'm going to stay calm now."

He did, to an extent. Moments after missing a sitter in the stoppage time in a 0-0 draw at Villa Park on a bitter March afternoon, Grimandi was sent off for a second bookable offence, but that was his final red card for Arsenal and the yellow cards dried up.

His contribution to Wenger's second double is often overlooked, but he made 40 appearances in defence and midfield, often as a substitute to stabilise the team in the closing stages and see out a result (precisely the kind of player Arsenal so obviously lacked during the miserable end to the 2010-

11 campaign.)

At 31 however he reportedly wanted to play more and a curious lull followed his departure from Arsenal that summer, as he spurned a number of offers from Japan, France and Middlesbrough, before eventually accepting what looked like an attractive deal to play in the MLS for the Colorado Rapids in January 2003.

"Unfortunately it wasn't any fun," he reflected a few years later. "In my era Beckham hadn't yet arrived, the clubs lacked ambition and didn't have the structures they needed… there is something missing mentally. Football is not a passion for people in this country. The professional players have chosen soccer by default, having failed at other popular sports. They are not born competitors."

Nor did the political climate help. While Britain's ostensibly left-wing government was bending over backwards in an effort to help the US invade Iraq, France's right-wing administration was frantically trying to make both countries pull back from the brink.

While most versions of history vindicate Jacques Chirac's stance, what was seen as bravery (or just sanity) on one side of the Atlantic was interpreted as cowardice on the other.

The term "cheese-eating surrender monkey", originally coined by a writer from the television show The Simpsons as a joke, became the insult of choice for describing the French, among diplomats and rednecks alike.

A turkey of a comedy called "Slap Her She's French" was released, but not everyone in the audience realised this was a gag as opposed to an instruction.

Grimandi, who was writing an online diary for Icons at the time, revealed he'd been abused in the street just for being French and this added to the pressures he was under, having gone from being a utility player to the top earner in a matter of months.

The Rapids planned to build their entire sound around Grimandi, but he played just once, in a pre-season friendly, before agreeing to sever his ties with the club.

Although he initially said he wanted to continue playing, the brief experience with Colorado seemed to have made him realise just what a comedown playing almost anywhere else would have been after spending so many years alongside the likes of Vieira and Bergkamp.

He became Director of Football at Valence in 2004, but when they went bankrupt within a year he began scouting for Arsenal instead, taking on ever increasing responsibilities over time, even if he was never made Director of Football, as it was rumoured he might be in 2007.

The second incident that enshrined his status as a cult hero came four years after he retired, when he was asked to play in Dennis Bergkamp's testimonial against Ajax.

With a few minutes remaining Edgar Davids was bearing down on an empty net, when Grimandi, the covering defender, simply wiped him out from behind.

Again context is everything. In a competitive game he'd have been sent off and pilloried for giving away a penalty but the referee, Mario van der Ende, played along, by keeping his cards in his pocket.

Davids, cast in this pantomime as the villainous ex-Tottenham player, picked himself up to shake his assailant's hand and Grimandi, realising he'd got away with it, broke out into a rare grin, while the crowd were already on their feet laughing. Ajax entered into the spirit of things by missing the penalty.

It was probably one of the funniest things I've ever seen, in or outside a football stadium and it's also probably the most memorable image of his Arsenal career.

Grimandi didn't have the talent of Nasri or Fabregas, but he ended up winning more medals than either. More importantly, if you're an Arsenal fan, it's almost impossible to think of him without smiling.

11) DAVID GRONDIN

DAVID Grondin's claim to fame is that he is perhaps the first French player who didn't make it at Arsenal, his career following a similar trajectory to scores of Englishmen who had fleeting spells in the first team before drifting into lesser leagues after being farmed out on loan.

In five years at Highbury, Grondin made just four appearances for Arsenal, making a minimal impact.

Born in May 1980 in the satellite town of Juvisy-sur-Oise, Grondin was part of the St. Etienne team that won the Gambardella Cup in 1998, by which time he'd made three substitute appearances for les Verts and had captained the under-18 national team.

Arsenal had obviously seen enough to part with £500,000 for him, but as a left back he was behind Nigel Winterburn, Sylvinho, Ashley Cole and even the long-forgotten Brazilian Juan.

He made his debut in a 2-1 win at Derby in the league cup, but was then part of what was effectively a reserve team, wiped out in a gruesome 5-0 defeat to Chelsea in the next round at Highbury.

He had more joy in another shadow side that managed a 3-1 win over a Panathinaikos side still in with a chance of qualifying for the knock-out stage of the Champions League, but he was merely one of many prodigious footballers at youth level, who are overtaken by so many of their peers that the adjustment to the adult game is always likely to be a disappointment.

For the next three seasons he was loaned to St. Etienne, Cannes, Beveren and then into the netherworld of the Scottish Premier League with Dunfermline on a free transfer.

He briefly resurfaced with a goal against Rangers in the Scottish Cup, one he celebrated by ripping his shirt off and whirling it over his head in a display of what may have been primal joy or possibly just relief, but he made just 15 appearances with the Pars before heading to Brest in 2004 and Excelsior Mouscron in Belgium a year later.

The Belgian club had run out of money, but during Grondin's three seasons there they still reached a Belgian Cup final.

Grondin played 90 minutes in a 2-1 defeat to Zulte Waregem, though if this was showpiece occasion for Belgian football it was one that only managed to pull in 24,000 fans.

Excelsior were relegated the following year and if it was a surprise when Grondin, one of the better performers in a poor campaign, was released, an explanation arrived when the club folded within 12 months. Complaining he'd been "thrown out like a 'malpropre'" Grondin's experience was comparable to that of many journeymen, trying out with clubs like ZTE in

Hungary and the Dutch side Nijmegen before a season with Mons and 10 games with FC Brussels, whom he quit for "personal reasons."

By the age of 30 he was an unemployed footballer, though he lasted longer than many of his contemporaries and was admirably frank when he spoke about his experiences at Arsenal some years later.

"I was 18 when I left for Arsenal," he said. "It was a dream. I walked in with open eyes, (and) Wenger believed in me. I trained with Anelka, Vieira, Petit and Bergkamp. Anelka was even my best friend. Unfortunately, I just didn't have enough quality."

12) JEREMIE ALIADIERE

Jeremie Aliadiere's Arsenal career was a story of accidents of timing and the timing of accidents.

Aliadiere, born in Rambouillet in 1983, had the misfortune to emerge as a first-team possible when Arsenal already had Henry, Bergkamp, Kanu and Wiltord ahead of him.

The chances for any emerging striker at Highbury were dependant on injuries to those ahead of him and Aliadiere's career was plagued by badly-timed medical misfortunes.

Claude Dusseau estimated Aliadiere was, with Henry and Anelka, one of the best three strikers to have passed through Clairefontaine and when he joined Arsenal in 1999 there was a similar chorus of disapproval from France, with Wenger again accused of poaching.

"This cannot happen," the national coach Roger Lemerre said. "Otherwise I can go to the hospital and buy your newborn child."

Wenger shrugged off the barbs, saying that Aliadiere was an "exceptional" talent who he would have signed, regardless of whether he'd been a striker, defender or midfielder.

His initial progress suggested he could match both Henry and Anelka.

He scored nine times in Arsenal's victorious 2001 FA Youth Cup campaign, was top scorer for the reserves the following year and made his debut in a 2-0 win against Grimsby in the 2001-2002 league cup.

Later that season he made his "proper" debut as a sub for Thierry Henry in a 4-1 win over Fulham and though his total first team experience by the end of that campaign totalled just 43 minutes, when he scored as a substitute in the final minute of a 5-2 win against West Brom at Highbury early the following season there was every reason to believe he would overtake Francis "Fox in the Box" Jeffers, as the fifth-choice striker.

Instead he suffered a hernia injury and a season that promised to be his breakthrough year ended with Aliadiere making just three substitute appearances.

For the Invincible 2003-04 season Aliadiere was fifth-choice striker again, Jeffers having "earned" a loan move back to Everton, from where his career sank without trace.

His credentials as a Premier League striker in waiting were underlined by his form in the League Cup, where he scored four goals in the first three rounds Arsenal played in, including twice in a 5-1 win over Wolves in the fourth round at Highbury.

The manner in which he took one of these goals, shifting from one foot to the other to bamboozle his defender before rifling in a low shot from the edge of the area, drew comparisons with Henry. A long-term injury to Wiltord again suggested Aliadiere's time was nigh, but within a month Wenger had signed Jose Antonio Reyes from Seville and his next chance came in an FA Cup semi-final with Manchester United at Villa Park.

After four months it was a lot to ask of a 21-year-old and the game represented one of Wenger's few failed gambles.

Torn between the lure of a Wembley final and the need to rest an exhausted squad ahead of the second leg of the Champions League semi-final with Chelsea, Wenger did neither, fielding a near-full strength side but crucially one without the injured Henry and Ashley Cole, leaving Clichy to deal with Ronaldo.

It nearly worked. Arsenal hit the bar in the opening minute and should have scored from the rebound, but the game grew increasingly fractious as United used physical intimidation to close the gap between the sides.

Freddie Ljungberg suffered a broken hand, Roy Keane hacked Pires, Scholes damaged Reyes' ligaments and as usual Arsenal were lambasted for being graceless losers when they complained - a little too enthusiastically in the case of Lehman - after going down 1-0 to Scholes' first half goal.

This could have been Aliadiere's moment, but he was anonymous, ineffective to a degree that only highlighted how far away he was from Henry's level.

Given how rare chances were, he needed to score, or at least cause United's defenders some problems.

Instead he gave way to Reyes after an hour and his season was effectively over.

In 2004-05 he went backwards, injuries limiting him to seven substitute appearances with no goals and by the start of the 2005-06 campaign it was obvious he needed to go on loan for the sake of his career.

Life away from Highbury got no easier. He left for Celtic, but having played just three minutes as the Hoops were knocked out of the Champions League by Artmedia Bratislava, he almost immediately returned to London to join West Ham.

Wenger would later claim that West Ham manager Alan Pardew had "begged" him to let him have Aliadiere, in a withering put down after Pardew had complained about a lack of English players in the Premier League, but once again the striker found himself a substitute and this time behind the likes of John Hartson and Craig Beattie.

In his desperation to play he dropped down to the second tier to play for Wolves, but was back at Highbury for the 2006-07 season, during which he made his most significant contribution in an Arsenal shirt.

Aliadiere was still nowhere near a first choice, with Henry, Adebayor, Baptista and Van Persie all ahead of him, but in the League Cup he found a semblance of form, scoring in a 6-3 rout of Liverpool at Anfield that set up a memorable semi-final with Tottenham.

Aliadiere was on the brink of joining Middlesbrough on loan during the transfer window, but an injury crisis stayed Wenger's hand and he played a pivotal role in a tie that graphically illustrated some of the many peculiarities of the men from the Lane.

When Tottenham were 2-0 up after just 19 minutes of the first leg the home crowd seemed to assume the tie was in the bag and displayed the kind of cockiness that so endears them to rival clubs across London.

With over 200 minutes of football to be played they were almost begging for something to go wrong and Julio Baptista scored twice in 13 second half-minutes to level the tie.

With the second leg still to come, Tottenham's fans resembled a school bully suddenly confronted with his victim's older brother and they showed a staggering lack of belief in the second leg at the Emirates.

Needing only a goal to knock Arsenal out, a full-strength Tottenham line-up were outplayed by a virtual reserve team.

Emmanuel Adebayor's 77th minute opener was the least Arsenal deserved, yet with time running out the goal Tottenham never really seemed to believe was coming arrived, when Mido equalised with a header.

Under European rules that wouldn't have been enough, but in the League Cup away goals only counted at the end of extra time.

For a side containing a number of players who would later become part of one of Arsenal's most psychologically fragile line-ups in 2000-11 this could have been a crippling blow.

Instead the likes of Clichy, Diaby, Denilson and Rosicky rode the punch and continued to run rings round Spurs in extra time.

Seconds from the end of the first period, Aliadiere's moment arrived.

A cross from Denilson rebounded back to him just inside the penalty box and he lashed in Arsenal's second.

Even then a second Tottenham goal would have forced penalties, but Aliadiere's strike sent the away contingent streaming towards the exits, well before Rosicky made it 3-1.

It was a triumph and also the high watermark in his Arsenal career.

He played well in the final, but that was against a full-strength Chelsea side with none of the mental frailties displayed by Tottenham and he ended up with only a loser's medal after a 2-1 defeat.

Within four months of the final he'd been sold to Middlesbrough for

£2.5million but in three years there he scored just 12 goals, one of them at the Emirates towards the end of the 2007-08 season.

Even allowing for injuries, his strike rate of one goal every eight games put him in the Heskey class, and it was little surprise when Middlesbrough released him at the end of the 2009-10 season.

He described what happened next as a nightmare, with putative deals with West Ham, Blackpool and even Al Ain in the UAE collapsing.

Wenger welcomed him home as another prodigal son and he even played for the reserves at the end of the 2010-11 season.

While back at Arsenal he gave the club's in house television channel an interview that was most notable for his 'Fressex' accent.

Almost alone among Arsenal's French Foreign Legion, Aliadiere picked up a native accent and some of the idioms, even though every sentence contained a gallic wobble or two.

"It's like coming 'ome really, I've been 'ere so long," he said, dropping an 'h' in the way both English teenagers and Frenchmen speaking English often do.

He confirmed he saw Wenger as a father figure.

"I've came here when I was 16 and he brought me here so you know it felt like he's a bit of a Dad to me you know?" he said. "He wanted to help me in the bad situation I was in and I'm very grateful he's done that.

"I had a few offers and wanted to go to West 'am, as West 'am was back in London and back at 'ome."

He sounded exactly like an English player when he said he "did" his cruciate ligament.

"Every time I was getting through and playing some games I was getting a bad injury and I was out of the side for six months or three months and it's difficult to get back from that."

He said "yeah no," a peculiarly contradictory and meaningless construction deployed across the home counties, and he even went down the George Best route of dating a former beauty queen, all of which suggested his assimilation was almost complete.

The sad conclusion however, is that he wasn't quite good enough, even in the second tier.

Perhaps if he'd been willing to drop down another level his speed and technique would surely have allowed him to net 20-30 goals a season instead of the handful he managed at Middlesbrough, but Aliadiere would almost certainly have been better off staying in the less brutal Ligue 1 in France, where he eventually wound up with Lorient.

13) ROBERT PIRES

THE God Robert Pires fervently believes in moves in mysterious ways and few are more mysterious than the way he indirectly owes his life to a conflict in Africa, thousands of miles from his home in Reims, that left at least half a million people dead and was indirectly responsible for the deaths of possibly another four and a half million.

This extreme example of the butterfly effect dates back over five centuries, to when the Portuguese began to colonise Angola in 1482.

After nearly 500 years of general rape and pillage in the name of civilisation, a nationalist movement (the MPLA, namechecked in the Sex Pistols song "Anarchy in the UK") began a war of independence against the Portuguese, the success of whose mission to civilise the natives can be gauged by the fact that three decades of civil war and corruption followed their departure in 1975.

By then the Portuguese themselves had been learning a thing or two about being subjugated, having lived under a dictatorship since 1933.

If Portugal wasn't quite as repressive a state as neighbouring Spain or the Eastern European regimes of the same era, the risk of getting drafted to suppress the Angolan uprising was enough to convince a young Portuguese man by the name of Antonio Pires to emigrate.

There are some people who get upset by this kind of thing, calling it draft dodging, but Antonio clearly belonged to the Peter Cook school of thought, questioning the need for a futile gesture at this stage of the war and taking a shufti to France, where his brother was already living.

There he met his future wife, an exiled Spaniard, and Robert was born in October 1973. Within two years the dictatorships in both Portugal and Spain had ended, but the Pires family stayed in Reims, where Antonio worked in a car factory and played football as an amateur.

Although Pires idolised his father it was his uncle, Jose Fernandez, who had a more significant impact on his career.

Fernandez, who played a handful of games for Stade de Reims, was a classic case of a young footballer whose talent was let down by a lack of application.

Tipped for greatness by Raymond Kopa, star of the Stade de Reims side that reached the first ever European Cup final in 1956, Fernandez squandered his talent and ended up playing for the local steelworks team, a tale of waste that Pires's mother drummed into her son from an early age.

At first he played just for fun with the junior side Reims St Anne, although they were good enough to win a French junior championship in 1983, the final giving a nine-year-old Pires the chance to play at the Parc des Princes before the 1983 Coupe de France final.

By 14 however it was apparent he needed nurturing and he joined Stade de Reims, who were still the dominant team in the area, even if they were now a shadow of the side they'd been a few decades earlier (not unlike Tottenham in fact, minus the Norma Desmond element among their supporters).

When his commitment periodically wavered his mother would yell: "Do you want to end up like your uncle?" and he would grudgingly knuckle down again, earning his first professional contract as a 17-year-old.

He broke into the first team in the 1991-92 season when Reims were in the third tier of French football, playing five times and experiencing his first taste of stardom when he scored twice as Reims came from behind to beat Baumes-Isle.

Just as his star was ascending however, his team were approaching the lowest watermark of their 61-year history.

Stade de Reims had gone broke and the French Federation never did have any qualms about relegating clubs who were unable to balance the books, regardless of their history.

Reims had accumulated debts of around £5 million and spent the second half of the season knowing they would go down, whatever they did on the field.

They ended up in the Division d'honneur and the squad disintegrated. Pires went for a two-day trial with Valenciennes but was rejected, dodging a bullet given that they were about to embark on the disastrous season that culminated in the OM match-fixing scandal.

Instead he joined Metz, two hours' drive to the east in the Lorraine region which, like Wenger's Alsace, had been part of Germany just half a century beforehand.

The contrast between life at Reims, and FC Metz was acute. The former town is on the map because it is the headquarters of the world's champagne industry which implies a certain amount of glamour, but the centre aside it's flat, uninteresting and often grotty.

Metz meanwhile, with its reputation as a Germanic garrison town, is less well known, but arguably has more to offer, in football and much else besides.

The training regime was far more intense, but Pires, who by now had done his military service, adapted, as he would throughout his career, claiming that conscription helped him to adjust to the discipline needed to succeed as a full-time professional.

The man who recruited him, Robert Sarre, stuck his neck out almost immediately, telling his club chairman Carlo Molinari: "I would like to introduce you to Robert Pires from Reims. Mark my words, he's going to be a great player."

Molinari replied: "I look forward to him proving it." Before he'd even made it out of the reserves Benfica made a substantial offer for him, which Molinari rejected.

Many players - Anelka being the most obvious - would have resented being denied such an opportunity, particularly as Pires's father was a Benfica fan, but the player himself was happy to stay put and continue his development.

Towards the end of the 1992-93 season he made his first team debut in a 2-0 win over Lyon and the following year he was a regular, playing 25 times and scoring his first goal in a 3-0 win against a Marseilles side that included Barthez, Desailly, Deschamps, Stojkovic, Boksic and Rudi Voller - and Manchester United's second Frenchman, William Prunier.

He improved again in 1994-95, scoring nine times in 41 games, a ratio of roughly one-in-four that he would maintain for most of his career, including an 89th-minute winner in the derby with Metz's regional rivals Racing Club de Strasbourg, as the Lorraine side came from 2-1 down to beat their Alsatian neighbours 3-2.

A year later he scored 13 from 49 and picked up his first trophy, the French League cup, after a 0-0 draw with Lyon and a 5-4 win in the shoot-out.

Pires was under serious pressure when he came to take the fourth penalty. Metz were 3-2 down and while a miss wouldn't have been terminal he looked nervous to the point of terror as he walked to the spot. He barely celebrated after rolling the ball past a hyper-aggressive Pascal Olmeta into the bottom corner, but made up for it when Cyrille Pouget hit the winner, joining the general orgy, pretending to hide the trophy under his shirt and then stripping down to his underpants on the turf of the Parc des Princes before jumping into the communal bath alongside his fully clothed team mates.

Here was a very good player who was turning into a possible great.

Scoring vital goals in derby games was a habit Pires never lost and his ability to make Tottenham suffer was one of many reasons why he was adored at Highbury. The following year he hit the only goal against Racing at Meinau, then completed the double with hit his first ever hat-trick in the return fixture. Two poacher's goals sandwiched a brilliant volley from the edge of the area in a 3-1 win, that instantly vindicated Aime Jacquet's decision to hand him his first international call-up.

This was one of the French League's more interesting eras. The crop of players who would win the World Cup was emerging, Marseilles had been relegated for Tapie's criminality, Bordeaux were yet to fully recover from their own financially-induced relegation, Lyon were still emerging and at the start of every season half a dozen sides had a serious chance of winning the title.

Logically Paris St Germain should have built on their success in 1994, but they were distracted by Europe and squandered the chance to build a dynasty. In 1995 Nantes usurped them, followed a year later by Auxerre and then Monaco.

Metz meanwhile were improving to the same extent their star player was. For two consecutive seasons they qualified for Europe and in 96-97 they reached the quarter-finals of the UEFA Cup, losing 3-1 on aggregate to Newcastle, after which Pires was almost continually linked with a move to St James's Park.

In 97-98 the title was an almost unprecedented two-horse race between Metz and Lens, teams that by Pires' own admission were middle-ranking.

The player himself compared Metz in stature to Aston Villa and the last time the English League had experienced anything similar was when Villa and Ipswich fought for the title in 1981.

Metz started the season with five consecutive wins and didn't lose until October, in the derby at the Meinau.

When they went to Lens at the end of that month it was Pires who equalised after Stephane Ziani had put Lens ahead.

It was the kind of goal that hinted he could become an Arsenal player. He sprang the offside trap, raced on to the kind of pass Bergkamp used to thread through a defence and finished from an angle.

Metz however spurned a host of chances to win and the dropped points ultimately proved crucial.

With five games remaining Metz were top by a point ahead of Lens going into a showdown at the Saint-Symphorien.

This was Metz's shot at history and they blew it. Although there were only 18,000 fans in the stadium, they created the kind of atmosphere that belied the reputation of French crowds as staid and dispassionate.

A hefty contingent of Lens fans held up red and gold placards, while the home support indulged in some Newcastle United style fate-tempting by displaying a mock trophy and some giant letters spelling the words "Metz Champion."

23 minutes into the game Metz won a corner. Guillaume Warmuz, Lens' supposedly gaffe-prone keeper, gathered the cross and launched a counter attack that within seconds saw Vladimir Smicer cross for Anto Drobnjak to score with a stooping header at the near post.

Within five minutes it was 2-0 when home keeper Lionel Letizi was caught out by a cross from Smicer and palmed it straight to Drobnjak's feet for a tap in, killing the atmosphere even more effectively than the first diuretic strains of "Red, Red Wine" at a wedding reception.

Metz won their next three games, meaning they were still in with a shout on the final day, but they needed to beat Lyon at home while hoping Auxerre could defeat Lens.

After four minutes Bruno Rodriguez volleyed Metz ahead with a cleverly side-footed finish and within seven minutes Bernard Lamouchi drilled Auxerre in front against Lens, a lead they held until half-time.

For nearly an hour Metz were top of the provisional standings, only for Lens to equalise seven minutes after the break and hang on to win the title on goal difference.

"We're a little bit disappointed," Pires managed to tell an interviewer afterwards with heavy understatement.

The thousands of fans present still invaded the pitch, the fireworks were still set off and it was still Metz's greatest ever season, but Pires admitted years later that failing to win the league left such a sour taste that it was impossible to think of his time there without some bitterness.

He and almost everyone else knew the game was up for Metz. Manager Joel Muller knew the squad would break up and Pires joined Marseilles, against the advice of almost everyone close to him.

Seduced by OM's history and their coach Rolland Courbis, he spurned an offer from Monaco and signed a £6million deal during the World Cup, complete with an eightfold increase in his salary.

It says something about his level of self-belief that he wasn't convinced he was worth the money, when at the same time English clubs were spending similar amounts on players like Steffen Freund and Mikkel Beck.

Early in the season he was involved in a game that strained credulity even by Marseille's standards, after they found themselves 4-0 down at home to Montpelier at half-time.

"When you arrive at a club like OM it's a joy to play at the Velodrome," Pires said. "But there, in the space of 45 minutes, I felt like I was on a boat that was sinking little by little and becoming a wreck."

It was still 4-0 after an hour only for OM to score four times in the space of 23 minutes to equalise.

With a minute left Pires broke into the Montpelier area and was brought down by a tackle so clumsy even an away team at Old Trafford would have been given a penalty for it.

Laurent Blanc scored and OM had completed the comeback of a generation. There was never any evidence this was anything other than legitimate, but as someone who has since covered both the Tour de France and an England v Pakistan series that was disfigured by spot-fixing, I struggle to suspend my disbelief.

The most logical explanation is that Montpelier buckled, just as Arsenal would at Newcastle 12 years later, although Pires wasn't fooled.

He didn't forget the derision he and his team mates had been subjected to at half-time and could see through the adulation from the same people at the final whistle.

OM were neither the relegation fodder they'd appeared to be after 45 minutes, nor the heroes they were feted as after 90.

In reality they were a very good team, but not quite a great one. In the UEFA cup they claimed some impressive scalps, beating Werder Bremen, Monaco, Celta Vigo and Bologna in the semi-finals.

In the second leg in Bologna they were three minutes from elimination where another late Laurent Blanc penalty (and again an entirely legitimate one) sent them through on away goals, sparking a riot.

The first leg had been notable for some sporadic violence in the stands, but this time it took place in the tunnel, where Bologna's players were trying to exact revenge on Peter Luccin, a player who later developed a reputation as a wind-up merchant.

Whetever happened - and with Luccin involved it's not difficult to believe there was provocation - Bologna's players went well beyond the usual handbaggery seen when footballers fight.

This was proper "Motherwell rules" street violence. Luccin retaliated, Christophe Dugarry went flying in and a mass brawl broke out, with players and officials aiming kung-fu kicks at each other, the upshot of which was that both Dugarry and Luccin were suspended for the final.

With Fabrizio Ravanelli and Eric Roy also out injured for the Moscow showpiece, a shadow OM side were outplayed by Parma and lost 3-0.

In the league OM were also impressive and for a second consecutive season Pires went into the final day with a chance of becoming champion.

Pires' goal gave OM the 1-0 win they needed at Nantes, but this time the denouement was even crueller, with Bordeaux scoring a last-minute goal to win 3-2 at PSG and steal the title, (a match dealt with in greater depth in the chapter on Sylvain Wiltord).

Marseilles ought to have been better equipped than Metz to bounce back from this kind of disappointment, but instead of regrouping they sold Blanc to Internazionale and handed the captaincy to Pires.

Like many a nice guy handed suddenly handed a position of responsibility, Pires wasn't equipped to deal with the office politics involved.

As a decent man he lacked experience when it came to dealing with the kind of sharks, backstabbers and shits who infest every walk of professional life.

Although OM did respectably in the Champions League, their domestic form was awful and after a 5-1 defeat at St. Etienne in December, the club's owners set a trap for the playing staff.

Unable to leave their hotel because their own fans were waiting to lynch them outside, the players were forced to stay an extra night and then had to agree to a "crisis" meeting with a group of seriously unhinged supporters at the club's training ground.

Pires reluctantly agreed to go, along with Dugarry and four others, expecting to meet seven elected representatives of Marseilles' many supporters clubs.

It was an ambush. 200 fans were lying in wait and the moment Dugarry got out of his car he was attacked. Security stepped in and the players fled to the dressing rooms while the police were called.

Sebastien Perez's windscreen was smashed, a smoke bomb was hurled through Pires' window and the players genuinely had no idea if they were going to get out alive.

Understandably they refused to talk to the representatives, but they forced themselves in anyway. When they realised they were talking to actual human beings the representatives calmed down, with the thugs outside fleeing when they realised they might get prosecuted for criminal damage.

There are myriad examples of clubs failing to look after their talent, but Marseilles surely have to take the palme d'or. The incident meant the entire Marseilles squad had decided they never wanted to play for the club again.

Pires stewed on what had happened for a fortnight before he went to see Robert-Louis Dreyfus, the club's president and told him he wanted to leave.

It's a measure of how oblivious Dreyfus was that he thought Pires was after a pay rise and was genuinely stunned by the news, but to his credit he agreed to let him go at the end of the season, even though he could have forced him to stay for another five years.

A team that missed out on the title by goal difference 12 months beforehand, avoided relegation on goal difference after drawing 2-2 at Sedan. Pires, probably desperate not to think about it, forgot the scoreline in his autobiography, saying it was 1-1.

"Some people tried to ruin my time at the Velodrome, but I still had some good times and met some genuine, appreciative supporters there," he said. "It was for those fans that we fought to stave off the drop, not for the morons who know nothing about football and made our lives hell."

It was a liberated Pires who joined up with the French squad for Euro 2000.

He'd had a bit-part role at the 98 World Cup, but the part he played in setting up Laurent Blanc for the golden goal against Paraguay in the second round, quite apart from staving off what was perilously close to being a national humiliation, gave a foretaste of the impact he would have in Belgium and Holland.

Two years on he was a crucial part of France's success, albeit as an impact sub rather than a first choice starter.

In the final he was thrown on with five minutes of the 90 left to replace Lizerazu and he was goaded by Desailly during the pause between the end of normal time and the extra 30 minutes.

The central defender asked him: "What position are you playing in exactly?" and if the comment was designed to provoke a reaction, it worked.

In around nine minutes on the pitch during normal time Pires had made no headway at all against an Italian defence that believed it was about to win the championship, but the physical side-effects of the psychological blow Wiltord's injury time equaliser dealt them can't be overstated. Pires was now up against defenders who were effectively broken.

Four minutes into extra time he unleashed a shot that Toldo only just kept out with his nose, which started to gush with blood.

Nine minutes later the Italians' mental state could be gauged when they did the most un-Italian thing possible and gave the ball away inside their own half, then allowed Pires to beat two of them before cutting the ball back to Trezeguet for the winner.

It was a life-changing moment. From being a very promising player, he was now an A-list talent who would never be able to go 24 hours without somebody reminding him of his role in France's win.

Pires could have picked almost any club in the world, but his Spanish mother persuaded him not to join Real Madrid, reasoning that having just leapt from a burning deck at Marseilles he would be in an even more vulnerable position at the Bernebau.

The day after the final he travelled to London Colney, in a private jet paid for by Arsenal, and signed for a fee reported at £6 million, which now seems an absurd bargain.

In his autobiography Pires says Wenger had tried to persuade him to join Monaco in the mid-1990s, but that he was unwilling to compete with Henry for a role on the left of midfield.

Given that Wenger was sacked in 1994, when Henry would have been 17 this was either remarkably prescient or the product of a hazy memory, but when the two men did link up it was on the understanding that Marc Overmars would be joining Barcelona, giving Pires the left of midfield to himself now that Henry had evolved into an orthodox striker.

Wenger left him on the bench for the first game of the 2000-01 season, saying: "I need you to see how matches are played over here."

Half an hour into the game at the Stadium of Light Pires wondered, as Petit had before him, what the hell he'd let himself in for, as the game passed by in a blur of studs up tackles and swinging elbows, but although his late substitute appearance was powerless to stop Arsenal losing 1-0, he was smitten by both the atmosphere and the style of play.

His adaptation took some time. He initially lodged with Thierry Henry and although he was impressed with the city and particularly Colney, which was like a haven compared to what he'd experienced at OM, his first visit to Highbury, accompanied by Henry to an empty ground, left him underwhelmed.

The feeling was mutual.

Fans were initially sceptical about his work ethic, the suspicion stemming from his lack of physicality and the fact that he wasn't scoring goals.

The breakthrough came in his tenth appearance, when, two minutes from the end of a brutal Champions League match at Lazio, he raced onto a long ball from Wiltord and curled an equaliser over Angelo Peruzzi.

This was, at the time, one of Arsenal's biggest ever results in Europe. During the 1990s Italian Football was shown live on terrestrial television in England with a solid audience of a million, while the Premier League was shown only on Sky, then a channel only a small percentage of viewers could either afford or be bothered to subscribe to.

The upshot was that many Italian teams and players were better known than their English counterparts to UK viewers.

Lazio were among the most popular clubs even after Paul Gascoigne had left them and even Arsenal's most experienced players had played very few games at grounds like the Stadio Olimpico.

The Lazio bubble had yet to be burst by owner Sergio Cragnotti's mad "investments" and they began the game with both Claudio Lopez and Hernan Crespo, £54 million pounds' worth of attacking talent, relegated to the bench.

Pires' main emotion was relief. By his own admission games were still passing him by and although he scored again four days later in a 2-1 win at Upton Park, another 15 games went by before he struck again, in a 1-1 draw with Chelsea at Highbury.

At this point the doubters probably outweighed the believers. "He's too worried about his hair," was the assessment of the bloke sitting next to me during one game, but by the end of the season the crowd were swinging behind him.

Nothing endears a player to the Arsenal faithful more than scoring against Tottenham and after getting a breakthrough goal in a 2-0 win at Highbury, just when it looked as though a woefully understrength (even by their standards) Tottenham might hang on for a draw, he tapped in the winner, from a Wiltord cross, in the FA Cup semi-final against the same opponents at Old Trafford.

Squaring up to David O'Leary at Elland Road didn't hurt either, given how despised the Irishman had become among Arsenal fans since taking over at Leeds, but in his own words Pires knew he had to better the following year.

Saying that was one thing. Several hundred professionals were probably thinking the same thing across the English league, but Pires' 2001-02 season was possibly his best ever, even allowing for its cruel curtailment, the knee injury perhaps inevitable after playing 110 games in 18 months.

Raw statistics don't really do justice to the contribution he made. He averaged a goal every three games which was impressive enough and he also led the league in assists with 15, two more than his nearest rival Ryan Giggs, even though he'd missed the last two months of the season.

More importantly he was becoming one of that elite category of players with the ability to turn key matches at times when the team was in danger of losing.

Midway through the season the title race was uncharacteristically open with half a dozen sides still in theoretical contention. Leeds, Newcastle and United were all within range while Liverpool looked Arsenal's most dangerous rivals.

In a pivotal game at Anfield, just before Christmas, Liverpool were battering Arsenal after Giovanni van Bronckhust had been sent off.

However, Henry gave Arsenal what looked like a fragile lead from the penalty spot and Pires then made a superb counterattack down the left flank to set up Freddie Ljungberg for a crucial second.

That 2-1 win was cited by Wenger as the moment the squad began to believe it could win the league.

A week later at Leeds, Pires scored to give Arsenal a valuable point from a 1-1 draw (which the BBC reported as "a great result for Manchester United") and from a personal point of view he helped avert a cataclysmic result when he came on with half an hour to go against Gillingham in the FA Cup and helped turn a 2-2 scoreline into a 5-2 win.

A defeat against the detested former rivals of my local team Maidstone United might have tested my belief that football puts life and death into some kind of perspective.

Pires of course, wasn't the only match-winner in that side. Henry, Bergkamp, Wiltord, Llungberg, Kanu and Parlour all made contributions, but just as importantly there were no weak links in the 01-02 squad, no players who you looked at and thought they could cost you the match.

At the back Ashley Cole was becoming an exceptional defender and going forward the way he dovetailed with Pires would cause right backs horrendous problems for the next four years.

It's arguable that Pires peaked at Villa Park, a week before the injury that nearly ended his career.

With an hour gone and Arsenal a goal in front he was one-on-one with Peter Schmeichel when he executed a precise lob over the head of one of the biggest goalkeepers in the game, before wheeling around to celebrate with his now trademark wagging finger.

For a man articulate in so many languages he was still remarkably reticent in English. After the Villa game reporters inevitably wanted to question a player who was by now one of the hottest properties on the circuit, but after agreeing to be interviewed live on air, he suddenly went shy when the first question was asked.

"He speak, me non," he said, pointing to David Seaman and running away.

Six days later he was experiencing a new kind of despair, the kind a footballer only feels when he realises that he can suffer far more on the field than he ever would after losing a championship in the final minute.

With just two minutes gone of an FA Cup replay with Newcastle, Pires curled in Arsenal's opener in now characteristic fashion. On 15 minutes he set up Dennis Bergkamp for a second.

Ten minutes later he felt the most agonising pain of his life. He jumped over a challenge from Nikos Dabizas and landed on his right leg.

The boot became entangled in the grass, there was a crack, a tear and his knee crumpled in front of the visiting fans in the clock end. Some of them applauded him as he was taken off on a stretcher, others jeered in that way that proves football remains a haven for the terminally inadequate.

Pires cited the physical and mental fatigue that came from trying to deal with a schedule that had included trips to Chile and Australia with the French national team as a possible cause, feeling that a weariness had contributed to his failure to land properly.

If so it means the injury was likely to happen sooner rather than later. At first he hoped it was just a repeat of the problem that kept him out for a month when he was at Metz, but it quickly became obvious this was more serious as the pain started to take over.

Wenger arranged for him to see a consultant in Strasbourg who told him he would need an operation and a minimum of six months to recuperate. He sought a second opinion and decided to wait three weeks to see if there was a chance of avoiding surgery, but although the rival consultant offered him a glimmer of hope, in his own mind Pires already knew his chances of making the World Cup were over.

If his life were ever to be made into a film, the next six months would have to be covered by an A-Team-style montage of Pires waking up at dawn to cycle 40k, running up steps, eating fish and being screamed at by a grey-haired coach, all set to a song performed by either Kenny Loggins or ideally David Hasselhoff.

In his absence Arsenal, then with a squad capable of coping with injuries to big players, won the double, and when the trophies were presented after a 4-3 win over Everton on the final day of the season, his team mates all bowed in front of him, in a "We are not worthy" tribute, the humour of which couldn't mask the sincerity.

In 12 months Pires had become a footballing equivalent of James Bond. Approximately 50 percent of the population wanted to sleep with him, while the other 50 percent wanted to be him and as with Emmanuel Petit four years earlier there was presumably a fair bit of overlap.

The Football Writers Association voted him their player-of-the-year, although his fellow professionals voted for Ruud van Nistlerooy, which at least proved the accolade wasn't a glorified popularity contest.

One of the many excellent and compelling reasons for loathing van Nistlerooy was that he "went down easily" to use the apologists' term for diving.

A year after completing his recuperation this charge was levelled at Pires.

By almost any standards he had been excellent in 2002-03, returning in October and making 49 appearances for club and country. He improved his goals-per-game ratio to better than one in 2.5 by scoring 20 times and he hit the only goal in the FA Cup final, a slightly uncomfortable 1-0 win over Southampton that could easily have been a three or four-goal trouncing but equally could very easily have gone wrong during a worrying finale.

In 2003 winning "only" the FA Cup was seen as a relative failure for Arsenal, but Pires' successful rehabilitation (especially when compared with the less successful versions of Rosicky and Diaby) was a major consolation.

In the Invincible season he played 51 times and scored 19 goals, but for some his halo slipped after an incident in a 1-1 draw with Portsmouth at Highbury, early in the season.

It was a game Arsenal were expected to walk, simply because Portsmouth, a newly promoted side, were felt to be cannon-fodder by the uninitiated. In fact Portsmouth were an excellent unit, packed with experienced, quality players assembled at what would eventually prove to be a cripplingly high price by Harry Redknapp, the self-confessed world's worst businessman.

While Portsmouth were on the rise however, they were tricky opponents and a nightmare scenario unfolded for Arsenal when Teddy Sheringham gave the visitors the lead midway through the first half.

Losing to Portsmouth would have been embarrassing enough, but even several years after the event the idea of the Invincible season being undone by Sheringham is enough to induce a cold sweat.

Which is what makes the events of the 37th-minute a little uncomfortable to write about even now, because it raises the idea that the team's greatest ever achievement was partly built on a piece of deception.

Pires cut into the area, knocked the ball past Dejan Stevanovic and then appeared to run into the defender.

"Everyone thought I had dived and no-one believed me that the defender had touched me a bit," he said years later. "If he touches me I'm going to fall, as if I was diving into a pool, but he's touched me so it was a penalty."

This much is true. He was touched and a penalty was awarded, which Henry scored after a retake. But was it a foul? The most generous way of looking at it is to say that Stevanovic obstructed him.

Another, sadly more plausible, interpretation is to say that he ran into the Serb's leg and dived over it. The replays aren't entirely conclusive but on balance it does seem that at best he was looking to induce a foul, which isn't quite the same as going down as if you've just been hit by an assassin but isn't far off.

In the court of public opinion, Pires was branded, his fall destined to be revived for use in lists of epic dives for years to come.

Nearly a decade after the event it was obvious this still rankled with Wenger, who complained people kept bringing it up after Nathan Dyer dived to win a penalty for Swansea against Arsenal in early 2012.

Pires continued to protest his innocence and it did seem an isolated incident. He was accused of falling easily at times, but the clips used in evidence against were fairly feeble.

And as he pointed out, there were times in England when a player knew he was going to get hit and had to take evasive action to avoid getting injured - Ronaldo, known as a serial diver, could mount the same defence.

Arsenal fans, whether they felt he'd dived or not, were prepared to give him the benefit of the doubt, because he never stopped performing.

Three weeks after the Portsmouth incident he scored a superb winner at Anfield to complete a 2-1 comeback, cutting inside and producing a wonderful curling shot that beat Jerzy Dudek at the far post.

He scored against Tottenham, again, in a 2-1 win at Highbury and hit the fourth in a 5-1 rout at Inter Milan.

All this took place against a backdrop of significant turmoil in his personal life. In his autobiography, published at the end of 2002, Pires painted a grounded picture of his home life and, without ramming the message down anyone's front in the manner of some players, he seemed to be completely at ease with his wife Nathalie.

With a year they were divorcing. An "exclusive" story in the Sunday People described the duo as the French Posh and Becks, which was clearly bollocks, but also quoted an Arsenal "insider" saying: "Bobby and Nat were seen as rock solid. No one knows what's behind it."

That was the trouble with the tabloids. Just because they were written, edited and owned by sick, twisted and morally bankrupt liars it didn't mean they were always wrong. However, a classic example of the way they manipulated the facts to suit their own agenda came when the Sunday Mirror ran a story in October 2005 saying: "My Divorce Ruined Me Says Robert Pires."

The quotes, which it seems probable were translated from an unattributed French source given the language used, didn't back up either the headline or the intro, which read: "Robert Pires has blamed his divorce and contract wrangles for his poor form over the past two seasons."

He did confess to making a bad start to the 2005-06 season, but the idea that he'd been underperforming in either of the previous two campaigns was risible.

In 2004-05 his scoring ratio remained as consistent as ever, (17 goals in 48 games) and he ended the campaign with an FA Cup winners medal.

Whatever the chronology, Pires was soon with the woman who became his second wife, a model called Jessica Lemarie, and he became a father in October 2005.

That season proved to be his last with Arsenal. At 31 he was approaching the end of his peak years and Wenger's reluctance to put anyone over the age of 30 on a long-term deal meant his departure seemed inevitable.

Dennis Bergkamp, settled in domestic bliss in Hertfordshire, had repeatedly agreed to single-year contract extensions after hitting 30, supposedly for ever diminishing financial returns, but Pires was still being offered big money elsewhere.

The favoured destination was Villareal, whom Arsenal had been paired with in their first ever Champions League semi-final.

He played the whole of the first leg and came on as a sub for the second.

Although he didn't really do a lot in either, the same could be said of almost every Arsenal player during that tortuous tie and no one was questioning his professionalism.

His appearances were becoming more and more sporadic however and he seldom played the full 90 minutes.

After Bergkamp he was always the second most likely candidate for a substitution and this was how his time with Arsenal ended.

When Wenger named him in the starting line-up for the Champions League final in Paris it was a pleasant surprise.

I, along with many Arsenal fans, thought Wenger was likely to start with Jose Antonio Reyes and leave Pires on the bench and I was delighted to be proved wrong.

Perhaps Wenger had finally realised Reyes wasn't going to be the player he thought he'd be when he signed him two and a half years earlier.

Against an exceptional Barcelona team he evidently decided it was a bigger gamble to wait for Reyes to come good, than to pick a player who had repeatedly delivered when it mattered over six seasons.

Arsenal, realistically, had a less than fifty-fifty chance of winning, but in the opening exchanges they looked capable of at least giving as good as they'd get.

With 17 minutes gone however, Ronaldinho split Arsenal's defence open. Samuel Eto'o, a player Wenger had previously attempted to buy, skipped past Jens Lehmann, who caught his trailing leg and brought him to the floor.

The ball rolled to Ludovic Giuly on the right and he rolled it into an empty net, but only after the referee, Terje Hauge had given the free-kick.

Given that Lehmann had self-evidently denied Barcelona a goal-scoring opportunity, or in this instance, an actual goal, the only way Hauge could atone for failing to play the advantage rule was to send Lehmann off.

Whether Arsenal would have been better off 1-0 down with 11 men remains one of the great imponderables, but for Pires the argument was clear cut.

Someone had to give way for Manuel Almunia and Pires was, in Wenger's eyes, the most dispensable of his 10 outfield players.

It was a decision that came within 13 minutes of paying off, but it nearly ruined the relationship between the two men and though they later enjoyed a rapprochement the episode left permanent scars.

Not long after the final Pires gave an intriguing interview in which he hinted there was a far more obvious candidate for substitution, but that he would never reveal his identity.

It might have been better if he had, because by letting this cat only partly out of the bag he posed the question: which of his team mates did he think so little of?

Presumably the back four would have stayed on and it's inconceivable he meant Henry, so that left Hleb, Llungberg, Gilberto or Fabregas - and he certainly got on well with the latter.

Two days after the final he sought out Wenger for an explanation and claimed he was told the manager was worried the team would be too defensive if he stayed on.

Perhaps he was being kind. Pires was the most attack minded of the quintet Wenger had to select from, but he was also the oldest and given the way he had been used that season it seems likely he would have eventually made way for either Flamini or Reyes, had Lehmann not been sent off.

Pires' response was to tell Wenger he was leaving for Villareal, where time did eventually heal the wounds, and more effectively for the player than the manager.

Pires had a better work-life balance than Wenger and thrived at Villareal, where he wound down his career over four seasons that included a second-place finish in La Liga and a Champions League quarter-final appearance at the Emirates, where he was showered with more adulation by the home fans than any of the Arsenal players on show.

That was possibly because having won 4-1 on aggregate they were in a generous mood towards a former legend, who hadn't done anything to tarnish his legacy (he'd promised he wouldn't celebrate if he scored).

In 2010 both men were asked about the final. Pires was able to joke about it. "When I saw it was my number it killed me," he said. "I didn't want to kill Wenger but Jens? Yeah I'd have killed the German bastard!"

Wenger by contrast still sounded haunted. "11 v 11 it would have been a fantastic game but we had to take Robert Pires off and he still hates me today," he said. "We had to take a great player out who could have contributed to the quality of the game. It was the referee's fault basically, because we went down to 10 men in a final that promised so much and it became a 'no' game. When a referee makes a decision like that he has to be absolutely sure, you do not kill a final that one billion people watch if it's not really correct."

He went on to blame UEFA for picking a referee from a minor league who was unused to the big occasions, but the impression given was of a man who never would come to terms with what had happened.

Perhaps Pires softened towards Wenger because his relationship with Raymond Domenech made him appreciate how lucky he was to have worked with him.

Pires had no history of being a difficult player for any of his club or national managers but as a man of above average intelligence, he was always going to find it difficult to mask his contempt for some of the stupefying things Domenech did.

Having missed the 2002 World Cup through his knee injury, Pires played in every game at Euro 2004, a tournament France might easily have won had they not picked the wrong day to have what cyclists in the Tour de France call "un jour sans" against the Greeks in the quarter-final.

He and his fellow Arsenal players took the piss out of the coach Jacques Santini when they learned he was going to manage Tottenham, but this was hardly an insurrection and it was tame compared to what was to follow.

When Domenech took over from Santini in the wake of the Greek defeat he picked Pires for his first five squads, but with 79 minutes gone of a World Cup qualifier in Cyprus, with France winning 2-0, he replaced him with Daniel Moreira of Toulouse and never selected him again.

As the exile endured, Domenech was pressed on why he'd excluded Pires and replied, in apparent sincerity, that he didn't trust Scorpios.

The episode recalled Ray Parlour's exclusion from England's 98 squad, allegedly because he'd quipped "short back and sides please" when sent to Glenn Hoddle's faith healer, Eileen Drewery.

Yet although Parlour confirmed he had made the remark, Hoddle, for all his faults, wasn't stupid enough to publicly cite that as a reason.

Parlour, with respect, was a fringe contender for that squad and while the decision to leave him behind was arguably the wrong one, he wasn't as obviously superior to some of those selected as Pires was to the likes of Vikash Dhorasoo and Sidney Govou.

Alarm bells should clearly have been ringing at the French Federation when Domenech went public with his astrological beliefs.

Astrology, like certain branches of religion, might be considered harmless enough if it helps deluded simpletons get through the day without slashing their wrists, but the idea that this charlatan's faith should be used in any professional decision is risible.

"When I've got a Leo in defence I've always got my gun ready as I know he's going to want to show off at one moment or another and cost us," Domenech said. "All parameters have to be considered and I have added one by saying there is astrology is involved."

Domenech did have a dry sense of humour and a sharp wit that didn't always endear him to people he needed to stay on good terms with, but in this case, if he was jesting, one can only salute the brilliance of the joke's disguise.

It's also possible there was another, underlying reason. Plenty of managers have excluded players they disliked and concocted a fictitious justification for doing so.

In the finest French tradition, a story that did the rounds was that Pires had slept with Domenech's much younger and implausibly attractive wife, Estelle Denis.

There was certainly a precedent for that in the national team, when Jean-Francois Larios from St. Etienne was banished from the 82 World Cup squad over a rumoured dalliance with Michel Platini's wife.

Nor was Denis without admirers in the squad. Ludovic Giuly, another player who would, on merit, have been picked for the 2006 squad (and who had just won the Champions League with Barcelona) was banished after sending her a text message asking for a dinner in Paris.

To use the classic formula newspapers deploy when they want readers to infer something that they can't prove, no matter how blatantly obvious it is, there is no suggestion that Giuly's motives were anything other than platonic.

In his autobiography he claimed he didn't know the two were an item - not an unreasonable deduction given that if you'd seen them in the street you'd assume Domenech was Denis's father - and he tried to clear the air when he found out.

"Don't worry, it was just professional," Giuly said. "I wanted to tell you so there was no misunderstanding."

Domenech replied that he'd read the text in question and was "au courant" with what had happened, a statement which could be taken in any number of ways.

"Without wanting to sound like a cad, I'm not attracted to Estelle Denis. We never had a relationship, nor wanted to," wrote Giuly, sounding not unlike a cad, but also like a teenager trying to persuade his friends he never liked a girl who'd just knocked him back.

The Pires story was, it seems, bollocks. Like the Paris substitution he was able to laugh about it at the end of his career, possibly because the dynamic of the relationship between Domenech and Denis was so inherently funny - like that between Ernest Borgnine and the former playmate Stella Stevens in the Poseidon Adventure and a dozen other comic couples from films.

And if everyone who hated Domenech had really had designs on his wife she'd have been even busier than Stevens' character Linda Rogo was in her early days.

It was easy to laugh at Domenech, or at least it was if you didn't have a vested interest in the success of the French team, but he wasn't always a laughing stock.

Like many architects of epic disasters, Fred Goodwin perhaps, or to take it to another level Robert Mugabe, Domenech's early career was actually quite promising.

As a left-back he'd won the title with Bordeaux and Strasbourg (where he was a contemporary of Arsene Wenger and sported a vibrant moustache) and he won the French cup with Lyon, earning the nickname, "the butcher".

He also won eight caps, albeit without ever playing in a major tournament, and as a coach he'd taken Lyon, into the first division before joining the FFF.

Domenech couldn't have achieved all this without some residual ability, but that was a problem.

A congenital idiot would never get near a position of such authority. Yet some of the most dangerous men in the world are those who feel that a round of applause in a provincial theatre means they can steal the show in the West End.

Thus it proved with Domenech. He was hardly the dream ticket when he was named as Santini's replacement and within three months of taking the job he had already embarked on a relationship of mutual loathing with the media, one that rapidly spread to become a menage-a-trois of contempt with certain of his players.

A conversation he had with his rugby union counterpart Bernard Laporte in 2007 was instructive.

"I talk with my players," Laporte said. "I prefer to be transparent so the player knows why he hasn't been selected."

"Moi?" Domenech replied. "I explain, errr ... nothing. At the end of the day you're not credible anymore. The first time you can tell him to hold on. The second time you say, yes, you deserve to play, it'll come. But at the end of the day he tells me 'you must think I'm a cunt.' And he'd be right."

There may have been a certain, brutal honesty in this, but it was sad that he'd never learned the value of pastoral care from Wenger, a man whose record he publicly disparaged.

He also had more in common with Pires than was immediately obvious. His father, a Spaniard called Raimundo, had also fled a dictator, in his case Franco, having fought for the republicans in the civil war. His interests - astrology aside - also went well beyond football.

Like Cantona he dabbled in acting, but he was never able to use whatever skills he picked up with his theatre company when it came to masking his contempt for players, fans and journalists - or female tennis players, of whom he once said: "80 of the top 100 women are sows."

Pires, by that point, was resigned to never playing for the French team again. Ignored for Euro 2008 and realising there was no point in being diplomatic anymore, he described Domenech as a "madman".

He said he felt "ashamed to be French" when the French squad went on strike in South Africa, but he made it clear his sympathies lay with the players, defending Anelka and pinning the blame squarely on the coach.

"I speak from experience, they were managed by a madman," he said. "When I was called up to play for France when he was in charge I felt I was going to a madhouse, I was physically sick. Arsene Wenger used to ask me what was wrong. I would reply that I didn't want to go there, the man is insane."

Pires had long ago said that before he retired he wanted to play a season with Stade de Reims, but when he was released by Villareal in 2010 he went back to London, where he'd bought a flat at the old Highbury, and started training with Arsenal to maintain his fitness levels.

Wenger said that from what he had seen Pires was good enough to play at top flight level and for those who hate seeing old friends fall out it was a tonic for the soul to see them on good terms again, but Wenger also had around eight midfielders he was trying to keep happy and instead recommended him to his old friend Gerard Houllier at Aston Villa.

At 37 it was unrealistic to expect him to perform to the levels he could five years beforehand and the sixth months he spent at Villa Park amounted to little more than a coda.

He never played a full 90 minutes, made only a handful of starts and scored just once, in an FA Cup tie with Blackburn. It was inconsequential but inoffensive, a bit like Villa in fact. In one of the few games he started he played the first half against Arsenal, did virtually nothing but still earned himself another ovation, albeit from the visiting supporters.

A year later he once again returned to the Emirates, announcing via twitter that he was off to training at London Colney.

This caused a flutter of excitement, coming as it did in the same week that Thierry Henry agreed to make a temporary return, but no offer was made, either from Arsenal or any other club in Europe that he could countenance playing for.

For some players the need to keep playing for as long as possible is born of desperation, either financial or a raging against the dying light.

Had Pires wanted to he could have followed a trajectory common among top-flight players before salaries multiplied enough to give them financial security.

He was linked with Doncaster Rovers and Crawley Town, but instead he agreed an eight-week deal to play in the first ever Indian Premier League, an eight-week competition designed to ape the sub-continent's multi-million dollar cricket league.

This was uncharted territory. The money on offer, up to £750,000, was presumably a lot more than Crawley were offering but Pires was always someone open to new experiences and India offered him something West Sussex and Yorkshire couldn't.

He gives the impression of being someone who will cope well with life as an ex-footballer and he seems to have coped a lot better without the Arsenal than Arsenal coped without him.

A succession of even faster, technically brilliant players tried to replace him, but none ever did. For Pires the exception can be made - the word legend has been well earned.

14) SYLVAIN WILTORD

ONCE compared by Arsene Wenger to a French version of Ian Wright, Sylvain Wiltord never quite achieved the hero status of Henry, Vieira, Pires and Petit among Arsenal fans.

Lacking the swashbuckling style of some of his compatriots, Wiltord was also notoriously taciturn, spurning opportunities to engage with supporters and requests for interviews from the English press, thereby cultivating a reputation for being difficult that wasn't entirely fair.

Unwilling to play the PR game, or perhaps just totally disinterested, Wiltord was still voted 33rd in the list of Arsenal's all-time greatest players when the club conducted an internet survey and while these polls always throw up anomalies it's surprising he finished behind both his predecessor in the moody Frenchman category Nicolas Anelka (29th) and his striking contemporary Kanu (13th). Even the pantomime pariah Ashley Cole (25th) rated more highly and given Wiltord's relatively high level of achievement this is something of a surprise.

Wiltord was born in the nondescript East Parisian banlieue, in an area called Neuilly-sur-Marne, long ago swallowed up by the city.

His parents were émigrés from Guadeloupe, which made him another source of aggravation to Jean Marie Le Pen and his intellectually stunted disciples, but a source of enduring pride to the islands of his ancestors.

He began his career with Stade Rennes, who took him on at the age of 17, believing he had a natural eye for goal.

After making his debut as a substitute at FC Bourges in September 1992, Wiltord's breakthrough arrived the following season when he scored nine goals in 17 second division starts, helping Rennes to promotion.

He established himself as a top-flight striker in 1995-96 earning a call-up to France's Olympic squad.

By this stage however, the seed in his mind that he had outgrown his surroundings had taken root and this feeling that would resurface several times during his career.

Wiltord began agitating for a move to Bordeaux but he instead signed for Deportivo La Coruna in a bizarre and frankly suspicious deal that saw him loaned back to Rennes. There he regressed.

Sulking and going AWOL from training, Wiltord's scoring rate dropped from 15 goals from 29 games in 1995-96 to just 3 from 33 a season later.

After that campaign he finally got his wish, signing for Bordeaux in a deal that saw Depor benefit from a 40 percent sell-on clause, an interesting piece of business for a player who'd never kicked a ball for them.

If the method behind transfer was dubious, Wiltord proved an excellent acquisition for the Girondins, where he proved he was a player who thrived on the biggest of stages.

His second season at Bordeaux produced one of the most nail-biting finishes ever seen in a major European league, with the Girondins needing to win at the Parc des Princes to hold off Marseille for the title.

On 19 minutes Wiltord sprang the offside trap and reached the corner of the six-yard box before curling the opening goal past Bernard Lama, in a manner that later became a Thierry Henry trademark.

The man who would become his great friend, Robert Pires, had given OM a 1-0 lead at Nantes, so when PSG equalised on 57 minutes the title was heading for the Velodrome, but within three minutes Wiltord volleyed in from six yards.

It was a poor goal for the Parisians to concede and Bernard Lama's refusal to come off his line to snuff out an innocuous looking cross fuelled accusations that PSG were intent on throwing the game.

Given French football's track record it would be naïve to rule that scenario out completely, but Lama was overrated as a keeper in any case and if PSG were that intent on fixing the result nobody bothered to tell Adailton, who headed a second equaliser with just 13 minutes left.

Adailton's muted celebrations have been cited as evidence of a conspiracy by the Marseillaises, who were admittedly experts in the field.

So was the fact his team mates failed to mob him after the goal, but this doesn't square with the celebrations that followed Bruno Rodriguez's first equaliser, or the point blank save that Lama made five minutes from time.

And if they really were trying to throw the game they were cutting it fine. With 88 minutes and 50 seconds on the clock, Wiltord advanced on goal in support of the substitute striker Pascal Feindouno, who'd raced onto a pass from Lilian Laslandes.

The angle was against the Guinean and Wiltord was arguably better placed, but Feindouno, who was just 17 years old, steered the ball past Lama with his first touch.

This was Bordeaux's equivalent of Anfield 1989 and in the bedlam that followed Wiltord was filmed deep in the bowels of the Parc des Princes, wearing a pair of oversized headphones and rapping into a microphone for the tv cameras. He repeatedly bellowed: "Shagga! Shagga! Shagga!" in a breaking voice, a side of his character that was seldom seen in England - though he did break out some Elvis wigs in the wake of the Old Trafford win in 2002.

If that was dramatic, it was eclipsed by events 12 months later, by which time Wiltord had forced his way into France's Euro 2000 squad.

Ever since Juste Fontaine's record-breaking performance at the 1958 World Cup, the French had a tendency to go into major tournaments, when they qualified for them, without a world class centre forward.

It hadn't done them a lot of harm in 82, 84, 86 or 96 when they reached the semi-finals or better. In 1998 they won the World Cup while carrying the lumbering Stephane Guivarch, so it was sod's law for Wiltord that his emergence should coincide with that of Anelka, Trezeguet and Henry when France rolled into Belgium and Holland in 2000.

It was a formidable looking squad and Wiltord's chances looked limited, but in a portent of what was to follow in the final he scored in the last minute of the opening game against Denmark, having replaced Anelka in the 82nd minute.

In the second game, a 2-1 win over the Czechs, he was used purely as a time-wasting substitute, though with both teams through to the last eight he was given 80 minutes against the Dutch in a game that many people saw as a dress rehearsal for the final, albeit one that doubled as an audition for Lemerre's fringe players.

Although they lost 3-2, the French played well enough to suggest that if this was their reserve line-up, they had far more options at their disposal than they'd had even two years beforehand.

Wiltord was therefore ignored for the quarter-final win over Spain, but he was brought on for a flagging Anelka with 18 minutes of the semi-final with Portugal in Brussels remaining and in another pivotal intervention won the golden goal penalty in extra time that sent France through.

With three minutes remaining Wiltord broke free on the right wing and played in Trezeguet. The striker's heavy second touch denied him a chance to shoot, but when Portuguese keeper Vitor Baia dived at his feet he failed to gather the ball. It broke to Wiltord at a ludicrously acute angle on the right and with a minimal target to aim at he hit a hard low shot that was steered behind by Abel Xavier's arm.

From the television replays it's impossible to say whether the ball would have gone in, but it was an unquestionable penalty, albeit one that the Portuguese spent several minutes protesting about hysterically both before and after Zidane slammed the ball into the top corner.

Xavier's arm may have denied Wiltord his moment of individual glory, but that would come five days later in Rotterdam.

The Italians had produced a defensive display for the ages to win their semi-final, on penalties, against the Dutch and they looked almost watertight after taking a 55th minute lead in the final through Marco Delvecchio.

Wiltord came on three minutes later, the BBC's commentators John

Motson and Mark Lawrenson both calling him Viltord, presumably because they thought this was the correct pronunciation (in fairness to both there are hardly any words in French that begin with a w - even the bigger dictionaries can't fill a page of A4 with entries and most of those are adopted from other languages).

Against an Italian defence that was as well organised as the famous Arsenal back four but with greater technical expertise, the French attacks were frequently strangled at birth.

Even when Del Piero spurned an easy chance with minutes remaining it looked like proving academic, until with 75 seconds of added time remaining the Italians made a minor but crucial error when Vincenzo Montella strayed offside and ceded possession.

Barthez, throwing out all sophistication, opted for a kick straight from the coaching manuals of the FA's controversial strategist Charles Hughes and hoofed the ball into the "Position of Maximum Opportunity."

Trezeguet won the header and the ball was deflected into Wiltord's path.

Chesting the ball down, he put himself in a position to shoot. The angle, this time from the left, once again seemed unfavourable but Wiltord took the chance with his left foot and drove the ball fractionally past the trailing leg of Alessandro Nesta and just under the keeper, Francesco Toldo, before running to the corner flag where he celebrated by grinning and wagging his finger.

You could argue it was a lucky goal and it was in terms of its timing and the sense that the margins were wafer thin. In terms of percentages it was a shot that would more often than not have either flown off the striker's boot and either wide or over. Even a shot on target would more often than not have hit either Nesta or Toldo, but Wiltord deserved credit both for perseverance and the precision of his effort.

It was probably one of the most psychologically destructive goals ever scored, as although the Italians stood a theoretical chance in extra-time, they were broken well before Trezeguet's golden goal.

It also proved that Wiltord had the temperament for the biggest occasions - it's easy to forget that while he was never as prolific as Henry, his record in games that decided titles, or semi-finals and finals was clearly superior.

By now Wiltord felt, with some justification, that he had outgrown French League and in an era when the top French players almost naturally seemed to gravitate towards Highbury a move to London seemed a natural career progression, to the player, if not his club.

By later standards his move was hardly protracted, but the deal dragged, with Arsenal offering Bordeaux a deal they initially dismissed as derisory, doubtless because they knew 40 percent of the fee was heading for La Coruna.

Wiltord finally signed after watching a 5-3 win over Charlton at Highbury, for a fee that was as ever undisclosed but reported as a club record £10.5 million.

His first season was a qualified success, bringing 15 goals including six in Arsenal's run to the FA Cup final. Two of these came against Chelsea in the fifth round and he provided the assist for Pires in the semi-final with Tottenham at Old Trafford.

He was preferred to Bergkamp and Kanu for the final with Liverpool and should have had a winner's medal, denied by a combination of Arsenal's profligacy, Stephane Henchoz's handled goalline clearance and the kind of late intervention from Michael Owen he himself had inflicted on the Italians 10 months earlier.

Within weeks of his arrival at Highbury however, stories were already appearing linking him with a move away from the club, stemming from his failure to secure an automatic starting role alongside Henry.

Nor was he universally popular with the crowd. From my semi-regular vantage point in the Clock End, Wiltord was a regular target for dissatisfaction.

"He is not good enough to play for this football club," was the indignant view of one regular, which was hardly a shaft of insight into his quality as a player but did illustrate how a player's popularity with the crowd didn't always reflect his value to the team.

Bergkamp remained the fans' choice to partner Henry, despite him seeming to go AWOL for much of the season, partly because of his past deeds and also because he was better at PR than Wiltord, whose limited English didn't yet allow him to show off his "Shagga!" personality.

One journalist who did succeed in getting him to open up was the Observer's Amy Lawrence, who, like Wenger, likened him to Ian Wright.

Wiltord's apparent surliness and the stream of stories that claimed he was unhappy meant this wasn't an immediately obvious comparison, but it was one the player himself clearly liked.

"Yes!" he apparently sang when Lawrence mentioned the name to him. "Me, I love to be alive. I love to have fun in the dressing room and have a laugh with everybody, but I also like to give a performance on the pitch."

Admitting he'd been tempted to join PSG that January, Wiltord said he declined for fear of being tagged a failure and also revealed he'd rather win the FA Cup than the Champions League because he was hardly ever picked in the latter competition - his exclusion from the 1-0 win in Lyon when his family were in the stands had particularly hurt him.

"I'm used to playing more than 50 games a year, as I have done for the past seven years in France. I'm used to that rhythm. When you are in and out it's hard to make progress," he said.

"My game is all about stamina, tenacity, outfoxing your opponent, and when you don't have enough playing time it's difficult to do that on a regular basis. You haven't seen the real Sylvain Wiltord. You see the real me over a season."

A few more interviews like that might have helped him win people over. Instead the Mail on Sunday reported he stormed out of the country following the Liverpool defeat and refused to play in the final league game at Southampton.

This was, to nobody's surprise, a heavily exaggerated version of what happened. At the time Wiltord had his own now-defunct personal website which he used to give his own version of events: "Basically I screwed up," he said, referring to the final. "We can consider the season a failure. I had an average season but that shouldn't call into question my future at Arsenal. I'm very happy here, I just wish I played more often."

This was picked up by fan sites like the also now-defunct and sorely missed www.arseweb.com, but for some reason individual player websites never took off in a way that twitter later would.

Players initially liked the idea of having a platform to talk straight to their fans, but the number of followers they had was negligible and the novelty faded when they realised their quotes were still being twisted for nefarious purposes by tabloid news organisations.

And in the eyes of the more easily led supporters, the damage was done.

He was as good as his word the following season, when Arsenal won the double, even if he only scored 11 goals.

His attitude and work rate were beyond reproach, but while he was appreciated by the crowd, he was never loved like a Wright or a Bergkamp and his name was rarely sung.

People in the know saw him differently. Wenger lauded his work ethic and Roger Lemerre claimed he was the "perfect" squad player: "First he has ability but also he always has the team in mind. He never complains whether I ask him to be on the bench with the substitutes, play up front or as a wide man."

This was demonstrated as Arsenal closed in on the double, following the injury to Pires.

For most of the run in Wiltord played on the right wing, a role he professed not to like but one he fulfilled superbly, a spinning top of energy, creativity and unceasing effort.

Then, when injury ruled Henry out of the trip to Old Trafford for the penultimate league game of the season, he switched back to a central striking role and once again delivered at the key moment.

On a night when United literally went down fighting (Ruud van Nistlerooy incredibly escaped scot free after punching Freddie Ljungberg in the stomach) Wiltord showed the kind of resilience his eventual replacement, Jose Antonio Reyes, conspicuously lacked when United repeated the same roughhouse tactics a little over two years later.

Arsenal looked comfortable, but a United win would have taken the race to the final game of the season and the frequency with which accidents happen at Old Trafford made it an evening of high tension.

On 57 minutes Ray Parlour robbed Mikael Sylvestre of possession near the half way line and rolled the ball 10 yards forward to Wiltord, who took three touches and aimed for Ljungberg on the edge of the area.

The Swede enjoyed a fortunate deflection off Laurent Blanc and hit a low shot that Barthez was only able to parry straight to Wiltord on the left of the area.

With his now familiar composure he drilled the ball into the far corner and then slightly fluffed his celebration by running to the wrong corner, away from the travelling support. Kanu somehow managed to hurdle over him and he was mobbed by his team mates, who slammed the door shut on United for the rest of the evening.

The following season Wiltord's statistics were almost identical (10 goals in 34 league games, as opposed to 10 from 33). He made an excellent start, faded a little, revived in the time for an ultimately unsuccessful title run in but was left on the bench for the FA Cup final win over Southampton, coming on for Bergkamp in the final 13 minutes.

His contract had, largely unnoticed, run into its final 12 months, leaving him free to speak to other clubs and the periodic stories of his unhappiness began to resurface more frequently during the Invincibles season, during which he was a peripheral figure after picking up an early injury.

By the time he'd returned Arsenal had signed Reyes, who initially looked like becoming a sensational player and Wiltord was free to talk to whomever he liked, including his national team manager Jacques Santini, who was keen to take him to Tottenham.

Although Wiltord said that would be a "difficult move" he didn't rule it out.

Wenger declared he wanted Wiltord to stay, but when he joined Lyon for free there was no outpouring of grief.

By then Wiltord had become a fringe player, but his subsequent career suggests the club might have made more of an effort to keep him.

He scored in France's penalty shoot-out defeat to Italy at the 2006 World Cup, won three consecutive titles with Lyon and although he later fell out with the management there, he enjoyed spells with Rennes, Marseilles and Metz before retiring in 2010.

After a year's sabbatical he wanted to make a comeback.

"I still want to play for fun," he said. "Maybe not in League 1, but in League 2 or the Nationale (third division) for the right club. It's not a question of money, but I'd like a nice challenge."

He found a bigger club than he expected in the shape of fallen giant Nantes. At the start of the 2011-12 season he was seemingly enjoying life as much as he'd ever done and still scoring goals at the age of 37.

In France his hero status was never in question following his goal at Euro 2000. In England perhaps it's time the role he played for Arsenal was reassessed, particularly in the light of the subsequent self-deification of players like Flamini and Nasri, and a glut of dissatisfied players for whom the failure to win trophies always seemed to be somebody else's fault.

15) PASCAL CYGAN

PASCAL Cygan always looked like one of the more vincible members of Arsenal's Invincibles, a player whose appearances were sometimes dreaded by Arsenal fans, but who was later regarded with more affection when it became clear with the passing of time that he was far from the worst of Arsene Wenger's central defensive signings.

When Cygan uses the age-old line about having no regrets it carries more of a ring of truth. It's a cliché usually deployed by players who are blatantly in denial about poor decisions, horrendous errors or lapses in fortune, but with Cygan the impression given is that of a man who can't quite believe his good fortune.

Cygan was a "Nordiste", or a Ch'ti to use the local argot, born in Lens in April 1974.

He was a late developer, which, if you believe the stereotyped view of the rest of France, isn't a surprise, given how far the north is said to lag behind the rest of the country.

In 2008 a film called Bienvenue chez les Ch'tis was released in which a post office worker was punished for pretending to be disabled by being sent from an idyllic post in Provence to the supposed hell of the north.

(L'enfer du nord is also the nickname for the Paris-Roubaix cycle race, acknowledged as the world's greatest one-day race and an event of almost unparalleled suffering for its riders as they churn their way through nearly 200 miles of mud over cobbles the size of bricks).

The film was an unsubtle, warm-hearted way of debunking certain myths about the nord and part of Boon's acclimatisation programme, designed by his fellow workers, was a trip to see RC Lens, where he found himself in the middle a deafening group of good-natured ultras.

For a section of PSG supporters however, the myths were reinforced rather than disproved.

At the French league cup final with Lens at the Stade de France a few weeks after its released, they unveiled a banner that read: "Unemployed, inbred paedophiles: Welcome to the Ch'Tis" earning the condemnation of both Boon and President Sarkozy, who threatened to walk out of the stadium if it wasn't removed.

The Nord is undeniably bleak compared to certain parts of the Hexagone and it's often described as industrialised, although its sheer size means that while it might be compared to English mining areas like Durham in some regards, there are still thousands of flat, windswept square miles devoted to farming.

At that time Lille was an emerging city, the fourth biggest in France, but some way behind a number of smaller provincial capitals in terms of its influence and with as much in common architecturally with parts of England as the south of France.

Lille's image began to change when the Eurostar turned it into a rail hub, but the Dogues (Mastiffs) of that era were still a long way from reclaiming the glory days of the post-war era, when they were one of the most powerful clubs in France.

Lille Olympique Sporting Club, a merger of a number of local sides, won the double in the first full season after the liberation under an English manager, George Berry, a Hackney-born striker who'd played for Gillingham and Crystal Palace before moving to France in 1934, where his first name acquired an additional S.

In a move that would make Roman Abramovich look like a soft-hearted senitmentalist, the club's president, Louis Henno, rewarded Berry for his league and cup success by sacking him, though for the next decade they remained pre-eminent, winning a second title in 1953 before they were turned into a laughing stock by "l'affaire Zakaraias".

Henno, believing he was omnipotent, pulled off what he believed was a transfer coup by signing a player who claimed to be Jozsef Zakarias, one of the Magical Magyars who reached the 1954 World Cup final.

The player turned out be an impostor who was in reality a foreign legionary from Czechoslovakia who had just returned from the Indochine war and, in the words of Lille's historian Jacques Verhaeghe, "didn't even know how to tie his own shoelaces."

Lille's credibility was shot and their decline accelerated when Henno stupidly refused to give Cor van der Hart, a superb Dutch international, the meagre pay rise he'd demanded.

LOSC spent the next half-century as a yo-yo club, a far-flung provincial outpost like Sunderland perhaps, with obvious potential but little chance of breaking back into the elite and often forced to play second fiddle to its neighbours Valenciennes and Lens.

Its stadium, the Metropole, doubled as an athletics venue and was therefore devoid of atmosphere, which may have been why Cygan, the son of a police officer, grew up supporting Bordeaux (making him the equivalent of the Kent children who grew up supporting Liverpool, which accounted for around 50 percent of the people I grew up with).

As a junior he played for Lillle, but he moved on to Wasquehal, a suburb between Lille and Roubaix where the British cyclist and die-hard Arsenal supporter Sean Yates won a time trial stage of the Tour de France in 1988.

He made enough progress with the local club, Entente Sportive Wasquehal, to earn selection for the Flanders under-17 side and a move to Valenciennes, who were then the dominant team in the region before the match-fixing scandal hastened their demise.

After three years in their reserve side Valenciennes decided Cygan would be a semi-professional at best and he headed back to Wasquehal, who played at an annexe to Lille's Stade Metropole.

This slightly unusual arrangement meant he was right under the noses of Lille's scouts and after two strong seasons as an amateur, during which he and his younger brother Thierry helped Wasquehal win the Division Four, the top flight club decided to take a chance.

Lille had nearly managed to bankrupt itself through a policy of fielding highly-paid has beens. Under the new regime, the modus operandi was to buy promising young players and sell them on for a profit.

In the short term it got them relegated, but in the longer term it proved a visionary move.

Cygan's top-flight debut came at the relatively late age of 21, in a 1-1 draw for Lille against St Etienne in August 1995.

He made 27 appearances in his debut season, but just 14 the following year when they dropped into the second tier.

It was one of Lille's darker hours, but it preceded a glorious dawn. For the next three years, while Lens were winning the title, Lille found themselves in the second division, playing local derbies with Wasquehal, who were experiencing one of the best eras in their history just as their neighbours were in one of their deepest troughs.

It was a once-in-a-generation convergence of the kind Tottenham supporters live for, although the rivalry was hardly comparable, as for many LOSC supporters Wasquehal were a second team and vice versa.

In one fixture three sets of brothers played against each other. The elders all appeared for Lille, including Pascal, while the juniors, including Thierry all turned out for Wasquehal.

Parity between the two neighbouring clubs couldn't last and under the tutelage of a slave-driving Bosnian called Vahid Halilhodzic, who made the players train while carrying ruck-sacks full of rocks, Lille experienced a dramatic upsurge, while Wasquehal drifted back down the leagues.

Cygan was a key member of the Lille team that won the Division 2 title in 1999-2000 and he had little trouble adapting to life in the top flight.

His performances in Lille's first season back in Ligue 1 won him France Football's player-of-the-year award and attracted the attention of West Ham, although having met with him at Lille they never bothered to call him back, a decision both parties might have lived to regret.

Within two years the Hammers were relegated despite having a supposedly stellar squad, one in which Cygan might have flourished away from the scrutiny his every mistake attracted at Arsenal.

While he was too well adjusted to be scarred by that experience, Cygan was slightly reticent when he became aware Wenger was interested in him a year later in 2002.

By this stage his profile had risen after two decent performances against Manchester United in the Champions League, but the fee, £2million, seemed low for someone billed as a replacement for the retiring Tony Adams.

Early in his Arsenal career he gave an interview to Henry Winter of the Telegraph in which he compared the contrasting styles of football across the channel.

"The difference between France and England in terms of the physical game is that in France only the defenders kick you, pull your shirt or are tricky. In England it is the whole of the team who do that."

Winter was impressed, as was Wenger, who claimed it was a matter of time before Cygan would go on to play for France.

But that never happened and Cygan suffered by comparison with his predecessors. At 6'5 and 28 years of age he was physically imposing and mobile, but it was asking a lot to expect him to seamlessly replace a player like Adams, who had given the club nearly two decades of excellence.

Instead he found himself behind Keown, who had just signed a two-year contract extension, and Campbell and when he did play he struggled to meet the exacting performance levels needed.

He scored a vital goal in a 2-1 home win over Everton, but as Arsenal frittered away an eight-point lead in the title race, Cygan was seen as symptomatic of Arsenal's new vulnerability.

A red card for two bookable offences in a gruelling 3-1 win over Chelsea in an FA Cup quarter-final at Stamford Bridge didn't help and injury kept him out of both the semi-final and the final.

After a year to adjust to the English game Cygan might have been expected to replace Keown, who was just beginning to fade, but instead Wenger opted to convert Kolo Toure into a central defender, to brilliant effect. That limited Cygan to 18 appearances during the Invincible season and the following year was little better.

By now the word "characteristic" was habitually being added to sentences about Cygan errors, such as the own goal he scored at Highbury against Panathinaikos in a 2004 Champions League game, an accidental deflection that saw the previously admiring Henry Winter revise his opinion of Cygan to "perennially hapless".

Cygan claimed he didn't read the papers and that he was therefore unaffected by the criticism he was getting.

This is another standard line from embattled players through the ages, although Cygan's relative age might have hardened him slightly and with the side still winning more often than not the criticism away from the media was usually limited to groaning from supporters.

There was an uncomplimentary chant: "He's bald, he's shit, he plays when no one's fit," and while it was seldom sung loudly enough to be audible on the pitch, the second line held more than a ring of truth to it.

Cygan had been overtaken by the emerging Swiss centre back Phillippe Senderos, a player who in time would rival Cygan in the bald, error-prone defensive stakes but who in 2005 kept Campbell out of the FA Cup final line-up.

Cygan made even fewer appearances in his final season with the club in 2005-2006, though he did score twice in a 4-1 win over Fulham at Highbury, prompting the PA man, who had been updating the crowd on how many goals Henry needed to overhaul Ian Wright's record, to drily announce that Cygan needed another 183 goals to overhaul the mark himself.

He wasn't even in the squad for the Champions League final and the only surprise when he left to join Villareal that summer was that Arsenal managed to secure a £2million pound fee for a player who was then 32 years of age.

He played fairly regularly in his first two seasons in Spain, covering for the injury-prone Gonzalo Rodriguez and helping Villareal to a remarkable second-place finish in 2007-08, behind only Real Madrid.

That earned him a one-year contract extension, though by now he was fading and he made just four appearances in what turned out to be his final season with Villareal, playing no part in the Champions League quarter-final with Arsenal.

At the end of the season he was left looking for a club and made the mistake of speaking to the Daily Mail.

"(Wenger) told me that if it all went wrong in Spain the door would still be open," Cygan said, with the anonymous reporter who was interviewing him noting he was laughing as he did so. "Now I'm awaiting his phone call."

By the time the sub-editor had finished with the story it had the headline: "Save me Arsene! Calamity Cygan makes a pitch for a return to Arsenal."

Given that Wenger signed Mikael Silvestre that summer this wasn't as ludicrous an idea as the Mail implied, but Cygan, who might have been tempted to return to Lille had they offered, ended up 230 miles down the coast with the mid-table Spanish second division side Cartagena.

He spent two seasons there but somewhat incredibly tried to commute every day, meaning he needed a six-hour round trip just to attend training sessions. His reluctance to move closer to the workplace was down to the fact he and his wife had opened a fashion boutique near to their home in Castellon, but their business never took off and they were forced to close it.

There was no obvious bitterness from Cygan when he reflected on the episode, or anything else that happened during his playing career.

"My coaches told me I wasn't good enough to play higher than the CFA (France's fourth division)," Cygan said, although he did lapse into false memory syndrome when trying to recall how man trophies he'd won. "In the end I played for Lille and Arsenal in the Champions League. My time with Arsenal was the best of my career. We won the championship in the first two years I was there, it was intense." (In fact Arsenal finished runners-up in his first season).

Cygan said he was hoping to embark on a coaching career, which seemed to give the lie to two of the more outlandish stories that appeared on his wikipedia page: that he was running a charity called "Faibless Mentale" somewhere in London (obviously false) and that he'd once doubled up as Arsenal's mascot Gunnersaurus because he was the only person they could find who fitted the suit (doubtful but at least possible).

"I have only great memories of that era," he said, as a parting shot. "You know when you're playing with players like Vieira, Henry, Bergkamp, Kanu, Pires and Wiltord you can only have good memories. I learned and enormous amount. I was playing with the best players on the planet and I think for that reason alone people must envy me."

16) GAEL CLICHY

"Gael Clichy, Clichy
He's better than Casherly
He should have been number three
Gael Clichy, Clichy …"

THROUGHOUT the Wenger era, Arsenal repeatedly came close to winning the League Cup by accident.

Virtual reserve sides would make electrifying runs to semi-finals, or even the final itself, by obliterating top or second tier sides who were often at full strength.

During these games stars of the "future" would often emerge, producing displays of such dazzling brilliance their progression to the first team was deemed inevitable and the days of whoever was ahead of them in the pecking order would appear numbered.

In some cases these players would flicker like fireflies, never to shine again. For every Fabregas and Wilshere there was a Quincy Owusu Abeyie, Jay Simpson or Arturo Lupoli, all of whom looked like world beaters for a few minutes and then drifted into lesser leagues.

Gael Clichy was one of several Arsenal players to use the League Cup as the platform for a durable career. In terms of playing time he was one of the most successful graduates, making 234 appearances in eight seasons and the decision to swap Ashley Cole for William Gallas and make him first choice left back in 2006 seemed the right one on almost every level - except if one uses the hard currency of medals.

Although the two men seemed to enjoy a genuinely warm relationship both before and after Cole's departure, the contrast between the pissy and permanently aggravated Cole and the mild-mannered Clichy is jarring.

Cole plays football in a permanent state of agitation, outraged at the injustices, perceived and real, foisted on him by opponents, referees and sometimes both.

In the face of the intense provocation Premier League footballers face, Clichy remains poker-faced and it's possible to draw the depressing conclusion that this is what gives Cole a slight edge over his successor, who may have been a part of a "nicer" second wave of French imports.

Clichy had an apparently stable and middle class upbringing in the Toulouse banlieue, the son of a teacher and a nurse who channelled any aggression he had into his football.

Although he ended up as a left back, Clichy was a naturally right-footed player, coaxed into developing his weaker foot by his father Joel, who as a referee once disallowed a legitimate goal his son had scored in a junior game purely because he'd used his right foot.

At the age of five he began playing for AS Hersoise and a decade later he turned professional with AS Cannes.

Unlike Gallas and Petit he kept out of trouble with the law, although he nearly died at the age of 15, when, in his first season on the Cote D'Azur, he took a shortcut over a metal fence at Cannes' training ground and a ring on his right hand became ensnared, ripping the end of his finger off.

"I had a seven-hour operation to sew everything back on but at some point I had a problem with my lungs and my heart stopped for 30 seconds," he said, several years later.

Although Doctors claimed it was a miracle that he survived there was no lasting physical or mental damage.

The episode did however give Clichy a lasting appreciation of how fortunate he was and the resolve not to spurn his talent. That meant not rejecting a personal overture from Arsene Wenger when he came to visit the family home.

Clichy had at that point played in a handful of French third division games for Cannes, but he had attracted international recognition for his age group and the attention of the supposedly visionary scout Damien Comolli - a man who in Xavier Rivoire's biography had claimed to be a confidant of Arsene Wenger even when he was in his teens.

In an interview with the match day programme before a 2-1 win over Manchester United in 08-09, Arsenal's Chief Scout Steve Rowley made an almost throwaway remark about Comolli's track record at Highbury once the latter had been named as Tottenham's Director of Football, supposedly on the seam of talent he had personally mined for their north London rivals: "He was a hard-working member of my staff for about seven or eight years and the player (sic) he found for us was Gael Clichy."

And even if Comolli did discover Clichy it was Wenger who persuaded him to leave France when he was still only 18.

Clichy later admitted he could barely believe Wenger had been sitting in his living room, but he was quickly given a reality check when he arrived at his new flat in Enfield, a London borough about as far removed as it's possible to be from the Cote'D'Azur while remaining in the same continent.

Unaccompanied by the kind of entourage many foreign players bring to London to help them adjust, Clichy taught himself how to cook and wash-up, skills unmastered by many professionals well into their thirties.

In his first season, 2003-04, he showed glimpses of phenomenal potential while Arsenal progressed to the semi-finals of the League Cup, as a left-back who could attack with breathtaking speed and self-control.

He was held partially responsible for conceding the decisive goal in the 1-0 FA Cup semi-final defeat to Manchester United, but given his age, 18, this was forgivable and he ended the season with a Premier League winner's medal, having made a total of 12 starting and substitute appearances.

In the short term Clichy's problem was how to break into a team that had just gone an entire season undefeated.

Ahead of him, in his favoured left-back position, was Ashley Cole, the England international billed by the English media, for once with some justification, as the best left-back in the world.

Wenger said openly that the time would come when he would have to play both Clichy and Ashley Cole and put one of them in midfield (he'd said the same about Cole and his predecessor Sylvinho), but when Cole was caught red handed by the tabloids speaking to Chelsea at the Royal Park Hotel during the 2004-05 season, the equation changed.

Cole's fatuous explanation that he just happened to be meeting his agents when: "The door opened and Jose Mourinho and Peter Kenyon walked in," was believed by precisely no one and his claim to have jumped off his chair in surprise was rendered risible given his later track record, despite the lengthy protestations to the contrary in his execrably ghosted autobiography.

From then on Clichy's ascension was just a question of timing.

Cole lamented his portrayal as the "Judas of Highbury" but this was a revisionist view.

It's true that some fans thought he should be sold to allow Clichy to take over - at one game at Highbury Cole's family were sat within earshot of a group who were loudly cheering Clichy's every touch and saying how much better a player he was - but a full-scale demonisation only occurred after his departure.

There were chants of Judas when Arsenal played at Stamford Bridge later that season, but by the time of the Champions League final a year later, when Wenger pointedly chose Cole ahead of Clichy, the tapping up saga had been largely forgiven, if not forgotten.

It was obvious that Cole was the right choice for that game because, as hindsight would prove, he was simply a better defender.

I watched that game from the vantage point I usually seemed to be allocated for cup finals, in the top tier, behind and slightly to the side of the goal Arsenal were attacking in the second half.

The sample may not have been entirely scientific, but from the people sitting around me Cole attracted only praise for the way he was defending. Against a Barcelona side of that quality everyone seemed to accept that what mattered was having the best possible defence on the pitch and if that meant including a player who apparently no longer felt he had a future with the club at the expense of someone who did, so be it.

None of which is to say Clichy was in any way a bad player - he just wasn't quite as effective against the very top players, eg Cristiano Ronaldo.

He made 24 appearances in total during the 2004-05 season and was outstanding in midfield during 120 minutes of an FA Cup quarter-final replay at Sheffield United which Arsenal won on penalties.

A breakthrough beckoned the following season when Cole fractured his foot, but instead Clichy suffered an almost identical injury and was out for four months.

With Mathieu Flamini playing as an emergency left-back Arsenal outplayed Real Madrid and Juventus to reach the semi-finals of the Champions League, but the suspicion that the position was cursed grew when Flamini pulled up with a hamstring injury nine minutes into the second leg with Villareal.

With minimal warning Clichy was pitched into the tensest game in Arsenal's history, a second leg spent almost entirely on the back foot as they struggled to defend the 1-0 lead Kolo Toure had given them at Highbury.

Given the attacking talent at their disposal it was a desperately disappointing performance, redeemed only by the sense that it would end in the kind of old-fashioned "1-0 to the Arsenal" result.

Instead, with a minute left of normal time, Clichy did exactly what Nigel Winterburn never had in these situations and conceded a penalty.

Jose Mari dived as he passed Clichy who was trying to shepherd him away from the six-yard box.

The multiple replays unavailable to the officials later proved his innocence but in real time it looked fifty-fifty and the "evening-up" principle applied given that Villareal had had a strong claim turned down during the first leg. At that exact moment it felt as though Arsenal's entire world had imploded and the only consolation was the knowledge that there was a German in goal.

Lehmann's subsequent save may well have spared Clichy from the awful burden of being the man who cost Arsenal a European Cup final and though he had the strength of character to recover it wouldn't be the last time he would fall victim to a faulty decision in the dying moments of a key game.

Although he was an unused sub in the final with Barcelona, Clichy spent the next five seasons as Arsenal's undisputed first choice left back, seeing off challenges from first Armand Traore and then Kieron Gibbs.

In 2007-08 he played in all 38 of Arsenal's Premier League games, a feat rarely equalled in the Wenger era, but he was also at the centre of that season's most controversial moment, again when he was punished for a crime he didn't commit in the 2-2 draw with Birmingham.

Having overcome the trauma of Eduardo's injury and a 1-0 deficit, Arsenal were 2-1 up in the final seconds of added time when Clichy was caught slightly off guard by a run into the box by Stuart Parnaby.

Setanta's pompous and posturing commentator Jon Champion derided the defender as "slack and casual" but while Clichy was fractionally slow to react he did recover the situation, nipping in front of Parnaby to win the ball cleanly.

The problem was that Parnaby then either fell or dived over his leg convincingly enough to persuade referee Mike Dean to award a penalty and this time there was no Lehmann around to get Clichy out of the jail he didn't deserve to be in.

While Gallas was busy showing everyone exactly how much he cared by sitting on the pitch crying, Clichy reacted stoically.

In his final three seasons Arsenal were good, without ever being quite good enough, which some observers might argue also sums up Clichy's career there.

More than one Premier League manager felt he was a weak link, with Martin O'Neill claiming he'd been "roasted" by Ashley Young after a 0-0 draw at Aston Villa.

His defending was also criticised, not entirely fairly, during the epoch-defining League Cup final with Birmingham City, though the suggestion that he was bullied appeared a lazy conclusion, based on his size relative next to some of City's bruisers.

Unlike some of his colleagues and - just as depressingly - hundreds of Arsenal supporters who began streaming for the exit, Clichy refused to chuck in the towel when City scored their freak 89th-minute goal.

Although Wenger later said that Koscielny had been destroyed by the incident what appalled me was the gutless reaction from some of the supporters where I was sitting, again in the upper tier, slightly to the left of the goal.

Unlike in Paris where everyone stayed put until the final whistle even though the chances of ten men scoring against a world class team were minimal, Martins's goal for Birmingham was the cue for a mass tantrum.

I became embroiled in a stand up row with someone who was blocking my view as he made for the door, telling him he should stay and support his team, given that there were still a full five minutes left.

Nor were Birmingham anything like Barcelona. Clichy at least continued to maraud forward in stoppage time, but this was probably one collective failure too far for him.

In eight years with Arsenal the mystifyingly overworked pundit David Pleat never once managed to say his name correctly, always calling him Cliché, which was something Gael resorted to when he spoke of needing "a new challenge".

Yet when he left, he did so with consummate dignity. His departure was a classic Arsenal parting. It was stage-managed perhaps and his profile was deleted from the club's website almost instantly, but it was otherwise done with the kind of class too often taken for granted: compare and contrast with the way the departures of Gallas and Berbatov were handled by Chelsea and Tottenham respectively.

In the build up to the deal Clichy didn't at any point criticise the club, nor did sources "close" to him tell the tabloid press he was worth more money, he merely issued a tweet, saying: "I am leaving Arsenal within the next two weeks. Thank you for all your support and great memories. You all will always be in my heart."

When the deal was finally done Wenger issued a heartfelt tribute: "We would like to thank Gael for eight years of terrific service, during which time he gave absolutely everything to the club. He has grown and developed so much since joining us in 2003 and he has been a crucial part of team over recent seasons. Gael leaves with our respect and best wishes."

He responded to individual correspondents on his twitter account and went out of his way to avoid giving offence.

However, in an innocuous interview he gave to Sky Sports, Clichy gave an honest assessment of where the previous season had gone wrong, saying the team had struggled without Van Persie and Fabregas and citing the League Cup final as the point where things had gone wrong.

Sky and several other media outlets duly went for the Clichy-criticises-Arsenal angle in their headlines, all of which proved that no matter how frank and truthful a player tries to be, when he deals with certain branches of the media he cannot win.

It said something about the nature of Arsenal's support that Liverpool fans seemed more outraged by Clichy's destination to join City.

He had been linked with a £7million pound move to Anfield, or Roma, but despite rejecting those clubs to join a side who had just won the FA Cup, and who unlike Liverpool, had qualified for the Champions League, he was inevitably accused of going for the Arabian riches he was offered.

Who wouldn't turn down a 60 percent wage hike? Sadly, from the Arsenal point of view, not Clichy, even though he'd been quoted on the subject of Adebayor's transfer two years earlier, saying: "I really believe if you are a player who thinks only about money you could end up at Manchester City."

17) MATHIEU FLAMINI

IF we ignore the strong claims of Nicolas Anelka, who arguably defies any attempt at categorisation, Mathieu Flamini was perhaps Arsenal's first and most obvious mercenary, beating William Gallas to that title by a couple of seasons.

For three of the four years he spent in London he struggled to establish himself as a first choice and by the time he did, for the 2007-08 season, it was common knowledge that his contract was about to expire and that he was going to make good on one of his repeated threats to leave.

Wherever he went journalists found it difficult to write about him without prefixing his name with the word "disgruntled" and this explains why he was never really loved at Arsenal. By the time he started to live up to his potential, it was obvious that somebody else was going to reap the benefits of the development he'd made as a player under Wenger, an irony that was not lost on Olympique Marseille, who he'd jilted in a near identical fashion four years earlier.

Calling Flamini, or any other player, a mercenary isn't necessarily detrimental. Although the word has pejorative connotations, implying that the player in question is motivated solely by money, the mercenary can also be a valued asset to a squad. A mercenary's interests usually coincide with those of his employer and at least Flamini didn't commit the ultimate insult and kiss the badge.

As a native of Marseille, albeit one who would have failed the Le Pen test due to his Corsican mother and an Italian father - if he felt any inherent loyalty to any team it ought to have been OM, where he spent 14 years and grew from a small child into a top flight footballer.

He was brighter than the average player, having spent six months studying law and though he abandoned his degree he'd already absorbed enough to know the law better than many club lawyers.

Flamini was 18 in December 2003 when he was given his Ligue 1 debut by OM's then-manager Alain Perrin (whose later attempts to manage Portsmouth were summed up by the way he repeatedly shouted the word: "Merde!" during a League Cup defeat at lower division side Gillingham).

Within a month of Flamini's debut Perrin had been fired, but his successor, Jose Anigo made Flamini an automatic choice for the rest of the season, which saw OM reach the UEFA cup final.

In a now familiar story however, the officials hadn't done their paperwork properly and Flamini knew it.

Before the UEFA cup semi-final with Newcastle he was put on the spot by a reporter about his contract situation. He blurted out that he would soon sign a deal with the club he loved, but as Anigo later noted: "He's intelligent and he knows the system. He's more calculating than you would think."

An underpaid apprentice, Flamini was legally bound to sign his first professional deal with Marseilles, under the rules of the French Federation.

What he knew and what OM seemingly didn't was that he could leave to join another side in the EU provided a derisory sum in compensation, set by FIFA, was paid. By the time OM actually made him an offer Wenger had already turned Flamini's head.

"Above all else Mathieu had a personal project," Anigo said in 2008. "The club's project he just doesn't care for. That's a respectable position but I think it's possible to have a good career, remaining elegant, while leaving clubs in the right manner."

Four years down the line, Flamini's departure evidently still rankled with Anigo, whose club received £320,000 instead of the £10,000,000 they'd coveted, though he had evidently calmed down a little since accusing his player of a "belle trahison" at the time.

The direct translation of that phrase, "beautiful betrayal", is jarring in English but it leaves no one in any doubt as to just how angry Anigo was, both with his staff for leaving a loophole open and with the player for exploiting it.

News of the deal broke in July 2004. Marseilles initially tried to block the move before realising they were powerless, though by this stage the picture had changed for Flamini, when the player whose boots he was supposed to be filling, Patrick Vieira, pulled the plug on his move to Real Madrid and decided he was staying at Highbury.

With the prodigious 17-year-old Cesc Fabregas becoming Vieira's first choice partner in midfield, Flamini found himself limited to cameo appearances while waiting for players to get injured or suspended.

His big chance came in December when Vieira, Edu and Gilberto Silva were all out of action for the visit of the leaders Chelsea to Highbury. He was impressive in the 2-2 draw, fitting in alongside Fabregas in a way that suggested the young duo might star for years to come, but he remained fifth-choice in his preferred central midfield role and wasn't even on the bench for the FA Cup final with Manchester United at the end of the season.

With Vieira and Edu gone the following season should have been easier for Flamini, but he was often overlooked in favour of Hleb, or even Pires and Ljungberg. He only found his way into the side after a spate of injuries saw him pressed into service as an emergency left back, where he was unexpectedly excellent.

Part of a back four that didn't concede a goal in the knock-out stages of the

Champions League, Flamini was back on the bench for the final after Ashley Cole recovered from a long-term injury.

He was introduced with a quarter of an hour to go, supposedly to shore up the defence in place of a tiring Fabregas, but within a minute of taking the field Barcelona had equalised and within another five they'd hit the winner.

This was hardly Flamini's fault as any side in the world would have struggled to resist an attack of that class with only 10 players, but once the bitterness of the defeat had subsided he asked for a meeting with Wenger, where he told him he no longer wanted to be considered a defender.

Wenger acquiesced but that meant a return to the central midfield queue and another season of sporadic action, with injuries also limiting his chances to just nine starts in league fixtures.

It was in 2007-08 that his career took a sudden and spectacular upwards turn, after a summer in which he proved that quite aside from being lapsed lawyer he might also have a future career as a PR agent.

Finding another then little-known loophole, Flamini realised he could buy his way out of the final year of his deal and offer himself to the highest bidder.

Usually footballers who agitate for a move get their agents to leak stories to the press. Flamini simply picked up the phone to a series of journalists offering them a series of first-hand quotes saying he was thinking of leaving. The man who took the call at l'Equipe, Vincent Duluc, was initially dubious about the caller's identity, especially when Flamini wasn't able to tell him when he'd lasted started a game for Arsenal, but he was eventually persuaded to run a story, as were the Gazetta dello sport, where Flamini's influence extended as far as having a say in the actual headline.

If this was further evidence of Flamini's shrewdness, there was one major problem with the campaign. At that stage in his career Flamini was a fringe player, unable to break into a team that finished third in the English League and unlikely to attract the kind of bid he felt he was worth.

To redress that he needed to become an automatic choice in a successful Arsenal side, something he did by brilliantly reinventing himself as Arsenal mounted their first serious title challenge in four years.

With Gilberto Silva away at the Copa America, Flamini seized his moment, securing the central midfield berth alongside Fabregas with a series of all action displays that earned him the nickname "Flattuso" from his team mates, after the AC Milan midfielder he would later play alongside, Genaro Gattuso.

That was selling him short. Gattuso played like the Tasmanian devil on amphetamines (interestingly in 2005 he refused to take a voluntary blood test), but Flamini had the same drive, minus Gattuso's borderline psychotic tendencies.

When the two came face to face at the San Siro in a Champions League second round tie in February, Flamini outran and outclassed Gattuso with a performance that surprised no one who'd seen the way he'd developed during the season.

In the following round at Liverpool a measure of his progress was offered when he went off just before half-time in the second leg to be replaced by a visibly less effective Silva, allowing Liverpool to wriggle off the hook and win 4-2.

The injury kept him out of the 2-1 defeat at Old Trafford the following Sunday, the loss effectively ensuring that Arsenal would end one of their most flamboyant seasons with nothing. It also ensured that Flamini would end his four years with Arsenal empty-handed, at least in terms of honours.

Arsenal offered Flamini a "substantial" new deal, but it clearly wasn't as substantial as that being offered by Milan, who had swooned for him after his audition at the San Siro a couple of months earlier.

The deal was reported before the season had even finished and Wenger, who'd vainly urged him not leave for a "few bucks" was left to face questions on why Flamini had been "allowed" to leave.

This implied he'd had some choice in the matter, which he hadn't. The only valid criticism was that Arsenal hadn't realised his potential earlier and much of that was down to the player.

History repeated itself. Flamini had said he loved Arsenal and wanted to stay, but this time few believed the former would ensure the latter. He probably did have a genuine affection for the club, but it was hardly the umbilical attachment of a fan and he parroted the desperate old line that he hadn't gone for the money, even though Milan had failed to qualify for the Champions League.

The departure was certainly a blow for Arsenal and it couldn't be considered an unqualified success for the player either.

For two seasons he seemed to have regressed and was used as a kind of luxury domestique, filling in when the real stars were injured and even ending up at full back again for a while.

In 2010-11 he was more heavily involved again in his preferred position and won his first serious medal when Milan took the Serie A title.

That season he was pilloried by the British press for a "horror" tackle on Tottenham's Vedran Corluka during a Champions League tie but he launched a charm offensive before the return leg at the Lane, giving multiple interviews in English to defend himself and reaffirm he was still an Arsenal man at heart, despite having been one of several thousand players linked to Spurs the previous year.

What might he have won had he stayed and provided a steadying influence to the kamikaze Arsenal side he left behind?

The word disgruntled continued to cling to Flamini at Milan but he doesn't seem to be the kind of player who will have regrets at the end of his career.

He has interests well beyond the game - bizarrely he is a friend of David Gest, a reality tv star whose fame mushroomed because he once took a turn as Liza Minelli's husband.

Flamini has both connections and the intellect to enjoy a number of possible careers after retirement and would clearly make an excellent agent. As such he may be distrusted but respected, admired but unloved. Almost certainly how he'll be remembered at Arsenal.

18) ABOU DIABY

It wasn't subtle, but it was accurate. Asked while working as a pundit for the BBC whether he though Abou Diaby could live up to the tag of "the new Vieira", Ian Wright said: "the only thing they've got in common is that they're both tall and they're both brothers."

Vasiriki Diaby, universally known as Abou, was perhaps the most disappointing of Arsene Wenger's signings.

Neither an unplucked turkey like Francis Jeffers, nor a card-carrying mercenary like Adebayor, who joined at the same time, Diaby was both tall and black and therefore drew immediate comparisons with Vieira - as did almost every other black midfielder over 6'0 in the Premier League.

Google helpfully produces 27,800,000 results for the "new Vieira", among them Momo Sissoko, Steven N'Zonzi, Yann M'Vila, Gueida Fofana and a host of non-entities peddled as the next box-to-box overlord by nefarious agents to credulous reporters.

In Diaby's case there were other similarities. Both men arrived at Highbury at a similar age having shown significant potential despite a limited amount of first team football, but there their career trajectories divided sharply.

Quite why still isn't obvious.

As a child Diaby worshipped Vieira, later saying: "He is a monument to French football and someone who inspires people in France. He inspired me when I was a kid growing up. I would watch him playing for Arsenal, playing for France and dream of one day playing for Arsenal too. All the kids I grew up with did, we would watch the way they played football under Arsene Wenger with some great French players like Vieira, Henry and Petit."

But he later admitted: "I accept that I do need to be more aggressive and more physical. I can tackle, I think I can anyway. I think I have the ability to have more of an impact in the middle, I am not lazy. People think I am because of the way I run, that I am not working as hard as I can, but trust me I am."

Was he though? He himself realised this perception was a problem. "I think the manager is still waiting for more to come from me," he said, to which the obvious response would have been that 60,000 people at the Emirates were also waiting. "I think he wants me to become a great player and I would like to become a man like Vieira," Diaby said, before adding: "I am not vocal like him. I am quiet. I need to work on that too."

If he did work on becoming more of a man the results never really showed. In interviews he came across as a slightly shy, but also charming and genial young man, a fundamentally nice person, which was something he could seldom afford to be when playing against the likes of Joey Barton or Darren

Fletcher.

An illustrative episode took place during his formative years at Clairefontaine, under the eyes of a camera crew filming for a reality tv show.

Diaby and his friend Hatem Ben Arfa were walking along a corridor to a room when the two suddenly start to argue. It seems that Diaby was the instigator, making a "mum joke". When Ben Arfa asks him why he's talking about mothers, Diaby suddenly explodes with rage, calling Ben Arfa a son of a bitch and threatening to beat him up. At that age, roughly 15, Ben Arfa was well under a foot shorter than Diaby and three friends had to hold the taller boy back.

It was classic bullying, the kind of incident that happens in a thousand playgrounds around France and England every day, but the aftermath was illuminating.

Ben Arfa, interviewed by the crew, seems completely unperturbed by what's happened. Diaby by contrast is on the verge of tears, suggesting he never really had the nastiness to dominate a midfield in a way that Vieira had.

Diaby was brought up in Aubervilliers, a suburb around three miles south east of the Stade de France (and almost exactly as far, in the opposite direction, from the ground as William Gallas' home in Villeneuve-la-Garenne).

The standard cliché is to say that as Aubervilliers is a suburb, it has to be a deprived area, but this is an exaggeration. It has some attractive areas and some less attractive high-rise estates.

It's true that some of his friends fell into crime, but that hardly makes him unique and while growing up there he developed a wide range of interests, including philosophy and religion (he is a practising Muslim).

This, while educationally commendable, paints the picture of a man a long way removed from the single-minded kind of destroyer beloved of English fans, the kind of player like Bryan Robson who will put his head where others are reluctant to put in a foot.

Diaby had better uses for his head. As a 16 year-old he was considered the best player in his position both at Clairefontaine and by his club Paris St. Germain, whose reputation for cack-handed administration proved well-earned when they forgot to send a contract to his parents, allowing an agent to whisk him off to Auxerre.

There he linked up with Bacary Sagna and Younes Kaboul and he made his full debut at the start of the 2004-05 season, though he made just a handful of appearances between injuries before signing for Arsenal in January 2006.

Diaby had by that stage won a number of influential admirers, including the then-Chelsea manager Jose Mourinho who tried to persuade him to go to Stamford Bridge.

The vice-president of Auxerre, Gerard Borgoin, said he had chosen Highbury "because Arsene Wenger was better than Jose Mourinho," but he also added a withering parting shot.

"We have always kept the younger players which our coach wanted to use. But Diaby did not play so this was a strategic sale for us."

At £2million it didn't represent a huge gamble for Wenger, but the warning signs were already there, particularly regarding Diaby's abysmal injury record.

His manager, the former French national coach Jacques Santini - who was fresh from a chastening spell in charge at Tottenham, was more explicit, effectively accusing him of not trying.

"Abou was one of the players I used at the start of the season and then he had to stop because of repetitive injuries," he said. "Maybe he was attracted by England and the money there. This probably did not force him to make all the necessary efforts to come back to his best level with us."

Perhaps Diaby was so naturally gifted that he didn't feel the need to display the kind of work ethic asked of most players, but if so he was destined to fail.

His debut, at Everton, came as a sub in a deflating 1-0 defeat. Three days later he made his first start in the second leg of a Carling Cup semi-final with Wigan that Arsenal lost in the dying seconds on away goals and to round off the week he was part of the side that lost 1-0 at Bolton in the FA Cup.

It was perhaps too early to judge him, but these were precisely the kinds of games that players with a genuine hunger used to win for Arsenal.

Ian Wright's put down aside, Diaby was just starting to show glimpses of the player he could become, scoring his first goal in a 5-0 rout of Aston Villa, when he fell victim to arguably one of the worst tackles ever witnessed in top flight football.

Subsequent injuries to Eduardo and Aaron Ramsey attracted a greater media outcry, but the tackle from Sunderland's Dan Smith that broke Diaby's leg was almost a criminal assault - it certainly would have resulted in a criminal prosecution had it taken place anywhere other than a football field, but the standard defence was that Smith was trying to make a legitimate attempt to win the ball.

Smith, who only made three appearances for Sunderland and was also sent off on his debut, was shown a yellow card, displayed little apparent remorse and never played for Sunderland again. He ended up on trial with Aberdeen (as opposed to on trial in Aberdeen as the Father Ted joke once had it) before drifting into non-league football with Blythe and training to be a hairdresser, which he may have considered a step up from the SPL.

In the short-term the injury ruled Diaby out of the Champions League final that was taking place a couple of miles from where he grew up.

The longer term effect of the injury was more difficult to quantify.

At the age of 20 he was told his career could be over. This may have been a case of the medical profession covering itself against a worst-case scenario, but for Diaby the psychological effect of worrying if he could ever play again must have been serious, and that was before you even take into account the sheer injustice of what happened.

After three operations and nearly nine months away he was back as a sub for the 6-3 League Cup win at Liverpool and he played an important role in the march to the final, where he ran the midfield for half an hour as Arsenal's nominal reserve side threatened to outclass Chelsea.

It was Diaby who set up Theo Walcott's opening goal and he also he kicked John Terry in the head as Arsenal faded in the second half, which didn't do his popularity with Arsenal fans any harm.

If that challenge was an obvious accident, his tackling wasn't always as forgivable.

In 2007-08 Wenger was accused of hypocrisy for failing to condemn Diaby for a shocking tackle on Bolton's Gretar Steinsson, five weeks after Eduardo's injury, that resulted in a straight red card.

Arsenal's official website described the 2007-08 season as Diaby's 'most productive to date' but in reality it was more of a damp squib. He seemed to have established himself in an exceptionally talented midfield when another injury saw him fade away.

His dismissal at Bolton ruled him out for a vital period in the run in for the title, but he was still eligible for the Champions League quarter-final at Liverpool, where he again showed a glimpse of his attacking potential with a goal that gave Arsenal a short-lived lead during the second leg.

At the start of the following season it seemed that Diaby was, at last, starting to make everyone see what the fuss was all about.

Inevitably a thigh injury kept him out for the first few games, but when he returned to a struggling side in October he seemed to be the missing link in a midfield that looked considerably weaker than it had 12 months beforehand.

Arguably his best game in an Arsenal shirt came in a 2-1 win over Manchester United in early November, a game it was widely expected Arsenal would lose.

Diaby was immense, dominating all over the pitch, using his physical power to shrug off multiple challengers in the way Vieira used to but also showing the kind of attacking flair and potential his predecessor lacked.

It's tempting to see this as his high-watermark, but Diaby still produced excellent performances. Sadly they were far more sporadic than the demands of a side with designs of winning trophies required - and in one specific case at Old Trafford, he did something that defied sanity.

Early in the 2009-10 season Arsenal were outplaying United and leading 1-0 thanks to some improvisational brilliance from Arshavin.

Early in the second period the referee, officially Mike Dean although Darren Fletcher appeared to have been acting as a surrogate official, gave a classic Old Trafford decision by awarding Wayne Rooney a penalty for a subtle dive over Manuel Almunia's arm.

It never takes a lot to shift the momentum at Old Trafford, but Arsenal were still comfortable enough at 1-1 when Diaby scored of the stupidest own goals Arsenal have ever conceded, an award for which there are plenty of contenders.

Watching replays of the goal over two years after the event it's impossible to work out what was going through Diaby's mind. With 63 minutes on the clock Ryan Giggs delivered a poor cross from the right wing that only Diaby had any chance of winning. With no attackers anywhere near him Diaby only had to head the ball behind for a corner or aim for a well-placed team mate. Instead he flexed his neck muscles and picked out the top corner of the net. It's possible he hesitated, but he couldn't have picked out the far corner with any more accuracy if he'd been a United agent (which, it's probably legally advisable to make clear given the number of conspiracy theories that appear elsewhere in this book, he wasn't and isn't).

Arsenal duly lost a game they had dominated and although Diaby made more appearances that season than any other, his influence remained limited.

He was one of France's best players in the 2010 World Cup, but that is almost the ultimate example of damnation by faint praise and he failed to use it as a platform, again spending an almost absurd amount of the following seasons out with a succession of injuries.

Diaby would spend three weeks on the sidelines, return for a substitute appearance, eg against Chelsea in the 3-1 win at the Emirates and then pick up an injury in the next game - in this instance after 27 minutes at Wigan.

Again he came back into the side and again he almost immediately forced his way out of it again, getting a particularly stupid red card in possibly the stupidest game Arsenal ever played, a 4-4 draw at Newcastle.

With Arsenal 4-0 ahead Diaby went in for a challenge with Joey Barton, who was, as was his custom, intent on winning the ball and not too worried about what happened afterwards.

Barton's chequered history has been well documented elsewhere but on this occasion he made a legal challenge and connected with the ball first before his follow through connected with Diaby.

Perhaps experiencing a flashback to the Smith tackle, Diaby reacted by giving Barton an almost effeminate push in the back, which he then followed up with a shove on Kevin Nolan.

On another day he might have escaped with a yellow card, but instead the referee Phil Dowd sent him off, meaning Diaby was widely blamed for the debacle that followed as Arsenal conceded four goals in the final 22 minutes.

This was only partly fair. The officiating didn't help. Dowd awarded Newcastle two contentious, but not outrageous, penalties and van Persie had a late winner incorrectly flagged offside, albeit after Newcastle had had a goal wrongly ruled out for the same infringement.

Had decisions evened themselves out Arsenal would probably have won fairly comfortably, but in Diaby's absence the ten remaining players should have been able to hold on in the way previous Arsenal sides defended far slenderer leads after red cards for Dennis Bergkamp and Patrick Vieira - both Arsenal players whose efforts for the cause meant they were forgiven for more serious lapses in discipline.

Had he been born a few years earlier a player like Diaby could have been mentored by more senior players, but in a team that lacked leaders he was cursed to be a perennial disappointment, after several false dawns.

By the end of the 10-11 season it was widely expected he would leave.

One report claimed Arsenal had turned down an offer of £10 million from an unnamed Turkish club, which would have represented excellent business, but Wenger apparently still wanted to keep him, even after a spectacular own goal was scored on his behalf that summer when The Sun ran a story headlined: "I own and wear a Tottenham shirt."

It's possible, probable even, that Diaby made a dry remark that was taken out of context.

The paper, never knowingly guilty of either underselling a story or observing the highest journalistic standards, "revealed" that Diaby owned a Tottenham shirt, which was given to him by his international team mate and friend Younes Kaboul.

This was hardly news. Diaby would almost certainly have swapped shirts with Kaboul at the end of a London derby, as would a number of his other team mates, meaning he would have any number of rival shirts in his collection.

The Sun claimed he wore it around the house, backing this up with the quote: "It's more difficult to wear in the street. There you are not safe."

That was probably a joke, though before the season was out L'Equipe had run an article casting doubt on his future, saying he hadn't ruled out a move and that he was coveted by Manchester City, Chelsea, Inter Milan and Juventus.

That may also have been a joke.

19) WILLIAM GALLAS

Jets of red and white ticker tape shoot from the podium into the sky. Arsenal players are cavorting. Nicklas Bendtner playfully stuffs some of the discarded tape down the back of Tomas Rosicky's shorts.

There is joy on every Arsenal face, because they have done it. They have won a trophy, felling European giants Juventus and Real Madrid in the process.

In the middle of it all stands their leader William Gallas, holding aloft the Emirates Cup.

It is the only trophy he will touch during his four years with the Gunners.

If there were a direct correlation between a player's talent and his popularity with supporters, William Gallas would have been ranked alongside the likes of Wright, Vieira and Henry in the affections of Arsenal supporters.

As a player, he ranks alongside Cruyff, Maradona and Bobby Moore, or at least he does in his own mind, the contents of which have regularly been spilled into the tape recorders of sympathetic French journalists and the ghost writer of his autobiography, Christine Kelly.

Unable to buy a copy in the UK, I ordered Gallas' autobiography from Amazon France and it arrived 48 hours later, wrapped in a red ribbon, with the words: "Il a Sauve les Bleus! (He saved the Blues!)" emblazoned in white in a giant font, a reference to the goal he scored in France's infamous World Cup play-off with Ireland.

Entitled: "La Parole est a la defence," which translates clumsily into English as, "It's the defence's turn to speak," it was released after Gallas's first season at Arsenal, when he nearly won what would have been his third title in four years.

Nearly, however, is the operative word. When one looks at Gallas' career, his greatest achievements were two Premier League medals, won with a Chelsea side bankrolled to the extent that the odds were stacked so dramatically against their rivals that they can hardly be equated to the titles won by, for example, Brian Clough or Howard Wilkinson with Nottingham Forest and Leeds, or even George Graham's successes with Arsenal.

He played, competently enough, in a World Cup final, but otherwise his is a modest return for someone who repeatedly delivered sermons about the importance of the team ethic, but who on even the most superficial of readings seemed self-obsessed - even by a footballer's own narcissistic standards.

Take for example the banner accompanying his book, an incredible perspective to take on a game that almost everyone else remembers for one of the most significant pieces of cheating ever to take place on a football field.

To Gallas's credit in the immediate aftermath of the goal he scored following Henry's handball against Ireland he seemed almost embarrassed and his celebrations were distinctly muted.

Perhaps the declaration that he had single-handedly rescued the French national side may have been the work of an over-excitable advisor, but he presumably could have vetoed this fate-temptingly premature statement, particularly in the wake of what actually happened to the French in South Africa. Elimination by the Irish might well have been the kinder fate.

The book's cover shows Gallas wearing a French national jersey with a tricolore painted on his right cheek.

The message, in case you didn't quite get it, is "I'm French and I care." The effect is to suggest he's slightly delusional.

And just when you're starting to harbour unkind thoughts about how far detached from the rest of the world these footballers are, you read that all proceeds have been donated to the handicapped and begin to feel just a little guilty.

This autobiography has yet to see the light of day in England.

There's a potentially fascinating book to be written about Gallas, but the man himself isn't likely to be the author.

"Parole" is the ghosted product of a series of interviews with the subject, with seemingly no input at all from other parties.

That in itself doesn't make it vastly different from any number of ghosted autobiographies but it seems slender and can easily be knocked off on a rainy afternoon. That represents a stark contrast to autobiography of the man he replaced at Arsenal.

Ashley Cole's "My Defence" is an almost toxic piece of work, a book that was intended to redeem Cole in the eyes of the public but instead made him look a dozen times worse than he would have done had he simply kept his mouth shut.

If we're being generous to Cole, a hefty portion of the blame for this has to go to his advisors, and to an even greater extent his ghost writer, whose jarring style represents arguably a far greater crime than the fabled line about crashing his car when he was only offered 55k a week.

Cole's ghost regularly deploys agonisingly contrived cockneyisms to suggest he's portraying the authentic voice of the East End Boy "done" good, as if he were writing a Graham Swift novel.

It's difficult to square the wounded soul who tells his wife Cheryl, "I've got too much pride for this shit babes, people are going to think I want to join Chelsea!" and "It's a carrot that don't belong in fair justice," with terms like "aided and abetted" that's it's almost impossible to imagine him saying.

And while his advisors may ultimately have secured him the kind of deal he felt he was worth, this was hardly the staggering coup you'd think they'd pulled off given the praise Cole showers them with.

If Mourinho rated Cole as the best left-back in the world, given the kind of money he had at his disposal it would have taken a congenital idiot not to have got him a lucrative deal.

And yet, even given the standard of the writing, what does come across is a desperate sense of sadness, that a player who was nurtured by Arsenal and obviously loved the club felt he had to leave.

And for all the temptation to dismiss Cole as a treacherous, money-obsessed tart, he made a number of points about the development of the Arsenal squad that had a discomforting ring of truth to them.

The Invicibles were a unit on and off the field, rarely leaving the training ground until mid-afternoon.

Cole was dismayed by the way the newcomers to the squad would leave as soon as training had finished and he named names, saying he knew nothing about Reyes, Toure, Eboue, Fabregas and Senderos.

Senderos in particular opened himself up for criticism by spurning advice from Martin Keown, blowing his cheeks out indolently to effectively snub a central defender who had won three titles and three FA Cups with Arsenal.

The way Senderos' career evolved after a promising start - he kept Campbell out of the 2005 FA Cup final winning side - suggests he should have paid closer attention.

He became, to use cricketing parlance, Didier Drogba's "bunny" and was bullied by the Ivorian centre forward in a way that Adams, Bould and Keown would never have allowed.

Sol Campbell's mystifying departure in 2006 - he was expected to move abroad but ended up at Portsmouth - marked the end of an era at Arsenal.

Campbell was the last Arsenal central defender opponents feared playing against and for the first time in 23 years, since Tony Adams made his debut, the Gunners looked vulnerable in that area.

At the start of the 2006-07 season, Arsenal's first choice central defensive partnership was Senderos and Toure, with the raw Johan Djorou as a back-up.

It was an area that urgently needed strengthening and with Cole by now desperate to get away, Wenger and Dein saw an opportunity to bring in a new "colossus".

It was perhaps surprising to see Gallas emerge as the makeweight in the deal, given the frequency with which stories linking him with a move to AC Milan had appeared in the press in the months running up to his departure from the Bridge.

Gallas will not be the last player to have his name linked with a move to a major club by an excitable agent and these stories had more credibility than some, but even the most committed Gunners fans would have conceded that at the time a switch to Arsenal was at best a sideways move.

These stories resurfaced four years later when the free-agent Gallas was once again linked with the continent's biggest clubs after his contract with Arsenal expired.

He joined Tottenham Hotspur.

The 2006 deal took a month to go through, as the usual posturing took place, with Chelsea at first saying the price was too high, even though Dein knew full well they could afford to pay almost anything Arsenal asked.

At one point Wenger asked an exasperated Cole if he'd heard any news on the deal.

"Shouldn't I be asking you that?" came the reply, as Cole himself seemed resigned to staying put, but the deal was finally revived on deadline day, presumably as it dawned on Gallas that he too might end up stuck at a club he had grown to resent.

The paperwork was eventually completed, but it was done so late the deal needed special ratification from the FA - the swap was announced at 1.25am, after deadline day had elapsed.

The Gallas era was about to begin.

Gallas is an occasionally infuriating character who also happens to be an exceptional player - albeit not one who you'd appoint as your team's morale officer.

As with Cole, there is a temptation to portray him as a mercenary villain, particularly given that he ended up at The Lane, but as ever Gallas' story is far more complicated and strewn with a number of "what ifs."

With better timing he might have joined Arsenal earlier in his career, with better luck he might have led Arsenal to the title in 2008 and but for a fleeting moment of insanity from Zinedine Zidane he might have won the 2006 World Cup.

Instead his four years at the Emirates coincided with Arsenal's most barren period, in terms of silverware, since the 1980s.

He was reported, fairly or otherwise, to be a major source of dressing room disruption and the overriding memory of his time with the club was his astonishing performance at Birmingham City when he at first threatened to walk off in protest at a late penalty that robbed Arsenal of two points and then sat crying on the pitch.

He will be equally remembered for being the first senior player to join Tottenham directly from Arsenal since Pat Jennings in 1985 and although this was hardly a defection on the scale of Sol Campbell's in 2001, his talent to popularity ratio was possibly the worst of any Arsenal player ever to pull on a red shirt.

Even when he was performing outstandingly well he was respected rather than loved, so did he ever stand a chance at the Emirates?

Gallas's crime is perhaps that he loves playing football more than he loves being at any one club.

He is a second-generation immigrant, whose parents come from Guadeloupe and returned there when he was just a teenager.

Gallas was raised in an "HLM" on the Allee St Exupery in Villeneuve-la-Garenne by his father Symbert, a plumber and his mother Viviane, a postal worker.

The suburb is about a mile north west of the Stade de France. Its name implies that it is a new town, but it was a hamlet at the time of the French revolution and given the status of a town in 1929.

By the time Gallas' parents arrived there in the mid-1970s it had been consumed by the banlieue.

To the outsider there is a certain sadness about the grey cubes but calling it a deprived area might be stretching things a little.

Parisians park as only they can, cramming Renault Clios into spaces barely big enough for scooters and the sight of a Lidl on one of the corners is enough to make the sternest of hearts sink a little, but the planners remembered to plant trees along the road sides and left in a reasonable amount of green space, meaning the area's rural past isn't an entirely distant memory.

Crucially they also included the kind of all weather, or rather fine gravel, football field where a generation of French players first learned how to kick a ball.

A measure of Gallas' early progress can be gauged by the nickname his friends gave him: Tigana.

In a throwback to the tales told by post-war era British pros of using tennis balls or bundles of rags as a substitute for a real football, Gallas would use almost anything as a ball, including yoghurt pots and boxes of cheese and either play in the hallway or stand by the window of his fifth floor apartment with his nose pressed against the glass until his parents yielded to his friends' demands for him to come and play with them.

In one of the more humanising passages in his autobiography, Gallas recalls how he would volunteer to take his baby-sister for walks, before parking her pram next to the pitch so he could play football.

As an incentive to keep checking on her, Gallas would rush over to give her a kiss every time he scored a goal.

When he once lost a toe nail, while shooting with his right foot, he decided to learn how to play with his left, developing the versatility that would become at the same time both an asset and a liability.

He would play for 14 hours per day, but while his parents were delighted to see him occupying himself and channelling his energies, it was his uncle Henri, who played at non-league level, who was the only member of his family to see the potential that was obvious to the more trained eye.

Jacques Gato, the coach at his first club, Amicale Villeneuve La Garenne, put Gallas' name forward for Clairefontaine, but the timing could hardly have been worse.

Having spent weeks waiting for news of his application, Gallas ripped open the envelope from the FFF, jumped with joy when he read he'd been accepted and screamed with delight as he told his parents.

Their response threatened to shatter his dreams: "We've decided to return to Guadeloupe, to live."

Given how Gallas habitually reacted to bad news when he was pushing 30, it isn't hard to imagine what followed.

The man himself said his world imploded and that his life was "broken" at the age of 13.

Gallas believed his chances of becoming a professional hinged on going to Clairefontaine, reasoning that a comparable apprenticeship would be impossible in Guadeloupe due to its infrastructure.

He refused to leave France, threw the kind of tantrum later seen at St. Andrews and hatched a secret plan to live with his uncle and kindred spirit Henri. Henri's influence eventually persuaded his brother and sister-in-law to take what must have been the horrendous decision to allow their boy to stay in France, on the condition that the slightest misbehaviour would result in him taking the next flight to Guadeloupe.

Yet for an individual as headstrong as Gallas and one entering the turbulent period between adolescence and adulthood, a level of misbehaviour was almost inevitable, particularly in the absence of his parents.

In his first year at Clairefontaine his coach Christian Damiano, who went on to work with Jean Tigana at Fulham and Gerard Houillier at Liverpool, warned him that while he was among the most gifted players of that year's intake, he was inattentive and lacked discipline.

Damiano attributed this to a lack of parental guidance and regularly covered up for Gallas, though after one misdemeanour too many he taught him a lesson in the art of humiliation by forcing him to muck out the dressing rooms for failing to pay attention during a speech on the need to respect the cleaning staff.

A lesser talent might not have got away with what was to follow.

In his second year his coach was a Brazilian, Franciso Filho, and it was Filho who decided that Gallas, at that point thought of as a striker, should play at the back.

Filho was a sharper tongued and altogether less sympathetic character than Damiano, but he commanded respect through his technical ability.

He reduced Gallas to tears when he was unable to perform one task, bawling: "You're nothing but a little cunt. If you can't control the ball go back to Guadeloupe. Do you think your parents left you here for you to fail?"

The words stung, but if they reinforced Gallas' professional determination, they did little to keep him out of trouble.

He was one of the last players in his year group to find a host club for his third year and was attracted to Caen where the regime was less stringent than elsewhere, notably Auxerre, which he described as a "prison".

At Caen Gallas found another kindred spirit in the under-18 coach Marc Dennis.

Instantly attracted to him by his performances on the field, Dennis was undeterred by (and possibly attracted by) Gallas' poor academic record, which mirrored his own.

One of the oddities of the relationship was that Dennis would often make racial remarks to Gallas, for example teling him "you blacks run faster than us."

To the outsider this can seem shocking, but context is everything when it comes to racism. Taken in isolation, Dennis's remarks could be viewed as racist and not dissimilar to the Spain coach Luis Aragones' rant about Thierry Henry, when he described him as a "black shit".

But between consenting adults the normal rules are sometimes waived, to the confusion of those of us who suffer from white guilt.

During the cricket World Cup in England in 2009, I travelled to one game on a Nottingham shuttle bus and sat behind four English supporters, all of whom were in their early 20s and two of whom were Asian.

At one point one of the Asians launched into a vocal parody of a Pakistani bus conductor ("Budbud, dingding, tickets please!") to the hilarity of his friends.

He then continued and pointed to his white friend: "You see I can say that, but if you say that it's racist."

The four men were obviously totally at ease in each other's company and I heard a similar story from a local football manager in Kent, who said that the only tribal divisions that existed at his club were those between his players and the opposition. He told me that his coach would use any and every term of abuse to banter with black players: "In the dressing room they call him fatty and he calls them anything he likes."

Consent was the guiding principle. If Jim Davidson or Ron Atkinson had claimed blacks ran faster than whites a tabloid furore would have erupted.

Gallas would have been outraged if someone had shouted this at him in the street, but he relished the banter with Dennis and their relationship gave him some leeway - perhaps a little too much.

It seems unlikely that Gallas would have been able to develop a fondness for whisky and coke if he'd been locked in Guy Roux's metaphorical jail at Auxerre, but at Caen he nearly found himself behind real bars when he stole a team mate's credit card.

The matter was dealt with in house, with Gallas demoted from the first team, for which he'd made his debut at 18, to the development squad by way of punishment.

Worse was to follow. He tested positive for cannabis and though he was cleared when the B test proved negative, an exceptionally unusual event, the saga contributed to an air of suspicion and it certainly cultivated his sense of paranoia.

Gallas was found innocent, unlike French national goalkeepers Fabien Barthez and Bernard Lama, both of whom smoked dope, but his career was still stalled, both by this and by an ulcer caused by his contact lenses.

There were, however, portents of the career to follow. He was part of a European "Espoir" title winning sqaud with Henry, Trezeuguet, Anelka and Mikael Silvestre in the summer of 1996.

At the end of the 1995-96 season Caen won promotion to the French top flight and Gallas's tear ducts, which would see a certain amount of use over the next decade and a half, began to leak with pride before he made his Ligue 1 debut against Lens on August 10.

There he was pitted against Titi Camara, who would later be regarded as something of a joke figure at Liverpool but who at the time was one of the most prolific strikers in French Football.

If the emotion of the occasion got to Gallas it didn't affect his performance and despite Caen's relegation and his own fractured campaign he did enough to earn a move to Marseille, where a different kind of prison awaited.

As a general rule in life it pays never to overestimate professional competence, more so when it comes to deal with the kind of people employed to run football clubs and especially when it comes to Olympique Marseilles.

During the VA-OM affair certain Marseilles officials proved exceptionally able at forgetting what they'd been doing and old habits died hard.

When Gallas signed for OM in 1997 he was the victim of the kind of administrative "oversight" that defies credibility.

Despite being one of the first players to sign a deal for that year, Gallas's name was not one of the 25 sent to the FFF for ratification.

With French clubs allowed to employ a maximum of 25 players, Gallas found himself in a kind of footballing purgatory.

Through no fault of his own he was classified as an amateur, which seemed inexplicable until one remembers the deal was concluded by Marseille's president Robert-Louis Dreyfus, who foisted the player on a sceptical coach, Rolland Courbis.

Whether this was accidental or not, Gallas was in a no-win situation. His options were equally unappealing, but he decided against what he saw would be the humiliation of a return to Caen on loan and bided his time, training during the week and drinking too much at the weekends in an attempt to stave off depression. In January 1998 he would have been cleared to play, but fate again intervened when he suffered a fractured big toe, turning him from a fit but ineligible player into an eligible but unfit one.

He made just three appearances for OM in his debut year, but the way he dealt with that misfortune converted Courbis from a sceptic into a genuine believer.

1998-99 was Gallas's breakthrough season. He established himself at left-back and began to attract the attention of people in the know, being voted "revelation of the year" by France Football.

He flagellated himself every time he made a mistake, although to describe himself as his own harshest critic would be inaccurate, given that the crowd at the Velodrome were merciless to any player who had the temerity to make a mistake - as Gallas once found out when he allowed a Rennes player to score an equaliser.

If the season ultimately ended in disappointment - Marseille were denied the title when Bordeaux scored their 89th-minute winner at PSG on the final day of the season - by finishing second OM had done enough to return to the Champions League after a seven year absence and it was here that Gallas announced himself on the European stage, in one of the most eventful weeks of his life.

On October 13 1999 he walked away, miraculously unharmed, from a crash on the autoroute but within 48 hours he had committed one of the worst errors of his career in a crucial league match with Lyon, when he allowed his concentration to drift and gifted a winner to Sonny Anderson.

Gallas was mortified and unable to look his team mates in the eye afterwards, but the following day his captain, Robert Pires told him: "Great players always manage to keep their heads up. It's at these moments that we see their true level."

Still furious with himself, Gallas chose the next match, a Champions League group game with Manchester United, to make his entrance.

Swearing he wouldn't make a single error, Gallas not only helped nullify one of Europe's most effective strike duos in Andy Cole and Dwight Yorke, he scored a stunning goal in the 69th-minute, surging through the United defence, playing a one-two with Stephane Delmat and then lashing the ball past Mark Bosnich for his first ever goal as a professional.

Gallas's self-belief rocketed as a result. Before taking on United he wasn't sure he even deserved to be on the same pitch as Yorke and Cole. Yet having scored a goal, something he seldom did even in training, and more importantly having kept the opposition at bay, Gallas began to develop the conviction that he was not only at home at the highest level, but that he was worthy of every column inch of praise showered on him.

He also started to feel he was a prophet doomed to go unrecognised in his own land.

Gallas might have been performing well, but Marseille, now under the former Spain coach Javier Clemente, were struggling to recapture the form of the previous season, Courbis having been fired after a poor start.

The OM supporters had little time for the distinction between individual and team performances and Gallas, who could only be as good as his team mates, badly missed Laurent Blanc, who had been allowed to join Internazionale. Instead of being mobbed by adoring fans, Gallas would now be abused if he walked round the city centre following a defeat: "you should be training, not shopping!" one fan scowled at him.

Clemente had little time for highly-strung players but the pair initially got on well, until Gallas objected to being asked to play at either left or right back and not in the "axe", leading to a furious row between the two and hardening Gallas's desire for a move.

"My versatility was becoming a problem," he wrote, with some understatement. It was an issue he never successfully resolved.

Raymond Dommench once said that Gallas was capable of playing in every position in the back four and of being the best player wherever he played.

Gallas was clearly flattered by this assessment, but asking him to demonstrate it would provoke a wounded, self-absorbed reaction.

He told Clemente he would rather be left on the bench than play "out of position" saying: "find a true left back or right back, but not me."

Clemente, a man who used to relax by hitting golf balls and pretending they were the heads of journalists, took this predictably well. By the end of the season Gallas was on his way, spurning an offer from Bayern Munich ("too cold") to join Chelsea for the 2001-02 season.

Like Petit and Pires, his first impression was that he would not be able to cope with the pace and physicality of the game, but with Petit and Desailly taking him under their wings, he flourished as Chelsea came sixth and reached the FA Cup final in his first season there - a reasonable achievement in the pre-Abramovich era.

At the time Chelsea were a club still trying to establish themselves among English football's elite, backed by the millions of the late Matthew Harding, who died in a helicopter crash in 1996 while travelling to a game at Bolton.

They were, however, already paying huge salaries to players like Desailly and Petit, who were arguably past their peak. For all the money invested, they still lagged significantly behind Wenger's Arsenal, making them clear, if not heavy, underdogs for the 2002 FA Cup final.

Gallas's recollection of this match again reveals much about his mindset. It was the biggest game of his career at that point, but he can't even remember the score correctly.

"This game will always leave a bitter taste … I had to play in three different positions!" he wrote, having started alongside his "big brother" Desailly in the centre. "At the start of the game we were 1-0 up and succeeded in blocking Thierry Henry as well as we could, so I don't understand why they bombed me out to left-back. At that moment we let in a goal. 1-1. 20 minutes later they told me: 'William, change, you're playing right back'. It was madness, I didn't understand anything anymore. At the end we'd lost 3-1, when we'd been comfortably 1-0 up. I would like to have discussed this with the coach but this wasn't the kind of thing we could bring up with him. But I told myself that if I wanted to play in a fixed position I would have to let him know."

Had he discussed this with Ranieri, the coach's first reaction might have been to remind him they'd actually lost 2-0 as opposed to 3-1. Ranieri might have added that Chelsea had never scored a goal, nor looked like scoring one, but that it had needed two exceptional goals from Parlour and Ljungberg to break down a highly efficient Chelsea defence that had, until the 70th-minute, completely nullified a formidable Arsenal attack.

Chelsea made progress the following season under Ranieri and they qualified for the Champions League on the final day by beating Liverpool in a game that was billed as critical to the club's future, as it sought to escape debts rising over £100million.

That figure was subsequently rendered irrelevant by the arrival of Roman Abramovich, but all the while Gallas, who'd been the subject of interest from Leeds and Arsenal that summer, was busy cultivating a sense of grievance over what he now referred to as his "versatility trap" and it seems unlikely his team mates were unaware of his level of self-regard.

Gallas compared Jose Mourinho's arrival at Stamford Bridge as the equivalent of being smacked in the face by a tornado and for the next two seasons they were one of the most effective forces ever seen in British football, ruthlessly exterminating all comers with a minimum of finesse and a maximum of efficiency.

It was seldom pretty to watch but it was impossible to argue with the results. The 2004-05 and 2005-06 campaigns were relatively joyless affairs for neutrals and Gallas, despite being in the most successful period of his career, seemed both unimpressed and apparently incapable of savouring his victories - or deriving any joy from them at all.

He devotes less than two pages of his book to the trophies he won (and two paragraphs to the 2006 World Cup campaign) but nearly 20 to his grievances, with Mourinho, Abramovich and the club.

These can be summed up as follows: he resented being asked to make use of his versatility; he resented being asked to play while not fully recovered from injury and he resented not being paid the wages the other star players, specifically Lampard, Terry, Makele and Drogba were being offered.

During the 2005-06 season stories linking Gallas to a high profile move to the continent - usually Milan - were an almost daily occurrence, appearing so frequently it was difficult to believe his representatives weren't just dictating them to their contacts in the tabloids.

When he instead joined Arsenal, on September 1 2006, the affair was handled with incredible ineptitude by Chelsea, whose director of communications was Simon Greenberg, a former Evening Standard sports editor who was later involved in England's doomed bid to host the 2018 World Cup and part of News International's post-hacking clean-up operation. Chelsea accused Gallas of "putting out misinformation" about Mourinho and claimed Gallas had threatened to score an own goal if forced to stay at Stamford Bridge.

It also accused him of refusing to play in the FA Cup semi-final against Liverpool and began to sound sinister, with its references to the Chelsea "family".

"When Jose Mourinho generously offered him a way back into the 'family' after the American tour, this was thrown back in the Chelsea manager's face.

"The manager told him that, even if he did not agree a new contract but returned to the 'family' and abided by the rules, he would still select the best players available and would not punish him playing wise.

"He threatened that if he was forced to play, or if he was disciplined and financially punished for his breach of the rules, he could score an own goal or get himself sent off, or make deliberate mistakes.

"However despite meetings to try and resolve the problems Gallas made it clear to Jose Mourinho he would never play for Chelsea again."

The episode proved Chelsea needed no help when it came to scoring own goals. This story would have been far-fetched by tabloid standards. That it came from Chelsea's own PR department handed Gallas the moral high ground.

"All this is very, very petty on behalf of Chelsea," he said. "But at the same time, coming on behalf of its new leaders, that does not surprise me. Even if Chelsea has much money, its new leaders lack class."

This was exactly what Arsenal fans wanted to hear. It allowed them to believe they had swapped a treacherous little turncoat, who had abandoned his boyhood team for a move to a jumped-up West London trailer park, for a man of honour, however far from reality that actually was.

The consensus was, after one injury-hit season, that Arsenal might have got the better of the deal and Wenger was certainly impressed enough to name Gallas captain for 2007-08, ahead of Toure and Gilberto.

The received wisdom on this campaign is that Arsenal were destined to win the league, but that they failed to recover from the physical and psychological damage sustained during the infamous 2-2 draw at Birmingham.

Gallas, while not trying to excuse his conduct that day, believed the warning signs were there after a 2-0 win over Wigan in November, when Gallas himself had broken the deadlock with an 83rd-minute header.

He felt Arsenal's opponents had begun to figure them out and were starting to lose their fear, while some of his younger team mates thought the title was already in the bag.

In the meantime however, Gallas continued to lead from the front. On December 16 he headed the only goal in a 1-0 win over Chelsea at the Emirates, a performance that appeared to underline the Gunners' title credentials as they beat the Russian's playthings for the first time since 2004.

Some minds were elsewhere however. Panicking at his inability to secure a first team place, Lassana Diarra jumped ship to join Portsmouth, while the two midfielders ahead of him, Flamini and Hleb, were already busily trying to engineer moves abroad, as was Adebayor.

Yet just as some standards appeared to be slipping, with two embarrassing defeats at Manchester United (4-0) and Tottenham (5-1) ending Arsenal's interest in the domestic cups, Eduardo de Silva began to emerge as the lethal finisher Arsenal needed, bolstering the league form to the extent that the Gunners had a five-point lead by the time they travelled to St. Andrews on February 23.

It's worth remembering, given the hysterical and paranoid reaction that followed, that Arsenal had been lucky to draw against Birmingham a month earlier, the 1-1 scoreline at home owing a lot to a fortunate penalty decision for a perceived foul by Stephen Carr on Eduardo, although it's not surprising that hardly anyone does.

"The match at Birmingham would sink a lot of ink," Gallas wrote, again with huge understatement, claiming to have detected signs in the pre-game warm-up that his team mates weren't showing sufficient determination.

The rematch was just three minutes old when the Croatian striker's life as he knew it changed forever.

Gathering a pass from Clichy just inside the Birmingham half, Eduardo spun on his heel and played a pass towards Adebayor.

It wasn't a dazzling piece of skill, but it was quick enough to deceive the lumbering Taylor, who had less than a split second to decide whether to pull out of the challenge or follow through.

His right leg, several inches off the ground, connected with Eduardo's lower right shin and the momentum saw the striker's leg almost snapped, his foot and the lower part of the leg pressed flat on the floor, while the remainder of the leg was upright.

The bone burst through the skin and only the rapid action by medical staff at the ground and later at Selly Oak hospital saved him from amputation.

"We were all affected," Gallas wrote. "I told my players not to think about it. It seemed to me in all honesty and having seen footage of it several times that Taylor wasn't really trying to commit a foul… I thought he was trying to play the ball and that Eduardo was too quick."

The perception at the time was that Arsenal were being bullied out of the title.

Gallas did what a captain should by instructing his team mates not to dwell on the incident but to use it as motivation and win it for their team mate.

And while he may have been right, this wasn't the first or last time his advice would go unheeded.

"A large part of our hopes went with Eduardo in the third minute of the game," Gallas admitted. "Our players were too young to handle the pressure. The average age was around 24, which meant we had kids of 20 or 22 years old and I sensed they would have trouble staying on the road. I'd been there and I knew what goes on in the head."

Eduardo's replacement, Theo Walcott, scored twice in the second half to make it 2-1, but in the last minute of injury time Gael Clichy made a clean tackle on Stuart Parnaby, only for Mike Dean to award a penalty, which James McFadden scored.

This was the incident that tipped Gallas over the edge.

The BBC's commentator Jonathan Pearce, never one to underhype an occasion, roared "Gallas is in a state of disbelief," as he raced to the touchline, seemingly intent on hitting someone and having to be restrained by an official.

He returned to the pitch as McFadden scored, slumped to the floor and started to cry, sitting on the turf alone, pointedly ignored by his team mates and manager.

For an Arsenal player it was a tantrum unparalleled in living memory. He made Ian Wright look like a Buddhist monk and in hindsight Gallas admitted it was "stupid" to let his emotions get the better of him.

"I'll never make a mistake like that again," he wrote. "Was it a good attitude for a player? No. Was it a good reaction from a captain? No. (But) it makes me think of Zinedine Zidane and I understand his reaction to Materazzi at the World Cup final."

Wenger ignored calls to strip him of the captaincy, on this occasion, but Gallas said the result was "the beginning of the end" and was later told by Manchester United players that the watching Alex Ferguson had used the result to galvanise his side.

Yet it needn't have been terminal for Arsenal's title chances. Had they won their next three league games instead of drawing against beatable opposition, (Villa, Middlesbrough and Wigan) the 2-1 defeats at Chelsea and United wouldn't have mattered - the Gunners would still have won the league by two points.

Gallas threw his shirt to the Arsenal fans after the unlucky defeat at the Bridge and continued his atonement a week later when he scored as Arsenal rallied from two goals down to win 3-2 at Bolton, with just 10 men after Diaby's dismissal.

Few Arsenal fans cared about Gallas's tantrums if he was doing the business out on the pitch, but circumstances often beyond his and Wenger's control meant they finished the season with nothing.

At Stamford Bridge Didier Drogba's equaliser was allowed to stand despite it being offside.

In the Champions League quarter-final with Liverpool Arsenal were denied a penalty in the first leg despite Dirk Kuyt clearly fouling Hleb in the area and in the second leg at Anfield Kolo Toure was penalised for a far less obvious foul on Ryan Babel, seconds after Adebayor's away goal had made it 3-3 on aggregate.

This made the suggestion that refereeing decisions even themselves out over the course of the season sound especially hollow, but the Babel incident illustrated two of Arsenal's frailties.

In the immediate aftermath Wenger could be seen gesturing for his players to calm down, knowing there were seven minutes left on the clock.

Walcott, whose staggering run from the edge of his own area, had set up the goal, was mobbed by Fabregas and Hleb, but from the kick-off Babel surged down the left flank, where injury had prevented Arsenal from fielding either Sagna or Eboue.

Had Gallas played at right back for one game, allowing Toure to remain in the central defensive role he'd performed throughout the Invicible season, Babel might never have been in a position to tumble over Toure's leg - assuming Gallas was as good at right back as he believed himself to be.

Instead, however unjustly, Arsenal were out and as they duly went backwards the following season, Gallas finally exhausted even Wenger's patience.

In November 2008 he sat down in Paris with Jerome Pugmire of the Associated Press and gave an interview, ostensibly to plug his autobiography.

The most controversial part of the book was a thinly-veiled attack on his team mates, including the newly arrived Nasri, who Gallas referred to as "Player S" in his book.

Nasri's crime was to have sat in Thierry Henry's seat during Euro 2008, a seemingly trivial incident that Gallas deemed worthy of two pages.

Gallas asked Nasri to move. He initially refused, so Gallas raised his voice, prompting Nasri to ask him to speak a little more quietly.

This apparently innocuous request enraged Gallas.

"Who do you think you are?" he snarled back. "You're only 20 years old. You're not my friend."

Nasri, now understandably getting angry himself, said: "You're not my friend either!" and Gallas threatened to "sort things out" during training.

"When the moment came I had a choice," he wrote. "Either I could say nothing and then during training I could take him down a peg by giving him a kick on the ankle, or I could tell him his fortune."

He took the latter option and Nasri supposedly backed down, but Gallas then produced a number of incendiary comments he'd left out of the book concerning another team mate.

"When, as captain, some players come up to you and talk to you about a player complaining about him and then during the match you speak to this player and the player in question insults us, there comes a time where we can no longer comprehend how this can happen," he said. "I am trying to defend myself a bit without giving names. Otherwise I'm taking it all (the blame). It's very frustrating. I'm 31, the player is six years younger than me."

Pugmire asked Gallas if he wasn't taking a risk by speaking out.

"There are things that can't be said and can't be tolerated," he replied, but he'd either failed to grasp the impact going public would have or he no longer cared.

It didn't take too long for people to work out who "Player S" was and by referring to "a" player six years his junior, Gallas was also casting a pall over Van Persie, Sagna and, the most likely candidate, Adebayor.

This time Wenger was finally forced to react, stripping him of the captaincy and replacing him with Fabregas, but even at this hour he still defended him with the patience of a weary but loving headmaster testifying on behalf of a wayward teenager, saying that he was both "a great player and a great man."

Gallas again achieved partial redemption. As a captain he was never capable of persuading his troops to follow him over the top, but as a player he was often exemplary and still able to inspire by his deeds on the field, to the extent that by the time he left at the age of 33 in 2010 his petulance had been largely forgiven.

As ever with Gallas however, there was a twist. During France's farcical World Cup campaign he managed to fall out with Domenech, who was one of his few remaining allies and when the long-awaited call from Milan failed to materialise, he spurned an offer from Panathinaikos to sign for Tottenham, for less than half the salary he was on at Arsenal according to Harry Redknapp, (admittedly not always the most reliable source when it comes to figures).

It generated only a fraction of the furore that greeted Sol Campbell's move in the opposite direction nine years earlier, given that Gallas was entering the twilight of his career.

While the odd lunatic may have tossed around the obligatory "Judas" insult, other fans reacted with relief and in some cases laughter.

Both sentiments were premature.

In the build-up to the first North London derby of the 2010-11 season a headline claimed: "Sagna declares war on Gallas" but this was journalism at its worst, with even reputable news outlets leaping on a PA story which took a remark the right back made to the club's official website and twisted it for whatever nefarious purpose.

It was Gallas, who revealed he had lost a child at birth in his autobiography, who had helped console Sagna following the death of his brother Omar in 2008, giving the two men a bond that would transcend a mere game of football.

Sagna did use the word war, but only to describe the way they would compete during the match: "On the pitch there is a war, but off the pitch we are all friends, I'm not angry at him because he signed for our rivals.

"He was always very professional and he always gave everything. Football is football; I'm not furious against him. He needed to leave to play football and that is what he loves. He deserves a good reception because during the time he played for Arsenal he always did well."

That sentiment was echoed by Arsene Wenger, but both men must have known there was more chance of hades freezing than Gallas getting an ovation.

Nasri churlishly refused his offer of a pre-match handshake and Gallas was roundly jeered by the home support as Arsenal took a 2-0 lead.

This was, however, was tame by comparison to the abuse Campbell was subjected to by Spurs fans for years, even after he left Arsenal.

In one game at Portsmouth the travelling Tottenham contingent managed to come up with a chant that was insulting on racial, homophobic and humanist grounds: "Sol, Sol, wherever you may be, you're on the brink of lunacy, we don't give a fuck if you're hanging from a tree, you Judas cunt with HIV."

It was sung by fathers with small children and it outraged Pompey's then-manager Harry Redknapp, the man who was in charge of Spurs when Gallas returned to the Emirates for the first time.

There was nothing inevitable about Spurs' second half comeback to win that game 3-2, their first win at Arsenal since 1993 and their first win away at a so-called Big Four side in 69 attempts.

What was inevitable was that Gallas was outstanding, feeding off the derision of the crowd to earn the man-of-the-match award.

It was victory in one last battle for Gallas, though in the greater fight, to feel at ease in his own skin, the outcome hangs in the balance.

Gallas has always been the child from Villeneuve-la-Garenne who above all wanted to play the game. His lack of skills when it comes to dealing with people counted against him as a captain and will probably preclude him from coaching at the highest level. When his body no longer permits him to play football he may struggle to cope with retirement.

Or perhaps not: when he appeared for an exceptionally rare press conference before Tottenham's Champions League game with Milan in the San Siro, he was asked how he felt about his opposite number being suspended.

"Oh, I'm sorry, I didn't know that," he replied. "But then I don't follow football."

20) BACARY SAGNA

THERE'S something reassuring about Bacary Sagna.

His nickname, for fairly obvious reasons, is Bac, which has a double meaning in French, as a word for a vessel for carrying things and as an abbreviation for the baccalaureate, France's equivalent of A-levels.

Sagna is like one of the few diligent students in a classroom full of unruly and disruptive pupils, someone whom a flailing teacher can go to for an answer when the lesson risks spinning out of control because the likes of Adebayor and Gallas are misbehaving.

He may look flamboyant with his blonde braids, but he's the kind of player who never causes his manager problems off the field, despite the fact that he had to endure the grief of losing his older brother early in his Arsenal career.

Sagna had an apparently stable childhood, raised by his Senegalese parents in Sens, a town of around 25,000 inhabitants in the Yonne department, where his father was a metal worker and his mother cared for the elderly.

He played for the local team, FC Sens and grew up supporting Paris St Germain, like many of the French players who would eventually end up at Arsenal, rather than the region's dominant team AJ Auxerre.

When Auxerre tried to sign him as a 13-year-old his father said no, feeling it was too early for Bacary to leave the family home, but a year later he joined Guy Roux's football factory, initially as a striker.

Sagna was still working his way through Auxerre's junior set-up when his father wrote to Senegal's manager Bruno Metsu, alerting him to his son's availability for their 2002 World Cup squad.

He didn't even receive a reply, an oversight the Senegalese would eventually live to regret. Two years later Metsu's successor Amara Traore contacted Sagna's father to arrange a meeting, but the day before the two parties were due to meet up, according to Traore, Roux held a knife to Sagna's throat (metaphorically one assumes although with Roux it's difficult to be sure) and told him he would refuse to renew his contract if he opted to play for his parents' homeland.

The 2004-05 season loomed and Sagna, who by now had been converted into a right back, was about to make his breakthrough.

He played in roughly half Auxerre's games, including the final half hour of Auxerre's 2-1 win over second tier Sedan in the final of the Coupe de France, coming on for the injury-plagued Johan Radet.

It was Roux's final game in charge and Auxerre scraped through thanks to a goal in the fourth minute of injury time.

Sagna looked so much younger than his team mates he could almost have been mistaken for the mascot during the post-match celebrations, but he was already 22 and this relatively advanced age meant Arsenal were in two minds about recruiting him.

Gilles Grimandi, who was now working for Arsenal as a scout, watched Sagna on 30 or 40 occasions over three seasons (depending on whose account you read) which suggests a degree of uncertainty that hindsight proves was ungrounded.

When the luckless Radet suffered another serious injury during the 2005-06 season Sagna became the automatic first choice and a year later he was named in the French League's team of the year, finally prompting Wenger and Grimandi to act.

He joined in July 2007 for the usual undisclosed fee, one that this time was allegedly undisclosed to the tune of £6million.

"I know Abou Diaby from our time together at Auxerre and also Gael Clichy and Mathieu Flamini from the French under-21 team," he said. "Also Arsene Wenger is a major reason why I signed for Arsenal. He is an excellent manager with a fantastic record and I am really looking forward to working with him."

He arrived just days after Henry joined Barcelona and delivered a fairly prescient analysis of the season ahead.

"The fact no one really rates us means that maybe we can surprise people," he said. "The young players want to prove what they can do and I want to prove what I can do. It's quite a French-speaking club, everybody has put me at ease right from the start."

Just how at ease he felt could be gauged by the way he immediately became the first choice right back, unseating Emmanuel Eboue.

At 24 Sagna was at the upper age limit for a player Arsenal felt they could develop (as opposed to the kind of off-the-peg recruit Wenger was reluctant to buy during his middle years at Arsenal), but his integration was far quicker than anyone expected.

As Arsenal surged into contention for the title, both Wenger and Grimandi remarked how at home he looked in the English league.

"It's very difficult to predict how a player will acclimatise," the latter said. "At the start of the season I thought it would take him six or seven months, but he's adapted very rapidly. It was a complete surprise for me because I didn't think he would make so many appearances so soon."

If he wasn't quite as effective as Eboue bombing forward, his defensive qualities were vastly superior. He was very rarely beaten for pace, seldom dragged out of position and went about his business with a quiet efficiency, much like Gilberto Silva or David Platt.

On February 11 2008 Sagna was part of an Arsenal side that beat Blackburn

2-0 at the Emirates to go five points clear at the top of the table, a night when for perhaps the first time since 2004 it felt like a league championship was a probability rather than a possibility.

Yet two days later, the day before his birthday, his world imploded, when his father called him to say that his brother Omar had suffered a seizure in his bath and died at the age of 28.

"I disconnected," he later reflected. "It was a childhood fear, losing someone close to me. As a result, I tried to avoid the subject. Not just forget about his death but go back to my life as it was beforehand, when he was there."

What happened next was an illustration of how even the best adjusted of men can suffer a psychological trauma in extreme circumstances.

The traditional football reaction to a personal or collective tragedy is to go out and win the next match to honour the victim because: "It's what he would have wanted."

In many cases this is the best and perhaps the only way of dealing with grief and it was impossible not to be moved by the tribute France and Cameroon paid to Marc-Vivien Foe, who died on the pitch during the 2003 Confederations Cup.

For some people this can help them achieve closure, while for others it's a way of escaping reality, but it's often only a short term remedy.

There are times when it seems morally wrong to expect a footballer to perform in the aftermath of devastating personal news, such as when a visibly stricken Shay Given kept goal for Aston Villa barely an hour after being informed of the suicide of his friend Gary Speed.

Sagna was due to miss Arsenal's next match anyway, when an under strength side capitulated 4-0 at Old Trafford in the FA Cup, but at the request of his father he played the following Wednesday when the Gunners drew 0-0 with Milan at the Emirates.

Sagna was flawless, as he was in the return leg when the Gunners produced one of their best ever performances in Europe to win 2-0, but when the intensity of the competition was less, his performances dipped, as did the team's.

"When a winger went by me I didn't give a fuck. As far as football was concerned I lost my concentration and tenacity," he admitted. "During matches I sometimes felt I was seeing things in slow-motion. I'd become a 'je m'en foutiste' (literally someone who couldn't give a fuck for anything) and after training I'd return home and would be unable to remember the journey. Things had lost their taste."

As one of Arsenal's most effective and unsung players lost his motivation, for entirely understandable reasons, so his team mates lost their way, drawing four consecutive games in the league including the Birmingham debacle.

"After Eduardo's injury things weren't the same," he said. "We lost something and I think it affected everyone. We used to think back to that game. Manchester United then joined us at the top and I think our confidence dropped. Our game changed, I think we lost patience on the pitch and from then on we wanted to do things too quickly. You can't forget something like Eduardo's injury."

Then came the trip to Stamford Bridge, where Sagna's season came to a premature end.

Games against the post-Mourinho Chelsea were habitually open, with the margins between victory and defeat slim and the winner usually the luckier side on the day.

Arsenal's luck seemed to be in when Sagna glanced in a near post corner from Fabregas just before the hour, but on 72 minutes he was forced off with an ankle injury that ruled him out for the rest of the season.

The effects of his absence were obvious in both the short and long term. Within a minute Chelsea had drawn level, by the end of the game they'd won 2-1 and for the rest of the campaign Arsenal's defence shipped goals at crucial times, never more so than when Kolo Toure, never entirely convincing at right back, conceded a penalty in the Champions League quarter-final at Anfield, seconds after Adebayor had put Arsenal ahead on away goals.

If the decision was debatable, Wenger later argued the incident might not have happened at all had Sagna been playing, while Sagna himself was so stressed from just watching the game on television that his skin started to come out in blotches.

The injury ruled him out of Euro 2008 and mentally Sagna was still struggling to cope with his brother's death. Ultimately realised he needed help.

The club's psychologist told him he had looked empty for sometime, but after talking about his issues he at least learned to live with what had happened.

As a player he returned to the levels he'd showed during his first few months at Arsenal and for the next three seasons he was remarkably consistent in a backline that was anything but.

He could have scored more often and there was the criticism, voiced by his predecessor Lee Dixon, that he didn't seem to have a relationship with Theo Walcott, who was usually playing on the right wing. Dixon argued that this contributed to Arsenal's structural weakness and there was also the temptation to conclude that if Arsenal were so flawed in defence then Sagna had to be at least partly responsible. This certainly seems to explain the attitude towards him in France and his antipathy towards a section of the French media.

"It's as if they are upset that some of us left the country which is quite crazy," he said. "They have made us out to be silly boys who wanted to leave early and that's bad.

"When I left they said I would be on the bench, that I wouldn't be in Arsenal's team. But what should I have done? I was playing for Auxerre and then Arsenal, one of the biggest teams in Europe, called me, but I am still expected to stay in France!"

This relationship didn't improve during the 2010 World Cup, even if Sagna was little more than a bit part player in the affair detailed in the chapter on Nicolas Anelka.

In the aftermath of the 2-1 defeat to Mexico Sagna wanted to keep his counsel, but he eventually addressed reporters, saying: "Do you realise that behind the players you are talking about there are individuals and that they have families?"

It was a rare, adult intervention in the debate, but once the post-tournament furore had subsided Sagna was treated like a child again, when the incoming manager Laurent Blanc suspended all 22 players who had made the trip, the equivalent of throwing the entire class in detention, regardless of who had actually been to blame.

It seems unlikely Sagna would have been a ringleader and more likely that he would have been a peacemaker - the fact that both Nasri and Gallas attended his wedding in Sens after the tournament attests to his diplomatic skills.

Yet the following season Sagna was actually sent off twice, once slightly unluckily against Partizan Belgrade in the final seconds of a Champions League game, the second, less explicably, after a clash of heads with Manchester City's Pablo Zabaleta.

"The guy who was sent off, that's not me anymore," he later said, admitting it had been out of character.

His press interviews were infrequent, but he became an enthusiastic tweeter, never more poignantly than after the League Cup final defeat when he said simply: "Just feel ashamed. Sorry."

Shame is a debased word in football, one that should only be used for cheats, thugs and match fixers and never because a team wasn't good enough to beat another team.

And yet somehow the fact that Sagna felt that way made the whole day seem even more heartbreaking.

21) LASSANA DIARRA

IF there's a question mark over the level of attachment some of Arsenal's French players had to the cause, there was none when it came to Lassana Diarra, who in six months at the Emirates never once looked bothered about anything other than his own interests.

If that sounds unduly damning, there were mitigating circumstances.

Diarra had just spent two years doing very little at Chelsea and expected to be a first choice at Arsenal, only to find himself in an almost identical situation, this time behind his compatriot Flamini, with Euro 2008 looming.

Diarra was brought up in the eastern banlieue of Paris near Belleville, although his family were originally from Mali (he shares a name with a Malian professional).

His parents did not speak French well and he was a quiet child who liked to steer clear of trouble and hang out with a trusted circle of friends.

Diarra himself described the area as "difficult" and said the schools "were not the best" but, almost as if reading from a script dropped in front of a thousand English players before him, he added: "I only thought about football. I liked it more than studying."

His first idol, as an African growing up in Paris, was the Liberian George Weah, who was part of the outstanding PSG team that won the title in 1994 and was narrowly beaten by Arsenal in the Cup Winners Cup semi-final that year.

When Diarra began to display some potential as a player Nantes took a look at him but quickly discarded him on the grounds he was "too short" and he had disenchanting spells with Le Mans and Red Star Paris before he joined Le Havre in 2003 at the age of 18.

After a year with their B squad in the equivalent of England's Conference, he was promoted to the first team, then in the second tier. A mere 29 appearances convinced Chelsea he could understudy Claude Makele, who took him under his wing, taught him something every day but also kept him out of the first team for the two seasons he spent at Stamford Bridge.

Mourinho's policy of picking his strongest possible team for every game, including the league cup, drastically limited his chances and when he did appear, as against Arsenal in the 2007 league cup final, he did well, without ever doing enough to unseat the man in front of him.

If it wasn't a surprise that he wanted to leave Chelsea, it was that he should join Arsenal, on the final day of the August 2007 transfer window.

"I have great respect for the manager Arsene Wenger and am attracted by the style of football the team plays," he said. "I am excited by what the future holds and keen to play my part in helping Arsenal fight for trophies this season and for years to come."

These quotes, from the official website, sounded suspiciously like they had been written for him, or at least translated as Diarra was a reluctant interviewee in any language and often looked ill at ease speaking English.

Wenger saluted his versatility, noting how well he had played for Chelsea at right back, but Diarra had clearly joined expecting to play in midfield, only to find his path blocked by another converted French defender in Flamini.

The season was already five games old when the deal went through and in that short time Flamini had made himself indispensable, leaving Diarra in exactly the same situation he thought he'd left behind at Stamford Bridge.

Stories of his unhappiness appeared almost immediately. When he played, as he did in 120 minutes of a 3-2 league cup win at Blackburn, he was happy, but it was obvious from the uncomfortable interview he gave after the match that this happiness was contingent on him getting something Wenger wasn't in a position to give him.

Less than three months after joining Arsenal he was actively seeking a move. It's almost not worth mentioning that Tottenham were interested but his actual destination, Portsmouth seemed an odd choice until one remembers the money the Hampshire club were throwing around at the time -and that on the very day he joined them Diarra made it clear he wouldn't be staying long.

Wenger felt Diarra had panicked, fearing he'd miss out on Euro 2008. "It was a disappointment to let him go because I fought to get him and to keep him," he said. "He was impatient, he put himself under a lot of pressure and that increased his impatience."

Diarra for his part was one of the very few players not to give Wenger a glowing reference, comparing him unfavourably to Mourinho.

"When I arrived at Arsenal I thought that he had a lot of experience in dealing with French players like me, but things didn't work out the way I expected them to," he said after leaving Portsmouth for Real Madrid.

"I didn't learn anything from Wenger. All he taught me was how to doubt myself, how to doubt everything. I'm not going to say I feel any rancour towards Wenger, but well, in life you can't get on well with everyone. I respect everything he's done, but to me his behaviour was not very good. These things happen in life.

"Mourinho showed me how to fight, He looked me in the eyes when he talked to me. If we had any problem we discussed it. Wenger never said a word to me until the day I left."

That sounds like an exaggeration. It doesn't tally with the experience of any other senior player under Wenger and it seems more likely that Diarra didn't get the amount of attention he felt he deserved and that this is darkening his memory of an undoubtedly unhappy time in his career.

With Portsmouth Diarra won the FA Cup in 2008 and at Madrid he did enough to suggest he would have been a handy player to have around.

But when Diarra talks about Arsenal he sounds unduly bitter. Wenger could have insisted he honoured his contract, but instead he let him leave and perhaps this explicit rejection is what really hurts.

"I feel like I never played at Arsenal," Diarra later said. "If people don't remind me of that fact I just forget it. It has been wiped from my mind." The feeling is mutual.

22) SAMIR NASRI

FEW players will ever make a better start to their club career than Samir Nasri's at Arsenal. Few will cause as much soul-searching when they depart.

In just over three seasons at the Emirates, Nasri sometimes hinted at greatness, but he was only ever destined to fulfil his promise elsewhere - if anywhere.

There were moments when it looked as if he could prise open any defence in the world with his low centre of gravity and two-footed guile, but on other occasions he faded from view when his team mates needed him and the manner of his departure overshadowed all of his limited achievements in an Arsenal shirt, following as it did a transfer saga that mushroomed out of all proportion to his actual worth.

It isn't fair to blame Nasri himself for this. The summer of 2011 represented an all-time low for British sports journalism, not a superlative lightly bestowed on a profession where the views of people like Graham Hunter and Lou Macari are presented as tablets of stone by Sky Sports.

To protest that Sky Sports lacks a sense of perspective is a bit like complaining the Church of England is repressed about gay vicars, a statement of both the obvious and the futile.

It is a network that believes Fulham bidding for a Den Haag winger constitutes breaking news, a station that treats the opinions of the of Frank Stapleton as if they were some kind of scoop and it shares the fatuous faith of many other media organisations that having presenters read emails aloud has some kind of journalistic merit.

To paraphrase what Clive James once said of David Coleman: anything that mattered so much to Sky Sports, you quickly realised didn't matter very much at all.

The Nasri saga unfolded just as Cesc Fabregas was making a tortuous deal with Barcelona and the salient facts in the Fabregas story were these: that the player, some time around 2008, became a target for his former club; by 2010 he had asked to move there and been rebuffed by Wenger - and a year later he was sold for approximately £35 million more than Arsenal paid for him.

That a player whose entire Arsenal career netted one FA Cup winners medal - fewer than Ray Parlour, Gilles Grimandi, Stephen Hughes, Andy Linighan and Ian Selley - should generate billions of words essentially recycling the three above facts, reflected the desperate poverty of imagination both from the sports editors who commissioned these stories and the journalists who churned them out.

Compared to this never-ending-non-story, Nasri's move was a sub-plot. He was a mere deckhand compared to Fabregas but one who nonetheless found himself targeted by clubs who thought nothing of offering over £100,000 per week to players for whom achievement was secondary to potential.

If one judges a star player on how often his individual brilliance can turn a game, Nasri's contribution was a fraction of that made by Arsenal's previous signing from Marseilles, Robert Pires.

In the space of six months Nasri was transformed in the eyes of the Arsenal faithful, from a thrilling attacking midfielder on the cusp of becoming a great player, to a pint pot Judas desperate to collect Manchester City's 160,000 pieces of silver per week.

At the height of his popularity the fans had rewritten the lyrics to KC & The Sunshine Band's "Give It Up" in his honour, but by the time of the of the first game of the 2011-12 season against Newcastle the chant had evolved, into something that made up for in sentiment what it lacked in either tact originality:

"Nanananananananana, Samir is a cunt, is a cunt, Samir is a cunt."

In 25 years of supporting Arsenal, this was the most vituperative collective outburst I'd ever witnessed from fellow supporters against one of their own players.

I had heard the c-bomb being dropped, obscenities shrieked at players and had twice witnessed the humiliation of seeing substitutes substituted - Chris Wreh and Emmanuel Eboue.

The latter's mortifying display against Wigan, when he was played out of position in left midfield, was shocking to an extent as it seemed the entire home support was on Eboue's back, but the mood was of exasperation as much as anger and Eboue later won the crowd back.

Arsenal fans are a relatively forgiving bunch, which was what made the Nasri chant all the more of a landmark. A fan will forgive you for being useless, but not if he sees duplicity.

Nasri broke his twitter silence of two months to complain about the disrespect he'd been showered with, but if this reminded the less unhinged members of the public that he was still a human being, it couldn't halt the tide.

Patrice Evra, who comes across on the field as a Gallic version of Gary Neville, openly said he wanted Nasri to join him at Old Trafford and the carefully orchestrated leaks started to link him with "Middle" Eastlands.

The Nasri transfer perhaps represented the moment when Arsenal fans could no longer pretend they were still on a level playing field.

From the moment the Russian sank his billions into Chelsea, football began its descent into a chess game for billionaires, who were able to throw as many queens as they liked onto the board.

On December 27 2010 Arsenal outplayed Chelsea to win 3-1 at the Emirates, an exhilarating act of resistance against an oppressive regime, but one that merely provoked another clampdown.

Abramovich's response was to abandon his umpteenth meaningless pledge to run Chelsea as a self-sufficient business and buy David Luiz and Fernando Torres in the transfer window.

A week later Arsenal outclassed Manchester City in an embarrassingly one-sided game in North London which somehow ended 0-0, but also illustrated the gulf between a team that had been cultivated over a number of seasons and a collection of more hastily-assembled mercenaries.

The response? City went out and spent even more money on the likes of Edin Dzeko and targeted Clichy and Nasri, unsettling both in the process.

The new Arsenal deal Nasri was reportedly "understood" - to borrow the BBC Sport term used whenever they weren't able to verify a story - to be on the brink of signing was ignored and as the months went by it became increasingly obvious that yet another turgid non-story was developing.

To Nasri's credit he at least seemed to realise this was no way to leave.

When someone claiming to be him on facebook published a status update saying he would be leaving "soon" and with "bitterness in my heart" Nasri issued a rapid denial, before restoring his reputation further when he showed an admirable level of commitment in a 2-0 home defeat by Liverpool.

His appearance in a midfield somehow already decimated by injury and suspension, for only the second game of the 2011-12 season, saw him applauded off the pitch at the final whistle.

That led to some forlorn speculation that he might stay. With Fabregas gone, Nasri had the chance to make the central midfield role his own, to become the side's key player, a number 10 like Platini and Zidane.

Instead, within 72 hours, he was gone, for what seemed like an absurd fee for a player with only a year on his contract - over £20 million.

Sky Sports News reported the news only fractionally less hysterically than their news channel was reporting the demise of Colonel Gadaffi at precisely the same time, treating a tweet from "Gary from Dublin" with the same reverence they gave to their luckless correspondent in Tripoli.

When Nasri gave his first press conference as a City player he tripped over his tongue, saying Arsenal fans were less passionate than their City counterparts, apparently on the grounds that they didn't have tattoos, though he quickly tried to row back from that statement, claiming that the atmosphere at the Emirates was less fiery than at Highbury - where he'd never actually played.

The damage was done though. And how had it come to this?

Nasri's biography follows a now familiar pattern. He was born and raised in the Gavotte Peyret quarter of a town called Septemes-les-Vallones, a few kilometres to the north of Marseilles and although he has Algerian heritage, his parents were born in France and his extended family all live there.

Only distant relatives remain in Algeria and the only time he ever visited the homeland was when he was very young.

All that made him significantly more Gallic than many of the England cricket team were English, but in the eyes of the lunatic fringe his non-practicing Muslim status and his inability to trace his routes directly back to Asterix the Gaul meant he would never be entirely French.

When The Sun wanted to find out more about Nasri's background it sent a reporter to "the notorious" Gavette Peyret and duly found a witness to paint it as a twin town of Baghdad beyond the Green Zone, illustrating the feature with a shot of a supposedly awful tower block that could in fact have been been taken in Manchester or Birmingham but for the fact that it showed the sun shining.

Officially a village of 1500 inhabitants, Gavette Peyrat actually looks like a typical Mediterranean settlement, with white concrete and orange rooftops strewn haphazardly around a hillside. There are some admittedly grim looking tower blocks, but for all the talk of gangs, high unemployment and drug dealing it's hardly the kind of territory that would drive Harry Brown to a purgative rampage.

At the local primary school Nasri is remembered as a happy, polite and punctual child with exceptionally neat handwriting and even neater ball control.

His first club was Jeunesse Sportive Pennes Mirabeau, based in the suburb where Zinedine Zidane's parents live.

After two years there he was recruited by Marseilles at the age of just eight and he evolved into an international class midfielder, scoring the winning goal for France in the under-17 European Championship in a team with Karim Benzema and Hatem Ben Arfa.

His first team debut came at the start of the 2004-05 season, in 2-0 win over Sochaux, dropping into a Marseille midfield recently robbed of the services of Mathieu Flamini.

Nasri scored his first and only goal that season in a 2-1 defeat at Lille, but he'd done enough to earn a nomination for the young player of the year award and he was already on the radar of Arsenal, Chelsea, Liverpool and Newcastle.

After two seasons he made his debut for France in a 1-0 win over Georgia and he picked up the Ligue 1 young player of the year award, but after 145 games - and just 11 goals – by the summer of 2008 he was angling for a move.

Nasri announced the deal on his own website, several days before the move was officially ratified and just as the French Euro 2008 campaign was unravelling due to multiple self-inflicted wounds, in an act of collective harakiri it was difficult to imagine any international side (even the Dutch) matching, until Domenech's 2010 vintage somehow managed it.

Nasri's tournament lasted for just 28 minutes. He had an ineffectual 12-minute cameo at the end of the opening 0-0 draw with Romania, missed the humbling 4-1 defeat to the Netherlands and then had a bizarre 16-minute spell against Italy when he came on as a substitute for the injured Franck Ribery, only to be sacrificed soon afterwards - in favour of Jean-Alain Boumsong of all players - when Eric Abidal was sent off.

When Gallas later delivered his post mortem on the tournament he depicted Nasri as a naïve, ignorant and arrogant young ASBO who had no respect for his elders' achievements, an attack that arguably said a great deal more about Gallas than it did on the player he referred to only as "Jouer S."

It didn't help that the attack came several months after Nasri had joined Arsenal, where Gallas was now the captain and one can only wonder what was going through his head when he agreed to publish the story when he did, for what must have been a negligible financial gain.

Nasri, who was already developing what would turn into an excellent command of English, responded in a manner that was a good deal more streetwise: "I don't think you can blame that (the Euro failure) on the fact that I sat in Thierry Henry's seat."

History repeated itself on the opening day of the 2008-09 season when for the second time in his short career, Nasri found himself drafted into a midfield vacated by Flamini.

Three minutes and 44 seconds into his Arsenal career, Nasri scored, steering in a Denilson cross from close range against West Brom.

A rout beckoned but instead Arsenal were limited to a 1-0 win and the rest of the season proved a similar let down.

Nasri's personal highlight came when he scored twice in a 2-1 win over Manchester United at the Emirates, a result achieved in the face of one of the periodic "crises" caused by defeats to Fulham, Hull, Stoke and an absurd 4-4 draw with Spurs, when the visitors scored twice in injury time, with two thirds of their own supporters having already given up and gone home.

Nasri's first goal came from a powerful shot that skidded in off Gary Neville, while the second was the culmination of one of Arsenal's best ever passing moves - Nasri rifled in from the edge of the area after 90 seconds of total football at the start of the second half that even moved Alex Ferguson to a tribute.

Gallas aside, Nasri seemed to integrate well, moving into a six-bedroom house in Hampstead with his partner, the tennis player Tatiana Golovin.

That led to some excitable journalists calling them the French Posh and Becks, but Golovin never made it past the last eight in a slam event and Nasri's Arsenal career similarly failed to glitter.

If the United win suggested Nasri had the big match temperament, he subsequently failed to deliver when it really counted.

During his three years with Arsenal the club challenged for the title twice, but in the pivotal games against direct rivals for the title he was often eclipsed. United may have wanted to sign him but they had little trouble in keeping him quiet.

His record in semi-finals and finals was equally underwhelming. On his departure he spoke of the mental damage inflicted by the League Cup final defeat to Birmingham, a comment that had most fans wondering where the hell he'd been during the 89 minutes that preceded Martins' winner - and more importantly during the five minutes after it when the team was crying out for a leader.

Again the contrast with a proven match winner like Pires is jarring. In the three months and 14 games that followed that defeat, Nasri played like a man who had already decided his future lay elsewhere, even though Arsenal were still fighting on three fronts.

He could be forgiven for his role in the Champions League defeat to a Barcelona side who were taking football to a new level and there was an element of bad luck in the FA Cup quarter-final at Old Trafford, but his overall contribution to the title run-in was negligible. He scored a solitary goal in a 3-3 draw at The Lane as Arsenal frittered away 19 winnable points, six more than they would have needed.

Nasri made his Manchester City debut hours before Arsenal's 8-2 debacle at Old Trafford and was instrumental in a 5-1 win at White Hart Lane.

The results had a grim symbolism. Barely 18 months beforehand Tottenham had beaten City to fourth place and qualified for the Champions League with a 1-0 win at Eastlands. Now they were being eclipsed, moving one observer to say this was the day the financially doped clubs made their definitive breakaway from those who tried to live within their means.

In a more considered interview with France Football, Nasri offered some insights into his time at the Emirates, one of the most pointed being that Wenger hated conflict - which can hardly have helped when Gallas and Adebayor were around.

"I know that training every day I will improve, there is a lot of intensity," he said. "It's the level above Arsenal. When we finish the session with a game it feels like a competition game." Which, given the size of City's squad, it clearly was, certainly by comparison to Arsenal, where injuries rendered competition almost non-existent for much of the Emirates era.

"I chose a club on the way up," Nasri said, willingly or unwillingly twisting the knife. "Arsenal remains a big club but the building of the Emirates changed a lot of things financially. It's the club politics, the officials, not Arsene. Arsenal don't have the same money to spend, they must sell their best players."

When Nasri left Marseilles for Arsenal the reaction among OM fans was one of resignation and pride with some anger.

When he left Arsenal for City the feeling was the same, minus any pride.

On his first return for City in the League Cup the following November he warmly embraced Marouane Chamakh and others in the tunnel, but he was booed throughout and played as if he was almost embarrassed.

After City had narrowly won 1-0 he became involved in a spat with Emmanuel Frimpong and in the league fixture at the end of the season at the Emirates the derision of the Arsenal fans was merciless when Mikel Arteta scored a late winner - a result that seemed at the time to have ensured Nasri would end another season without a medal.

He may have regretted it himself. On the day of Arsenal's 125th anniversary match with Everton he said it was an honour to have played for the club, but his rare forays onto twitter now just elicted abuse from embittered fans like Piers Morgan. Social network morons scattered words like Judas around as if he'd done anything other than act as almost everyone else would have done in the circumstances.

In the case of Thierry Henry Arsenal fans were prepared to accept someone could love their club even after abandoning it. Nasri was never extended the same courtesy and this was desperately sad.

City bought Nasri simply because they could. In his first season there he struggled to get into the team. They didn't always need him, but because the laws of economics didn't apply to them by signing him they picked up a useful option and weakened a rival team in the process.

Right up until the dramatic final day denouement, which saw City win the league with two injury time goals against Queen's Park Rangers, Nasri might have been happier if he'd never been placed in a position where he felt he had to leave, a little like the character Private Major in Joseph Heller's novel, Catch 22.

Major's only pleasure in life was playing basketball with other men of his rank. When he was promoted after a clerical error it ruined his life. His pay improved but he could never play basketball again, lost all his friends and worse still he was now known as Major Major.

During City's 2012 League Cup semi-final with Liverpool, Nasri was brought on for Mario Balotelli after a little over half an hour, but struggled to make an impression, or at least the kind of impression his fee demanded.

After the game he was youtubed by a carload of Liverpool supporters, who chanted "You fucking wanker" at him and goaded him into winding down his window.

"How do you like that you fucking Arsenal reject," one yelled. "You should never have left Arsenal, you had a better chance of winning the Champions League with Arsenal then you have with Man City."

"I'm top of the league," he replied, before putting his foot down, screaming away from his tormentors and then coming to a grinding halt seconds later at some traffic lights.

There was a metaphor in there somewhere.

23) MIKAEL SILVESTRE

SIGNING a player with as many medals as Mikael Silvestre would usually be regarded as good news, but when Arsenal paid Manchester United an undisclosed sum of money for him in the summer of 2008 it seemed like a symbolic move for all the wrong reasons.

At 31 he was far older than the average Wenger signing and although he'd collected plenty of honours during his time with United, so had the likes of Quinton Fortune and Phil Neville and nobody would have been queuing up to see them in Arsenal shirt.

But there was something more worrying than that and it wasn't the fact that he'd spent the bulk of the previous two seasons out injured.

There was an uneasy feeling that Arsenal were trying to plug a leaky defence with a United cast-off and that in itself was cause for alarm.

If United seriously saw Arsenal as a threat there was no way they'd sell them a valuable asset, which left two uncomfortable conclusions. One, Arsenal were no longer a threat and two, Silvestre wasn't much of an asset anymore.

Arsenal and United just didn't do transfer business with each other. Aside from a brief loan deal for Jim Leighton in 1991 which saw the troubling Scot spend some time at Highbury on loan, the last time a player had moved in either direction was when Alex Ferguson signed Viv Anderson for £250,000 in 1987, at a time when Arsenal were building their first great side for years and Anderson was jumping into a sinking boat at Old Trafford.

Before that you had to go back to 1981 and Frank Stapleton's defection from Highbury, a move that earned him the enduring contempt of Arsenal fans - a seam of loathing that is mined to this day every time Stapleton opens his mouth in one of his mind-numbingly pointless appearances on Sky Sports News.

Before Stapleton, United had offloaded Jimmy Rimmer and Brian Kidd to Arsenal in the seventies, with George Graham going in the opposite direction, but the only player to cause the selling club any genuine pangs of regret was Andy Cole, who was released by Graham and later became clumsily prolific at Old Trafford having called in at Bristol City and Newcastle on the way.

"We have a strong squad but a young squad and Mikael's versatility, experience and calibre will provide the extra depth we need to reinforce our challenge for honours this season," Wenger said, somewhat optimistically after inking the deal.

Silvestre made the right noises about "still having the fire" and "new challenges" but it was fairly obvious that the best years of his career were behind him.

"When Arsenal came in for me I couldn't turn them down," he said, which given his choices were to pick up splinters on the bench at Old Trafford or go even further down football's food chain wasn't the statement it might have been.

Silvestre was born in Chambray-les-Tours in the Loire Valley, part of a footballing family who'd emigrated from Guadeloupe. Their clan included the former French international Franck Silvestre, once of Sochaux, Auxerre and Montpelier, the Nantes players Xavier and Laurent, who shared the same surname and his Guadaloupe-born father, also called Franck.

His first club was Union Sportive St Pierre but his football education was at Stade Rennais, where he made his top-flight debut as a precocious 18-year-old in the 1996-97 season, before establishing himself as their first choice left back the following year.

It was a stage he quickly felt he'd outgrown.

Silvestre was one of the first of France's elite young players to realise that the contract he had with Rennes was barely worth the paper it was printed on.

At the end of his second season as a first division player, Rennes offered him a deal that he rejected. They then made the same mistake PSG had made with Nicolas Anelka by making threats he was streetwise enough to know were empty.

Angered by the directors he and his team mate Ousmane Dabo used the same loophole exploited by Anelka to join Internazionale, leaving Rennes with just a pittance in compensation.

Unlike Anelka, neither Dabo nor Silvestre had a clear path to the first team ahead of them and this was a time when Italian football was still dripping with money.

Silvestre made a respectable number of appearances in his one season at the San Siro, but Javier Zanetti, Taribo West, Dario Simic and Giuseppe Bergomi were just some of the names barring his route. When he was subsequently told by Marcello Lippi that he'd be understudying the enthusiastic but limited Greek international Grigoris Georgatos, he decided to bail out.

Silvestre was on the brink of joining Gerard Houliier's Liverpool when United, who'd first tried to sign him when he was still at Rennes, stepped in.

They wafted a £4 million cheque in Massimo Moratti's direction and the lure of a central defensive role in front of the player.

He instantly felt far more at home in England, where the game was less disciplined but also less predictable than in Italy and where he found

United's supporters willing to see any mistakes he made in the context of his overall contribution.

It's tempting to look at Silvestre's time with United and dismiss this contribution as peripheral, but he averaged around 40 appearances per season in his first seven years at Old Trafford before injuries sidelined him for the final two campaigns.

In 2007 he turned down the chance to join Newcastle on the grounds that he couldn't play with Joey Barton, the alcoholic-turned-philosopher who in his hell-raising days had once stubbed a lit cigar out in the eyeball of a trainee at Manchester City and then went to jail for an assault on Ousmane Dabo that left Silvestre's friend with serious facial wounds.

"I could not sign for Newcastle out of respect for Ousmane Dabo," he said. "Money is not the only thing in life."

This principled stand, it's reasonable to assume, would have cost him a hefty signing on fee and a lucrative contract, given that Newcastle were then so pitifully run.

By the time he'd joined Arsenal a year later his market value would have dipped and he was only offered a two-year deal by a manager not known for throwing money at ageing players. He was a long way from being a regular, having sat on the bench throughout the 2008 Champions League final and United was not the kind of place where an under-performing player could hang around for too long.

Yet if he wasn't at the same level as Ferdinand or Vidic he at least looked a better bet than Cygan, Senderos, Tavlaridis and others.

He had experience and medals, two qualities the 2008 Arsenal vintage conspicuously lacked, but he also had the kind of injury record which they conspicuously didn't.

He missed the first two months of the season, scored an own goal in his second game, an otherwise convincing 5-2 win at Fenerbahce and then took centre stage for the first time in a ludicrous 4-4 draw with Tottenham.

When Silvestre equalised David Bentley's freakish but brilliant early strike by heading in a Van Persie corner he instantly endeared himself to a sceptical crowd, but he was one of a trio of players supposedly lambasted by Wenger after the team squandered a 4-2 lead with 89 minutes gone.

If there was any consolation at all for Arsenal fans it was that two thirds of the visiting fans had long since gone home, and that they hadn't been around to see their most dramatic comeback in a derby in living memory.

None of that would have filtered through to the home dressing room however, which had allegedly turned into a pit of vituperative recrimination, finger-pointing and back-stabbing.

Or at least that was what "an insider" told the Daily Mirror, so it must have been true.

Silvestre was neither the kind of player to start whingeing in the press, nor a player who had a reputation for being difficult to get on with, though in fairness to the Mirror some of the personalities involved, Gallas, his best friend Nasri, Adebayor and Van Persie, weren't always known for their ability to cultivate team spirit.

The insider also claimed Silvestre was "facing the axe" for the next match, a trip to Stoke, possibly the last place on earth Arsenal would have wanted to go after that kind of a debacle, although he kept his place for another two months until a thigh injury forced him off after half an hour of an FA Cup win over Plymouth.

He returned for the final month of the season, but this was a bad time to be an Arsenal defender. Whichever combination Wenger used, against top opposition Arsenal always conceded, often heavily and usually when it mattered most, specifically against Chelsea and Manchester United in FA Cup and Champions League semi-finals.

This wasn't entirely down to the deficiencies of the backline. Behind them Wenger had to choose between Almunia and Fabianski in goal, which was a bit like trying to decide whether to amputate your left or right arm.

And ahead of them the midfield was packed with interchangeably brilliant but tiny attackers like Fabregas and Nasri, who were about as far removed as possible from the shield system offered by Petit and Vieira.

Not many defenders were going to emerge from that campaign with an enhanced reputation and Silvestre fared little better the following year, when Thomas Vermaelen was the first choice alongside William Gallas and Sol Campbell was brought back at the age of 35.

He made 20 appearances, none memorable for the right reasons. His only goal put Arsenal 2-0 up at Wigan, but the home side scored thrice in the last 10 minutes, past a keeper in Fabianksi who radiated panic throughout the side.

During the summer of 2010 he joined Werder Bremen as a free agent, but there he was castigated by the sporting director Klaus Allofs, who was quoted in the market-cornering trash tabloid Bild saying: "His playing style is remarkably slow and he makes too many mistakes."

Not many fans will remember Silvestre's time at Arsenal with any degree of affection, if they remember it at all.

Aside from his goal against Tottenham it was a forgettable two years for both player and club and it's also difficult to remember any incidents he was involved with while playing against Arsenal, though this isn't necessarily a bad thing.

Until I started researching this book I'd completely forgotten the red card he picked up for head butting Freddie Ljungberg at Highbury in 2005.

"He pissed me off so I butted him," was what Silvestre said to Ferguson as he walked off, according to the referee Graham Poll.

This was out of character though it did at least answer one question, namely what exactly a United player would have to do to get sent off against Arsenal - on the same night Wayne Rooney swore 27 times at Poll, who could have shown him 27 separate red cards.

The folly of Poll's leniency - and that of several other English referees - is obvious every time Rooney pulls on an England shirt. Rooney never learned his lesson and is doomed to repeat his error. Silvestre did learn his and to date this remains the only red card of his career.

For Arsenal he was probably the right man at the wrong time, but his career commands a significant amount of respect, as does the way he conducts himself off the field.

Stories about footballers and charity are easy meat for the cynical, particularly when newspapers and websites are contractually obliged to mention them in interviews in exchange for access to players. Unless a player renounces mammon completely like Roma's Damiano Tommasi, who agreed to play for the minimum wage, someone will always make a comparison with the amount they earn in a week and what they donate.

Silvestre gave time as well as money, setting up vocational training centres in Guinea, Niger, Laos, Senegal and Haiti, where he travelled after the earthquake.

It would have been a lot easier to sign the cheque and sod off to a seven-star hotel in Dubai for a holiday, but Silvestre was actively involved in trying to combat illiteracy and educate the victims of the earthquake.

"The goal is to tell them that we need them, that the country needs them, because foreign aid is coming," he said. "But now we really put the tools in their hands for the reconstruction of their country."

There's more to life than money and there's a lot more to Mikael Silvestre than not wanting to be Joey Barton's team mate.

24) FRANCIS COQUELIN

WHEN it was announced that Francis Coquelin had signed for Arsenal in the summer of 2008 it wasn't a cause for widespread euphoria.

It was no fault of Coquelin's, but with Flamini and Hleb on the way out fans hoping for a high-profile replacement would have been forgiven for rolling their eyes on hearing that Arsenal had signed yet another "promising" French youth international, this time from Laval, where his family settled after leaving La Reunion.

At 17 it was assumed, correctly, that Coquelin was some way from being ready for the first team and it was over a year before he made his debut in the League Cup, where he got an hour against West Brom in his preferred role in the centre of midfield, alongside Aaron Ramsey and Jack Wilshere.

He had to wait another four months for his next appearance, this time as a right-back in a miserable 3-1 defeat at Stoke in the FA Cup and at the end of the season he was farmed out to Lorient on loan .

There he was largely forgotten by Arsenal until he returned for the start of the 2011-12 season and found himself back in the first team squad owing to a spate of injuries and departures.

He somehow managed to emerge from the 8-2 loss at Old Trafford without his reputation in tatters and also impressed in a 2-1 defeat at Tottenham, but he was still some way from being a first-choice. Just when it seemed his future might lie elsewhere however, he agreed a new long-term deal with the club in January 2012.

25) GILLES SUNU

THE unwanted distinction of being the Frenchman with the shortest Arsenal career belongs to Gilles Sunu, whose total playing time with the first team amounted to 72 minutes in three seasons.

He did better than Clive Allen (playing time 0 minutes) and Jason Crowe (playing time 20 minutes and 33 seconds, the 33 seconds in question coming in a League Cup tie with Birmingham when he was sent off for a foul on Martin O'Connor moments after coming on), but for a player who was courted by some of Europe's top clubs before he joined Arsenal as a 16-year-old it can only have been a disappointment.

Sunu, the son of the Togo international Manu Sunu, was born in 1991 in Chateuroux, one of the more forgettable towns in Berry, one of France's more forgettable regions.

He started playing for the local club, Berrichonne de Chateuroux at the age of six and stayed there for ten years before joining Arsenal for a reported £700,000.

As he spoke very little English Gael Clichy and Armand Traore looked after him and his initial progress was encouraging.

He scored the opening goal in the 2009 FA Youth Cup final with Liverpool, finishing calmly after being played in by Henri Lansbury and Jack Wilshere and his all-round contribution impressed the veteran striker Steve Claridge, who was scouting the game for the Guardian.

"Playing up front on your own can be seen by some players as a licence to become lazy and not to do your defensive work," Claridge said. "But each time Sunu did lose possession he worked extremely hard to get the ball back.

"What I liked about his play was besides all the glitz and glamour of Arsenal's superiority he at times brought sanity to the proceedings by getting hold of the ball, shielding it and playing the simple pass. In areas of the pitch where he didn't need to complicate matters he was someone his team mates could rely on."

A few months later he made his first team debut, playing for an hour in the league cup against West Brom. He then came on at the end of a Champions League dead rubber at Olympiakos, but didn't really catch the eye and was sent on loan to Derby.

That summer Sunu equalised in the final of the Euro under-19 championship as France came from behind to beat Spain 2-1, but after receiving some tentative interest from Bordeaux, who were looking to replace Marouane Chamakh, he was injured.

When he returned, a couple of months into the season, despite scoring a couple of goals for the reserves he was a long way from first team contention and he joined Lorient on loan at the end of the transfer window.

His last act as an Arsenal player was to sit on the bench during the 8-2 atrocity at Old Trafford. Three days later, again on the final day of the transfer window, he signed for Lorient, this time for four years.

"My wish was to come back to Lorient so I could play," he said, fully aware that barring an epidemic this was never going to happen at the Emirates.

26) LAURENT KOSCIELNY

ARSENE Wenger has never been guilty of deliberately undermining his players, but he arguably didn't do Laurent Koscielny any favours when, doubtless in a pit of despair following the 2011 League Cup final with Birmingham City, he revealed his defender had been "destroyed" by the error that resulted in Arsenal's defeat.

Koscielny's career hopefully won't be defined by that one calamity, but by using such an emotive word Wenger nearly wrote a premature obituary for his defender's career.

The incident in question is one that it's difficult to recall without considerable emotional pain for Arsenal fans.

After 89 minutes against weak opposition, the score was 1-1 and even then Arsenal had been aided by a generous refereeing decision in the opening moments that might have seen keeper Wojciech Szczesny sent off and a penalty awarded, but for an erroneous offside call.

Had the Pole been shown a red card it might at least have spared Koscielny the indignity to follow, however.

He was outjumped in the build up to Birmingham's opening goal, a footnote that would have been forgotten had a team that had beaten the same opposition 3-0 away just a few weeks earlier been able to conjure more than a solitary Van Persie equaliser in reply.

Instead, with just over 30 seconds of normal time remaining, Koscielny and Szczesny combined to throw away a trophy that had gone from being regarded as an afterthought during Wenger's early years at the club to a potentially vital piece of silverware.

A free-kick was hoofed to the edge of the Arsenal box and although the initial header was won by Zigic, it seemed to be heading innocuously back to the keeper.

Looming into view was Koscielny, under no immediate pressure, but presumably unable to hear what, if anything, Szczesny was shouting at him.

The most obvious course of action was let the ball roll back to the keeper. The second most obvious course was, if there was any doubt, hoof the ball back to the mythical row Z.

Koscielny chose the "safety first" option, but instead of making contact he swished at the ball, which a distracted Szczesny was unable to gather. It bounced off his knees and rolled straight to the feet of Obafemi Martins, who accepted the easiest chance of his career.

The reaction was telling. Szczesny, who was at least as culpable for taking his eyes off the ball and must have been feeling a small death of the soul, jumped straight up, smacked his gloves together and immediately urged his team mates to go for an equaliser.

Koscielny meanwhile received a smack in the back of the head from Barry Ferguson, a classless and moronic act which nonetheless added to the air of victimhood that now clung to the defender.

For Laurent Koscielny in 2011, read Gus Caesar in 1988.

When Caesar had his moment of doubt and pain in a League Cup final against Luton, Koscielny was a two-year-old growing up in the sleepy Limousin town of Tulle, blissfully unaware that Wembley had just become a graveyard for a promising young central defender's reputation.

Koscielny was in fact something of a late developer, who, for all his apparent youth, was 25 when he had his Caesar moment and 18 when he turned professional with En Avant De Guincamp, a team who somehow managed to sustain Ligue 2 football despite coming from a Breton town of less than 8,000 inhabitants.

Some of Guincamp's success was due to its ability to unearth talents like Didier Drogba and Florent Malouda, though in the three seasons he spent in Britanny Koscielny did little to suggest he would ever be mentioned in the same company.

He made less than 50 appearances and, apparently unable to cut it in the second tier, dropped down a level to play for Tours, a team from a far bigger town where gates of a few thousand rattled around in the bowl-like Stade de la Vallee du Cher.

Here Koscielny began to catch the eye, winning the club's player of the year award in successive seasons and collecting the equivalent award for the entire division in the second of these.

Coveted by PSG he instead opted to go back to Britanny and join Lorient, on the grounds that he was more likely to be an automatic selection.

Koscielny had obviously done well at Lorient and earned a share of what passes for the limelight in Ligue 1 when he scored his first ever top flight goal against Bordeaux and then earned a straight red card, all in the opening half hour.

The dismissal came for the slightest of fouls on Marouane Chamakh, who hit the deck as soon as contact was made, a habit he hadn't grown out of by the time he'd joined Koscielny at Arsenal a few months later.

Poland, where the paternal grandfather who bequeathed him his surname hailed from, wanted to select him for their national side, but after initially saying he would take dual nationality, tempted by the chance of playing for the hosts in Euro 2012, he backed off when he realised a French call-up was possible.

12 months after signing a four-year deal at Lorient for a fee of 1.5 million

Euros his market value had increased by 11 million, which represented a major gamble by Wenger on a player who barely three seasons beforehand had been sitting on the bench at Guincamp.

Like Grimandi before him, he's a slightly unlikely looking footballer, although where Grimandi looked like an eternal student, Koscielny was more wiry, his harsh hair cut accentuating his large ears and giving him the air of a willing squaddie, or even perhaps a pterodactyl.

Three ageing centre-halves in Gallas, Campbell and Sylvestre were shipped out of Arsenal that summer, with Koscielny and later Sebastien Squillaci replacing them.

By then however Wenger was no longer in a position to compete for the top talent and had to make do with what was left when the richest clubs had filled their ranks. The net result was the replacement of a creaking but experienced backline with a confused, error-prone duo who it couldn't be argued represented any improvement.

None of which would have relevance if it didn't add to the air of helplessness Koscielny seemed to exude when something goes wrong.

There was a heavy hint of the defensive misery to come when Arsenal conceded five goals to Legia Warsaw in a comical pre-season friendly that saw them rally from 3-0 down, one of them a Koscielny own goal, to win 6-5.

Although he was sent off on his league debut at Anfield, Koscielny actually performed well and his dismissal for a second booking was harsh, as was the straight red he received in stoppage time against Newcastle a few months later.

Laurent Blanc, now manager of the French national team, was impressed. "I've been watching him since the start of the season and he's been making constant progress," he said. "He's looking more and more assured and I'm very pleased with the way he restarts play. He's a boy who plays with his head, he's intelligent and on a football field that's important."

As 2011 began Arsenal were resurgent, fighting on four fronts with Koscielny the first choice at the back. Although he was part of the collective 4-4 debacle at Newcastle, he scored in the League cup semi-final win over Ipswich, headed the winner in a gruelling league game with Everton at the Emirates and had his best game in an Arsenal shirt in the 2-1 win at home to Barcelona.

"In England all the strikers are six foot three or four and 90 kilos," he told the club's magazine, showing a suspiciously impressive grip of imperial and metric measurements - the suspicion is the first statistic was translated. "I had to progress physically as I was not used to that kind of opposition in

France."

Then came Birmingham. In a matter of seconds Koscielny learned that in football a single error at the wrong time can make you look like an idiot in front of millions of people.

That isn't an easy thing to live with, but the game also offers its victims multiple shots at redemption if they are good enough to take them and the way Koscielny grabbed these in the 2011-12 season was a joy to watch.

After an appropriately safe amount of time had passed, the club felt able to bring the subject up in an in-house interview.

"I do think about it sometimes," he said of the Birmingham incident. "Mistakes can happen in life. It was hard for the fans and for the club, but life goes on, there are things more important than losing a final. There will be plenty more finals to play and win. It was tough to swallow but it made me a better player and a better person."

This was the kind of thing an official Arsenal publication would only run if Koscielny had achieved a degree of closure. He admitted: "Afterwards I had a week where I was feeling really bad. It was my first final and the fans had been waiting for a trophy for a while. It was so hard to take. I needed time to digest it but I had to bounce back to come back stronger than I did."

It's a measure of how well he succeeded that by the end of 2011 Koscielny had become a reassuring presence in the most solid Arsenal defence since 2006.

Now all he needs to do is find a World Cup pantomime villain to lamp and his rehabilitation will be complete.

27) SEBASTIEN SQUILLACI

"WHO the hell was responsible for scouting him?" asked a member of Arsenal's French Supporters Club, midway through Sebastien Squillaci's fraught first season with Arsenal, showing a pointed lack of empathy for his fellow countryman.

Arsene Wenger couldn't often be accused of making "panic" purchases during his time with Arsenal, but he would intermittently try to plug a gap in the squad with a player who would prove a busted flush.

Even the most successful managers buy the odd turkey (and sometimes for their own nefarious financial reasons), but even Wenger's worst acquisitions had a certain logic to them at the time.

In the summer of 2001 Wenger had one of his poorer forays into the transfer market and yet Arsenal still ended up winning the double.

The £10 million signing of Francis Jeffers, the "Fox in the Box" is widely cited as Wenger's worst ever deal, but at the time, in the summer of 2001, Jeffers was one of the best young finishers in the game.

A second deal, quoted as anything between £2million and £6 million for the Ipswich keeper Richard Wright, also proved a disappointment and the way these two English players flopped explains Wenger's reticence to buy from the domestic league.

For a long time this made perfect sense. There was no point in paying an inflated fee just because a player was English, particularly if a player of equivalent value from abroad became available.

By the summer of 2010 however, this was starting to look like a misplaced article of faith, as "Toto" Squillaci followed Laurent Koscielny into the Emirates for a fee reported at £6.5 million but later, in the way Arsenal fees often seemed to depreciate with time, quoted as £3 million.

Even that seemed overpriced. When the last great Arsenal defensive partnership, Kolo Toure and Sol Campbell, began to deteriorate, fans looked at Pascal Cygan and Phillipe Senderos and began to long for a new Adams, Bould or Keown.

When Squillaci and Koscielny were playing together Senderos and Cygan sometimes seemed like a dream ticket and even the second vintage of Campbell alongside Sylvestre might have been preferable.

Given the hoops Arsenal had to jump through to secure his signature, Squillaci was expected to be a first choice alongside Thomas Vermaelen.

He allegedly refused to play for Seville in a Champions League qualifier for fear of becoming cup tied, his team mate Julien Escude claiming: "When the coach gave his team talk Sebastien was starting. Then I do not know what happened with the coach or sporting director but there was a change in the line-up. Later we knew Sebastien refused to play."

Squillaci's head had been turned by what he described as a "sensational" offer. "If a French player receives an offer from Arsene Wenger it's practically impossible to turn down," he claimed. "It was a difficult situation but I knew I had to take this chance. I knew if I played against Braga then I would not have been able to play for Arsenal in the Champions League."

When Carlos Tevez refused to play for Manchester City a year later it was considered an act of treason, but Squillaci's behaviour attracted little condemnation, for reasons that would later become clearer.

"Arsenal were always the team I watched out for, for any spectator like me you had to watch a squad with Henry, Pires, Vieira and Gallas," he said, before adding somewhat prematurely: "Now I'm happy to have my name in the history books. For me this a great new challenge and I've gone there purely to be a part of that."

Superficially, Squallaci looked like a logical purchase.

He was born in Toulon in 1980, his Italian sounding name coming from his Corsican parents, and he was raised in the agreeable Mediterranean district of La Seyne-sur-mer.

He played for the local team FC Seynois, where he is as fondly remembered as any successful old boy would be.

In 2007 the town renamed a stadium in his honour and interviewed after Squillaci's selection for the French squad for Euro 2008, Franck Seva, one of his first coaches, said: "He's difficult to beat one-on-one, a tenacious defender and excellent with his head, just as he was when he was younger. Above all he's an adorable, modest boy who hasn't forgotten where he came from."

From Seynois, Squillaci made the step up to second division Toulon, making his debut at the age of 17 in a team destined for relegation.

Within a year - and in another example of a south coast team failing to do its paperwork properly - Monaco poached him for nothing, but for the next four seasons they farmed him out, first to their reserve side and then to Ajaccio in Corsica before they finally trusted him enough to make him part of the first team squad in 2002.

He must have been doing something right. Playing alongside Gael Givet or Julien Rodriguez he was part of one of the best central defensive partnerships in France, memorably knocking out both Real Madrid and Chelsea on the way to the 2004 Champions League final.

He didn't play in the final, a 3-0 defeat to Porto in which Monaco were repeatedly thwarted by blatantly incorrect offside decisions (against a team coincidentally found guilty of match-fixing in the Portuguese League that very season), but won successive titles with Lyon after joining them in 2006.

For Squillaci that wasn't enough: "I wanted to leave Lyon and see something else," he said, in an eerily prescient quote. "Once I knew Seville were interested in me I didn't hesitate, even if it was difficult to begin with to leave Lyon."

After two seasons at OL he moved on to Seville, winning the Spanish Cup in 2010 and earning a call up to the World Cup squad for South Africa.

If all this suggests a steady career progression, there were clues as to Squillaci's suitability to the English game.

He himself admitted there wasn't much opposition in France and his medals with Lyon came at a time when OL were almost winning the French title by default.

At Euro 2008 he was left on the bench even though the French were in the middle of a defensive crisis so severe that even Jean-Alain Boumsong was given some game time.

His major tournament debut came in even more desperate circumstances, in the third game of the 2010 tournament against the South African hosts, with both sides facing elimination.

Given what had gone on before (the Va Te Faire Enculer saga) it would have been quite an achievement for the French to further disgrace themselves, but they somehow did, with Squillaci playing his part in a collectively shambolic 2-1 defeat.

Arsenal's official website described his debut season as "low-key but solid" which was certainly an interesting way of looking at it.

"I knew it would be physical with some good sides, playing good football," he said. "The strikers are big and strong and it is a big contrast with Spain, where the strikers are fast and not so strong."

Yet oddly enough it was Squillaci's positional sense that would be found wanting more often than his aerial prowess.

The official version also made the eyebrow-raising claim that "as with all new recruits, Sebastien took time to find his feet," which ignores the impact made by players like Vieira and Arshavin and also the fact that Squillaci's initial performances were reasonably solid.

It was over a month after his arrival that the alarm bells began to sound, during a 3-2 home defeat to West Bromwich Albion, a newly-promoted side who were expected to capitulate but instead raced into a 3-0 lead, running through the Arsenal backline as if it were an eight-lane motorway.

That, it was hoped, might have represented a one-off and Squillaci was surprisingly named captain for a disappointing but far from disgraceful 2-0 defeat at Chelsea a week later.

Yet for the rest of the season Arsenal's defence, minus the permanently injured Vermaelen and further hindered by a desperately out of form Manuel Almunia in goal, seemed to be permanently on the point of buckling, making the title challenge all the more remarkable.

Although he scored in a 3-1 win at Partizan Belgrade, it didn't help Squillaci that he had a goal ruled out for offside in the 3-2 defeat to Spurs in November, or when he missed the chance to head a late equaliser in the same game.

Arsenal's defence, for years one of the best in Europe, was now a toxic brand and Squillaci's name was contaminated.

His reputation for haplessness grew when he felt the need to commit a professional foul in an FA Cup tie at home to Huddersfield and although he partially redeemed himself by heading the only goal in a 1-0 win over the league's most obdurate opponents, Stoke City, for the rest of the campaign he was behind both Koscielny and Djourou, neither of whom looked any better than Senderos on a bad day, or would have figured in a list of the top 20 centre backs playing in England at the time.

After a year in England, Arsenal were reported to be trying to offload him, only to find there were no willing takers.

The following year he played even less and his reputation was hardly bolstered when unconfirmed reports suggested he was being paid £60,000 per week - and that the nine minutes he played in the Premier League triggered a 250,000 euro payment clause to Seville.

Squillaci comes across as a humble, modest and likable guy who may yet prove useful to someone. Both Tony Adams and to a lesser extent Martin Keown successfully rebuilt their reputations later in their careers, but the feeling is that at 32 the Toulonais may have left it too late and may lack the edge to do likewise.

28) THIERRY HENRY

Friday, December 9, 2011. Thierry Henry is in tears outside the Emirates Stadium. A statue has just been unveiled depicting Henry at his zenith in 2002, kneeling and glaring at the away end, after scoring arguably the greatest goal of many great goals against Tottenham at Highbury.

He is unquestionably the greatest player seen at Arsenal in my lifetime, a genius, and the most exhilarating player I've ever seen in the flesh with the possible exception of Ronaldinho.

There is no possible argument that he deserves this honour.

So why is something jarring? To some Henry's halo slipped after his infamous handball in the 2009 World Cup play-offs against Ireland. Others took umbrage about his alleged diving: the Independent's James Lawton, a man who would never use one word when 5,000 would do, excoriated him for an incident in the 2006 World Cup when he exaggerated the contact made by Carles Puyol, but this could be dismissed as a sour, pompous, overwritten occupation of the moral high ground.

Was it his sulking? At times, when things were going against Arsenal, Henry was like the kid in the school playground who knew he was better than everyone else and just had to let them know, unable to mask his frustration with their limitations.

There was also the question of his performances in the biggest matches.

After all, he never scored for Arsenal or France in a major final and missed two chances against Barcelona in Paris that were difficult, but that a player of his calibre should have converted.

But none of these things really bothered me. The handball was instinctive and he apologised for it afterwards, while his "diving" was a matter of opinion: anyone attacked by James Lawton has to elicit a certain amount of sympathy.

His outbursts at least showed he shared the occasional exasperation of the fans, of whom he still claims to be one and his lapses in the biggest games were unintentional.

But I wasn't able to fully subscribe to the cult of Henry for one reason. It was the fact that he left us, despite his repeated protestations of undying love, in 2007, at around the same time his marriage to the model Nicole Merry ended.

Merry wasn't alone if she felt jilted. Being dumped was an unusual feeling for an Arsenal supporter, although it was one we'd soon have to get used to.

Players almost invariably left on the club's terms. Before Henry's departure, only the deal that saw Marc Overmars and Emmanuel Petit join Barcelona in 2000 caused any pangs of regret.

Yet there was something unsettling about this stage-managed departure, with Henry continuing to say how much he loved Arsenal, while claiming he had to join Barcelona because he wanted to win the Champions League.

This is a common mantra among players, whose sense of entitlement to the game's honours apparently overrides all considerations of loyalty.

It also implies failure on the part of the team mates left behind.

Some fans swallowed this and when he returned for Barcelona in the Champions League he was warmly received. After another year had gone by he was treated like a lost Messiah when he reappeared with the New York Red Bulls for the 2011 Emirates Cup.

Yet for me Tony Adams, a man flawed in different ways, was a greater servant over a greater number of years, a man who stayed at Arsenal until he retired and never bemoaned the trophies he could theoretically have won elsewhere.

As captains both men led by example, but when Adams delivered bollockings he did so in a manner that left the recipient in no uncertain terms that a repeat wouldn't be tolerated.

Henry's approach was to sulk, to take a misplaced pass almost as a personal insult. In his final season at Arsenal his unhappiness was blatantly obvious.

That he left to join Barcelona, that most arrogant of clubs with their "Mes Que un Club" logo and belief in their own divinity, made it even worse.

During the 2006 Champions League final the Barcelona fan and self-proclaimed comedian "Jimmy Jump" - in reality a serial tosser who is about as funny as amoebic dysentery - evaded security at the Stade de France and tried to hand Henry a Barcelona shirt. It was the equivalent of going to a party and having to watch someone stick his hand up your wife's skirt, though in terms of its classlessness it was entirely in keeping with Barcelona's enduringly lecherous pursuit of the striker.

Internet polls, international plaudits, trophies and bald statistics all support the contention that Henry is the greatest Arsenal player of all time.

The club's record scorer with 226 goals, Henry is one of the most decorated players of the modern era, having won every possible trophy and possessing every possible attribute a footballer could need, from his searing pace, dexterity with either foot, guile, charisma and showmanship.

It would be immensely churlish not to be impressed by the contribution Henry made to Arsenal and when the club conducted a poll to determine its greatest players via its website in 2008 Henry almost inevitably won, ahead of Dennis Bergkamp and Tony Adams.

Even if one allows for all the usual caveats when evaluating these polls, he unquestionably deserved it, but when he first arrived at Arsenal he didn't look or play like a man who would rewrite the club's record books.

He was born right on the outskirts of the Parisian sprawl in 1977, just six months after his hometown, Les Ulis came into being, when it was split from the neighbouring districts of Orsay and Bures-sur-Yvette.

Henry is quoted as saying he could hear the occasional police siren when he played football. At a guess around 90 percent of the world's population lives within earshot of the occasional siren, but this is used as evidence that the area was rough, to perpetuate the idea that Les Ulis was a ghetto.

It's undeniably ugly compared to many parts of France, but it looks like Beverly Hills compared to parts of Stoke or Sunderland.

For once however, it seems that there is something more than just cliched myth-making when it comes to the backdrop to Henry's childhood.

He lived in an area where the skyline was dominated by HLMs and when darkness fell the local ne'er-do-wells congregated in the streets.

Quite what they got up to Henry was seldom in a position to tell. His parents, in particular his father Antoine, were strict, protective and refused to allow him to mix with the kind of people who could have led him into trouble.

Antoine was an émigré from la Desirade, an island just six miles long and less than two miles wide to the east of Guadeloupe.

He kept his son in an even more confined space, keeping him indoors at nights, in a flat where he could witness his friends socialising in the streets below.

Antoine later said some of these friends had had brushes with the law. Thierry went further, saying many of them were in jail.

That's possibly an exaggeration, but for Thierry football was, from an early age, his most plausible escape route, given that his intelligence was never obvious in his academic results.

There was a sporting tradition in the family. His uncle, Aurelien, was a 400 metre hurdler of some repute. Antoine said he was once a French champion in the discipline. Thierry wasn't sure when pressed on that point, but his uncle later worked as a fitness coach, physiotherapist and a nutritionist. He was briefly with Everton, where one of his clients was Abel Xavier, an association he'd probably want to leave off his cv.

Antoine was the family's footballer, an aggressive striker who played with the local team at the Pampres Stadium. He pushed Thierry into the local team, Club Omnisports des Ulis and moved him on again to Union Sportive Palaiseau when he felt his son had outgrown them.

It's perhaps this slight that explains why Henry's picture doesn't adorn the front of the CO website section dedicated to its former players.

That accolade goes to Patrice Evra, the Manchester United left-back who gives the impression of being desperate to start a fight in an empty room and was the captain of the doomed World Cup campaign in 2010.

Evra is not a bad player - but he was never in Thierry Henry's league and nor were the half-dozen other professionals who passed through his first club's ranks.

This may not be a big deal, but Henry's time at Palaiseau also curiously merits only a passing reference on their website, at the end of a page that proudly boasts of 12 others professionals and where top billing, bizarrely, goes to Jean-Alain Boumsong and Jonathan Zebina.

After a season there he moved on again, and again at Antioine's behest, this time to Entente Sportive Viry-Chatilon, a progressive amateur team, who at least put him at the top of their list of old boys, who include Zebina again and David Grondin.

The recurring theme from that era is that while Thierry was as charming as the adult he would grow up to be, Antione was the archetypal nightmare parent, genial one moment, the next a fulminating, raging touchline presence desperate to protect his son's bourgeoning career from the thugs who he felt tried to kick him out of the game.

He also had a habit of criticising his son's team mates, something that would become one of Thierry's few non-endearing characteristics during his final years at Arsenal.

Antoine separated from Thierry's mother, a university receptionist from Martinique called Marylese, at around the time Monaco first scouted their son, but both parents remained constantly supportive and the impact of the separation was lessened when Henry was drafted by Clairefontaine, despite the misgivings of the director, who felt he was too weak academically.

He emerged three years later, drastically improved, both as a footballer and a scholar, and joined Arsene Wenger's Monaco.

Like Emmanuel Petit before him his jaw nearly hit the floor when he saw what the principality had to offer compared to Les Ulis, but with a level of awareness not always obvious in footballers he also realised his career could be strangled at birth if he succumbed.

He made his debut as a 17-year-old in a derby with Nice, alongside Petit, Thuram and Djorkaeff, on August 31 1994 and played for 64 minutes up front with Sonny Anderson before he was replaced by Ben Bettahar, moments after Nice had scored the second goal in a 2-0 win. Within a month Wenger had been sacked, but Henry's sporadic appearances continued and at the end of the season he started to score.

Even by the standards of a man who would go on to score some outrageously brilliant goals, his first ever senior goal was an almost miraculous piece of improvisation.

Monaco were 1-0 up at home to Lens when Henry came on after 22 minutes for the injured Mickael Madar, sporting a trainee moustache and an afro-caribbean version of the curtain-haired indie kid look that was fashionable at the time.

Within four minutes he found himself through on goal but at a poor angle to the right of the penalty area. The keeper, Guillaume Warmuz, came out to narrow the angle and found himself stranded, but his charge seemed to have pushed Henry wide enough for the immediate danger to have passed.

Any coach would have screamed at him to hold the ball up and wait for support, but with five defenders between him and his team mates and Warmuz still trying to make his ground, Henry, barely a yard from the byline, curled the ball from an apparently impossible angle just inside the far upright.

It was a similar effort to the fabled goal scored by Kanu at Chelsea in 1999 and before the half had ended he'd added a tap in. Monaco went on to thrash a poor Lens side 6-0, but if that was relatively easy, Henry's next intervention showed he had an appetite for the big occasion.

Monaco were trailing 3-2 away to an outstanding Nantes side who included Claude Makelele and Christian Karembeu and were closing in on the title when Henry was thrown on as a sub, again for Madar, with 12 minutes to go.

He silenced a full house of 34,000 when he hit a 90th-minute equaliser that at least temporarily delayed Nantes' title celebrations, collecting the ball just inside the area to the right of the keeper and hitting what was either a terrible cross or a wonderful shot - with his "weaker" left foot.

The following season he progressed under Jean Tigana to the extent that he was named France Football's young player of the year for 1996 and as an impressionable and immensely promising young French player it was almost obligatory that he'd become embroiled in a contract saga.

By reportedly signing a pre-contract deal with Real Madrid and an extension with Monaco on the same day he earned himself a hefty fine, but he was confident enough in his own skin by now to defy Antoine's wishes and honour the latter agreement.

It's impossible to guess how he would have developed at Madrid, but it's reasonable to assume that by staying with Tigana he played far more than he would have done at the Bernebau, where his attacking rivals would have been Raul, Suker and Mijatovic, as opposed to Madar, Christopher Wreh and Victor Ikpeba, a player who was only at Monaco because his wife was so taken with the Cote d'Azur that she locked him in their house when he was on the brink of signing a deal with Reggina.

He was almost ever-present as Monaco won the league in 1996-97, scoring at a rate of exactly one goal every four games from the left wing position where Wenger famously told him he was "wasting his time".

That, however, wasn't enough to earn him a full international call-up, even though he was captain on the under-21s.

For the 1997 Tournoi, France selected Christophe Dugarry, which was fair enough, but also Nicolas Ouedec of Nantes, PSG's Patrice Loko, Florian Maurice of Lyon and Marc Keller of Strasbourg, all of whom were the footballing equivalents of flat-track bullies.

Yet with hindsight it seems clear that Aime Jacquet knew what he was doing. The quartet were all respectable enough attackers, but Jacquet needed to demonstrate that they lacked the qualities needed to open up international defences which, it rapidly became obvious during the following season's Champions League, Henry had.

In the group stage against Bayer Leverkusen he scored with a classic sidefooted finish that had the commentators purring about his "sang-froid extraordinaire" and then showed his athleticism by chasing an apparently lost cause and hooking a ball back off the touchline for Ipkeba to score as he hurtled into the advertising hoardings.

He curled in a third, Monaco won 4-0 and Henry was in the French squad for their next match with South Africa, the team against whom his international career would come to a disillusioning end 13 years and 123 games later.

If he didn't score in that 2-1 win at Lens, his performances in Europe were bringing him an army of admirers.

He scored twice in a 5-1 win over Lierse and twice again as Monaco overturned a 2-0 deficit to win 3-2 at home against Sporting Lisbon, his second goal coming in the 90th minute. He then got a late equaliser in a 2-2 draw at Leverkusen that won Monaco the group.

Although he'd played against both Leeds and Newcastle in the UEFA Cup (he was stamped on by David Batty during the latter tie), the first time he really came to the attention of a wider English audience was in the Champions League quarter-finals in March 1998 when Monaco thrillingly dumped Manchester United out of the Champions League, just days after Marc Overmars' goal had given Arsenal a pivotal 1-0 win at Old Trafford to alter the course of the title race.

That earned the Monegasques a semi-final with Juventus and although they were humbled 4-1 in the first game, Henry scored in a 3-2 win in the second leg, putting himself on Juventus's radar and breaking Raymond Kopa's goalscoring record for a Frenchman in the European Cup with his seventh of the campaign.

He hadn't played for France since his debut, but he was named in Jacquet's provisional squad for the World Cup and retained ahead of Anelka when the final 22 were announced.

When Jacquet selected him on the left for the opening game with South Africa it was quite a statement from the manager. It was France's first fully competitive international since the Euro 96 semi-final defeat and after two years of experiments it signalled that the manager presumably regarded the 20-year-old as his best option in his strongest line-up.

In fact he was the only player who started against South Africa who, for tactical reasons, wasn't retained for the final (Blanc was suspended and Stephane Guivarc'h owed his recall to an injury to Dugarry).

Henry scored in stoppage time against the South Africans, a brilliantly taken goal where he nutmegged the last defender and then clipped the ball over the keeper with his next touch.

In the next match with Saudi Arabia he opened the scoring with a close range tap in, then scored France's third after latching on to a huge punt downfield from Barthez.

The French won that game 4-0 to ensure qualification and Henry was left out of the starting line-up for the experimental team against the Danes.

However, he was hooked off 25 minutes from the end of the second round tie with Paraguay, having hit the post in normal time, and dropped for the quarter-final with the Italians, when Jacquet, opted for a more defensive approach by bringing in Karembeu.

Henry replaced him after 65 minutes and scored a penalty during France's shoot-out win, but he was again left on the bench for the semi-final with Croatia.

This time he came on when Karembeu was injured after half an hour and set up Thuram's winner, but he played no part at all in the final, when his hopes of a substitute's appearance were dashed by Marcel Desailly's sending off.

He dealt with the disappointment in a mature way, particularly when compared to Anelka, who wasn't even watching.

"I only felt sorry for myself for about a minute," he said later.

Henry could reasonably have assumed that his time would come and he'd done enough in the tournament to ensure it was matter of time before Monaco sold him to a bigger club.

The usual ritual was observed. "He's staying, full stop," Monaco's president Jean-Louis Campora said, but everyone knew this was bullshit.

Arsenal reportedly made an enquiry. Campora made a great show of saying that he wasn't for sale, but rather than just put the phone down he went all the way to London to tell David Dein in person.

Campora wasn't the only bullshit merchant at Highbury that summer. Arsenal made a great deal of enquiries in the off season if you believed the papers, with everyone from Fabio Cannavaro and Zinedine Zidane to Matt Jansen and Oxford City's Jermaine McSporran tipped to sign.

Henry himself openly said he wanted to rejoin Wenger and was clearly unsettled when he began the 1998-99 season still with Monaco, where the attraction of playing in front of 5,000 fans suddenly seemed a lot less obvious given what he'd experienced during the summer.

In mid-January Tigana quit and within a week Henry, who'd scored just once all season, was sold to Juventus for a reported £12 million.

His time in Italy is widely considered a failure, but Henry cited mitigating circumstances.

The sanity of the Juve fans could be measured by the way they turned against Marcello Lippi, whose crime was to manage them to three scudettos, three consecutive European Cup final appearances and a Coppa Italia and then say he'd like to step down at the end of the season.

A reasonable man would assume that he might have been allowed the occasional blip with a record like that but after a 4-2 defeat at home to Parma he decided to jump.

"If I am the squad's problem then I resign," he said. "Let's see if this team can get going if it no longer has Lippi."

It didn't and nor did Henry, who scored only thrice in his six months in Turin. Two of these came in a 3-1 win over Lazio and the first was down to the kind of goalkeeping error from Lazio's Luca Marchegianni that was almost a gift, if that isn't too loaded a word to be using when talking about the Serie A of that era.

The downturn in his form was so obvious he was demoted back to the French under-21 side, at exactly the same time that Anelka was starting to look like the striker who would lead the French line for the next decade.

As Henry's market value dwindled to the point that Juventus were seriously considering loaning him to Udinese, so Anelka became the subject of increasingly laughable bids from Real Madrid.

It's possible that Anelka looked a better prospect than Henry in August 1999 but the idea that he was worth over twice as much now looks almost absurd.

Wenger might have been genuinely scandalised by his departure, but with the £23.5 million he fetched Arsenal were able to buy both Henry and Davor

Suker and still had enough left over to build a new training ground.

Henry had instructed Juventus that he wouldn't countenance a move to any club other than Arsenal, which possibly helped to lower the fee, but in purely business terms it has to be one of the greatest ever transfer deals.

There's an often-quoted anecdote about Wenger telling Henry he was "wasting his time" on the left wing, but that's where he began his Arsenal career.

Signed too late for the Charity Shield (Anelka was incredulous and visibly affronted when asked if he'd watch the match in question), Henry was left on the bench for the opening day game with Leicester and brought on at half-time for Freddie Ljungberg.

His biographer Oliver Derbyshire wrote: "his electrifying pace made an instant impression on everyone present" but that seems an exaggeration. The impression wasn't universally favourable and he missed, by Wenger's estimation, three clear chances, all of which left him progressively less confident.

He was undoubtedly quick, but so was Tony Daley, the Aston Villa winger who was almost impossible to stop down the flanks, but who was easy to defend against because once he'd got to the byline he had almost no idea what to do with the ball.

According to Derbyshire, Nick Hornby's brother likened him to a French Perry Groves. (This wasn't intended as a compliment, although having once paid £5 for a ticket to a sportsman's dinner that featured a talk from the ginger Messi himself and a free plate of chilli, I'd have to interpret it otherwise.)

For the next few weeks he was shuffled from the starting line-up to the bench and from the flank to the centre and back again, never looking entirely convincing, but showing enough to suggest he'd probably come good.

His breakthrough came at Southampton on September 18, when he came on as a substitute for Kanu with 19 minutes left.

Eight minutes after coming and having already missed a one-on-one he collected a short pass from Tony Adams with his back to goal. Henry was a couple of yards outside the penalty area, he held off a marker who had a fistful of his shirt and curled a shot past keeper Paul Jones that swung inside the far post.

He celebrated by running to the corner flag, seemed to think about using it as a microphone for a second and then contented himself with just blowing a kiss to the travelling supporters.

On the following Wednesday he again got Arsenal out of jail when he came on as a sub against AIK Solna in the Champions League at Wembley.

As the game went into injury time Henry drilled in Kanu's lay-off to make it 2-1 and moments later he set up Suker's third, but a mini-drought followed as he went two months without a goal while Wenger tried various combinations of Suker, Kanu and Bergkamp up front.

Suker might have been a great signing for Arsenal had they got him a couple of years earlier, but he only became available after falling out with John Toshack at Real Madrid. At 31 and after a decent start he was injured too often to make an impact.

Wenger came to the conclusion that Bergkamp and Kanu "didn't really work" and for the home game with Derby County on November 28 he finally went with his instincts and put Henry up front.

He scored twice, set up both times by the brilliant Marc Overmars. The first, the equaliser from an acute angle on the left, the second a more orthodox forward's goal through the centre.

The next game, a league cup tie at Middlesbrough, convinced Wenger to make the move permanent. Arsenal lost in a shoot-out after Henry had conceded a late penalty with a handball, but Henry's goal, and more importantly his performance as the central striker arguably represented the start of a six-year period as one of the very best, if not the best, forward player in the world.

He scored goals of almost every possible description, though admittedly hardly any with his head.

Some were the result of pure pace. If left isolated with a single defender he could invariably either wrong foot them to carve out a yard of space, or just glide by, as he did twice in a 4-1 win over Sunderland that all but ended the career of Steve Bould, who was playing out a twilight season at the Stadium of Light.

Some were close range tap ins after a perfectly timed "arrive", to borrow a Ron Atkinsonism, in the box.

Others flew in from distance, like the waft of his right leg that saw him find the bottom corner against Bradford.

There were goals of pure power, like a shot at Nantes that nearly took the keeper's head off and against Deportivo in the UEFA Cup he even scored with a far post header from an absurd angle. There were penalties, usually struck low and as close to the posts as possible and there were the goals when he'd receive the ball Alan Shearer-style, backing into a defender, using his strength to hold off the tackle and then scoring with a minimum of backlift, such as the goal that settled everyone's nerves in the UEFA Cup semi-final at Lens.

But perhaps the most symbolic moment came towards the end of the season when Arsenal played Chelsea at Highbury and Henry was pitted against Marcel Desailly, perhaps the archetype for Stuart Hall's beloved term "the colossus".

For much of the previous decade Desailly had been one of the strongest and most effective players in Europe, a key part of the Milan team that won multiple trophies and the defensive pivot for France in 1998, when Henry was still a junior member of the squad.

Henry had already scored when, a minute into the second half, Bergkamp played him in on the right. With Desailly covering it didn't look that threatening a situation, but Henry brushed him aside like Jonah Lomu trampling over a random Underwood brother, leaving Desailly sprawled on the floor, wondering whether he'd just been run over, before rolling the ball through Ed De Goey's legs.

It was a phenomenal first season, though to judge him by the harshest standards, those elite players have to be judged by, in the biggest game he wasn't decisive. In the UEFA cup final with Galatasaray he set up chances for Keown and Overmars that should have been put away, but this only partly absolves him of his own guilt for the point-blank header he steered straight at the keeper in extra-time.

At Euro 2000 he started France's opening game with Denmark alongside Anelka and had completely usurped him by the time the final came around. He scored against the Danes and again in the semi-final with Portugal, but against the Italians in the final he ran himself to the point of exhaustion and saw Wiltord and Trezeguet steal the glory.

Hyper-critical? Perhaps, but within a couple of years he was being feted as the best player in the world by Arsenal fans when perhaps he may never quite have reached the same level as Ronaldo, Zidane and later Messi.

What isn't in question is that once he reached his top level he stayed there for a long time. 2000-01 followed a similar pattern of goals, the majority of which were well beyond the wit of the average striker, with no medals to show for them.

Against Manchester United at Highbury his turn and volley to chip Barthez had Ferguson muttering darkly about how often he'd pull the same trick off if he tried it 100 times, but a great goal is something that by definition can't be seen every week.

A lesser player might have scored a similar goal but would someone who hadn't already banked 30 goals for his club have had the idea, or dared to try it?

Against Tottenham at Highbury he picked up the ball near the halfway line and almost tortured the covering defender Chris Perry, forcing him to retreat like a cowering christian fleeing a lion for 40 yards before tiring of his prey, strolling past him and then nearly falling over but still finding the time to pick himself up to score.

Against Leicester he volleyed in Pires' corner, first time, from outside the box but in the FA Cup final with Liverpool he again failed to make the crucial difference.

Again the fault wasn't entirely his own.

In possibly the worst miscarriage of justice to befall Arsenal in the modern era, Henry was denied a goal by Stephane Henchoz's handball on the goal line in the first half.

With 16 minutes gone he waltzed round Sander Westerveld, went slightly wide but hit the target, only for Henchoz to make a decent save with a hand tucked under his stomach so the referee Steve Dunn couldn't see what had happened.

It was the kind of incident that would have merited a penalty try in rugby and while that sanction is unlikely ever to exist in football, a penalty and a red card would at least have compensated Arsenal.

Henry couldn't be blamed for that, nor for Ashley Cole's failure to put away an easy chance created by the striker's individual brilliance early in the second half.

Yet once Ljungberg had finally given Arsenal the lead Henry missed a sitter moments later and given that Liverpool possessed one of the few better natural finishers in the game in Michael Owen, that was almost asking for trouble.

In the aftermath of the defeat Henry coined the famous "fox in the box" phrase, which later became an anvil round Francis Jeffers' neck, but while it was a gut-wrenching way to lose it was arguably a freak result rather than anything more systemic.

If the match had been replayed ten times Arsenal would probably have won eight or nine of them, rendering Owen's exploits academic.

And Arsenal didn't really need a fox in the box the following season. Jeffers was signed, but he seldom saw action.

It was rumoured that he'd celebrated signing the deal with Arsenal by going out on the lash, thus incurring Wenger's displeasure before he'd even kicked a ball for him. He was also injury prone and destined to be the fifth-choice up front.

After a couple of patchy seasons Bergkamp was back to his best, Wiltord was beginning to peak, Kanu was still more than useful and Henry was almost unstoppable.

A volley at Middlesbrough on the opening day of the double-winning season set the tone.

For the first time he scored direct from a free-kick at Derby and there was a faintly odd celebration against Panathinaikos when seemed to be eyeballing the entire away end.

More significantly he scored twice in the home game with Manchester United, twice pouncing on errors by Fabian Barthez as Arsenal won 3-1, a performance Ferguson described as the best Arsenal had played against his side for years.

It was an oddly generous remark given that the game was basically decided by human error. Unlike the year before when he'd hit a brilliantly improvised winner, this time round United might have hung on for a draw had Barthez not had one of the worst 20 minute spells of his career.

David Beckham, looking to relieve some pressure, rolled a routine backpass back to Barthez, who was supposedly one of the best keepers in the business with the ball at his feet and who had played as an outfield player in a pre-season friendly.

Dennis Bergkamp put him under pressure but he was merely doing a striker's job.

At the highest level such a run might produce an error less than one in a hundred times, but Barthez sliced the ball straight to Henry, who took two touches and rolled the ball into an empty net. He celebrated by lifting his shirt over his head to reveal the latest in a series of slogans he wore on his vests; "For the West Indies." (Someone in authority soon decided T-shirt messages were a form of sedition and duly banned them).

Barthez greeted that error with a rueful grin but within 10 minutes he'd erred again and this time it hurt.

Again all that was needed was a routine piece of goalkeeping to smother a Vieira clearance, but he blundered, fumbling the ball behind his back where Henry was waiting to again roll it into an empty net.

Barthez howled and hitched up his shorts so high it was almost as he was inflicting some kind of public school punishment on himself.

Arsenal and Henry were entering a state of grace, winning both the biggest games (Liverpool away) and those against supposedly lesser opponents like Aston Villa, against whom Henry scored in injury time to complete a comeback from 2-0 down to win 3-2.

He missed a penalty at Juventus as Arsenal bowed out of the Champions League, the one black mark on the campaign and again he failed to score in a final when Arsenal beat Chelsea in Cardiff, but he was feeling so generous in the final game of the season against Everton he even made a point of setting up Jeffers for a goal. It seemed like an act of charity.

By the time the World Cup arrived, however, he was a spent force, like the rest of the French squad. He'd already had to sit out the title showdown at Old Trafford and after toiling to no reward in the shock opening defeat to Senegal he was sent off for a studs-up tackle in the second group game with Uruguay, ending his tournament.

Henry lost the ball in midfield and lunged into a challenge. His eyes seemed to be on the ball, but he went over the top and sent Marcelo Romero spinning, lucky to have escaped injury.

Witnessed ten years on it looks like a disgraceful challenge, the kind likely to inflict a serious injury. At the time it wasn't quite as clear cut, but that perhaps demonstrates how much the game has evolved even in a decade and had an opposition player produced the same kind of tackle on Henry, Wenger would doubtless have been outraged.

Had Henry stayed on the pitch he might have snatched a winner, but the 0-0 draw meant an exhausted side needed a 2-0 win against a relatively fresh Denmark in the final group game. In the space of a week France had gone from being one of the main favourites for the tournament to a rank outsider. Under normal circumstances a 2-0 win over Denmark was hardly out of the question, but something inside the French team had died.

The air of invincibility Wiltord's last-minute goal at Euro 2000 had given them had gone. The team included a number of players who were performing well below the levels they reached four and two years previously, not least Zidane whose inclusion against the Danes even though he was carrying an injury smacked of desperation.

Blanc and Deshamps had gone, Candela was no substitute for Thuram, who'd been drafted into the centre, Desailly was in decline and neither Dugarry nor Trezeuguet could compensate the French for the loss of Henry.

It might have been different if they'd scored the first goal but when Dennis Rommedahl volleyed in after 22 minutes the game was up. Against fitter, faster opponents France, for all their technical superiority, were as good as out.

The following season however, Henry was almost unplayable and he scored one of his greatest ever goals in the North London derby at Highbury.

Gathering the ball from just outside the Arsenal area he controlled it with his knee and a volley, making it look almost as if he was showboating. 13 seconds later he'd scored.

Matthew Etherington nibbled at his legs but couldn't catch him, Stephen Carr back-pedalled in front of him like Chris Perry had in the same fixture two seasons before and Henry left him on his backside, before rolling the ball past Kasey Keller.

He then galloped back up the field to eyeball the Spurs fans, a gesture that did nothing to lessen him in the eyes of many Arsenal supporters watching.

He was also flicking free-kicks over defensive walls with the ease of a specialist and by this stage of his career Henry was making the remarkable seem almost banal.

At Manchester City he scored what could have been dismissed as a route one goal, whose brilliance was masked by simplicity. The ball was hoofed out of defence, but 60 yards downfield Henry found a yard, took one touch to control the ball with the next found the bottom corner. Against Chelsea in the FA Cup he was clean through when a (relatively) poor touch made it seem that he'd lost the ball to Carlo Cudicini.

Instead he whisked the ball back, pirouetted around the keeper and then rolled it into an empty net.

One of the most memorable images of the season was at Anfield, when he appeared to be in a different time zone to Jamie Carragher as he left him trailing like an elephant trying to catch a gazelle's hind legs.

That game however ended in a 2-2 draw, after Emile Heskey scored in injury time from a wrongly awarded corner, and the wheels were coming off the title charge.

Perhaps the luckiest goal he ever scored was in the showdown with Manchester United when a shot from Ashley Cole ricocheted in off his leg. He knew nothing about it, but within minutes he'd scored a second (from an offside position), only to see Arsenal immediately concede at the other end and the game finish 2-2.

On this occasion at least Henry had risen to the occasion in the biggest game of the season, only to be let down by his team mates and by Mark Halsey's decision to send Sol Campbell off for a supposedly deliberate elbow on Ole Gunnar Solskjaer.

It was rumoured the Norwegian planned to support Campbell's appeal until he was told not to by his manager, who said he found the way Arsenal put pressure on the linesman "nauseating and absurd".

He effectively accused David Dein of running the FA's disciplinary process and added: "I think Arsenal need to have a good look at themselves and not accuse my player of getting one of theirs sent off. And as for Arsene Wenger to turn round and say if it was a Manchester United player he would not have got sent off, it is just ridiculous."

Of course it was.

Without Campbell for the run in Arsenal leaked goals at crucial times and were left with just the FA Cup final to play for, a 1-0 win over Southampton that was described as a "quarter-triumph" by Wenger's biographer Jasper Rees.

Within seconds of the kick off Henry was through on goal and hauled back by Claus Lundekvam. He stayed on his feet and attempted to score when he might have had a penalty and earned Lundekvam a red card, but he was later pilloried for diving after an incident late in the second half.

There was little argument over the yellow card. He'd cut between two defenders and still had control of the ball when he threw himself over Svensson's leg.

It was cheating and it did tarnish his image. He had crossed the line almost every top class sportsman is tempted to cross. He may not have been an habitual cheat, but he seems to have concluded that playing fair hadn't worked and was beginning to flirt with the dark side, a flirtation that would ultimately have serious consequences for his reputation.

This time the public largely forgave and forgot. Arsenal were almost ignored by pundits ahead of the 2003-04 season and Arsenal barely featured in the newspapers until Henry appeared in a photoshoot that illustrated his awareness of the club's history when he was pictured modelling the new away kit.

It was a classic yellow and blue throwback to the cup finals of the 1970s and Henry launched it by laying on the ground and mimicking Charlie George's 1971 celebration - something it was difficult to imagine Nicolas Anelka ever doing.

During the Invincible season his new trademark goal was the counterattacking sucker punch.

It typically started from an opposition corner or throw-in deep in Arsenal territory. Leeds, Middlesbrough or Inter Milan would lose possession and the ball would break to an Arsenal player. Ten seconds and approximately five passes later, Henry would score.

At Villa Park he played to the whistle and took a free-kick before the wall was ready. This amusingly exposed David O'Leary as a spluttering hypocrite when the Villa manager claimed it shouldn't have been allowed, claiming it was "totally different" to an identical incident when Ian Harte had scored when O'Leary was Leeds manager at Arsenal two years previously.

(O'Leary was actually shown footage of Harte's goal, just moments after he'd told a television interviewer what an outrageous decision it had been).

When the season was threatening to unravel after the FA and European cup exits, he scored a hat-trick, including another outstanding individual goal at home to Liverpool, then hit four against Leeds.

This was the greatest player I ever saw, playing for the greatest team I'd ever seen. Over the following three seasons both declined, but while Henry's dip was marginal, the team's was more acute, eventually contributing to his departure.

Thirty goals in 2004-05 wasn't a bad effort but the era of financial doping was now in full swing. He scored twice in a pivotal game with Chelsea at Highbury, one an outrageous volley, the other another quickly taken free-kick, but he alsomissed a clear chance of a winner in the dying minutes and although a 2-2 draw was no disgrace, something had changed.

The "sea change" Wenger talked about after Old Trafford in 2002 had happened, but not in the way he'd imagined.

In the Invincible season Arsenal played Chelsea five times, won three of them 2-1, drew the first leg of the Champions League semi-final 1-1 and lost the second leg 2-1.

In all five games there was little to choose between the two sides, with individual brilliance or errors making the difference.

A Cudicini error gifted Henry the winner in the league game at Highbury, while Reyes scored two superb goals in the FA Cup tie. But for Jens Lehman making a critical error Chelsea would never have equalised in the Champions League, but just a few months after that something was different.

Chelsea now had Arjen Robben, who was derided as an "old man" by the North Bank because at 20 he was already nearly bald, but the banter couldn't mask a worried admiration for someone was the outstanding player on the pitch, Henry included.

Robben had quite openly joined Chelsea for the money. They offered PSV nearly treble the figure Alex Ferguson had tried to buy him for, which even allowing for the fact the United manager almost certainly would have gone higher, blew him out of the water.

Arsenal weren't even mentioned as an alternative destination and from this point on the struggle was to retain their star players, rather than acquire any new ones.

When Vieira's long-rumoured departure was finally confirmed in 2005, the focus switched to Henry. His contract was due to expire at the end of the 2005-06 season and acres of rain forest perished as a result, as tabloids and broadsheets alike churned out thousands of articles, all of which said precisely nothing other than he might leave, or he might sign a new deal.

At first there didn't seem to be too much to worry about. Henry's love for Arsenal was genuine and obvious, but as the team deteriorated behind him so the anxiety grew.

His successful pursuit of Ian Wright's goalscoring record felt like a distraction, as had Wright's when he overhauled Cliff Bastin.

When he did equal the record it was with a brilliant goal, albeit one ITV's commentator David Pleat managed to dismiss as a fluke.

Having just recovered from an injury he started on the bench at Sparta Prague, with Wenger not wanting to risk his fitness after a month on the sidelines, but within minutes of the kick-off he had to come on as a sub for the porcelain-built Reyes.

Kolo Toure, roughly level with the centre circle in the Arsenal half, pumped the ball towards the edge of the area. It was due to land behind Henry, but he controlled it with a backheel, and while it bounced three times, Henry danced round it, into a position where he could volley it with the inside of his right foot into the bottom corner.

The goal that actually broke the record, from a pass by Pires, was routine by comparison.

Wenger said it was "nearly inexplicable that a guy who is not really interested in scoring goals can score so many," but he was probably relieved to get what was danger of becoming another circus out of the way.

The attention that record commanded wasn't entirely the fault of the media this time. The club were equally involved in making the event some kind of landmark but Henry, despite having reportedly vowed to overhaul the record some day, hadn't gone to Wright's lengths to mark the occasion.

He did receive an award from Wright at the next home game, but there were no Nike-sponsored vests to be unveiled. Maybe he felt a discomfort about individual accolades in a team sport and if so perhaps he could see what was coming.

Arsenal were enjoying their best ever European campaign, nearly managing a clean sweep in the group stages and making Real Madrid and Juventus look ordinary in the knock-out phase, but in the Premier League the top two finish that had been taken for granted had degenerated into a spat for fourth with, of all teams, Tottenham.

Henry was still performing at a level equal or above any attacker in Europe and his goal in the 1-0 win at the Bernebau was as good as any he'd scored. He picked up a pass from Fabregas in the centre circle, held off three central defenders and drifted slightly to the left of the area, resisting Sergio Ramos before planting the ball under Iker Casillas, who was to my untutored eye the best keeper in world football.

But something in the team had gone with Vieira and to a lesser extent Edu: a gutteral will to win that got the team through less appealing league fixtures.

There was no big mystery as to why. In European games Reyes was given greater protection from referees and he played to his maximum level, whereas in the league the likes of Gary Neville could "test" him with impunity. The word got around that he didn't fancy any kind of physical confrontation and the unkind but probably accurate assumption was that he was using the Champions League as a shop window.

It's a myth that Arsenal never lost in places like darkest Lancashire when Vieira was in the side, but they were freak results rather than the norm.

In 2005-06 Arsenal lost at Middlesbrough, West Brom, Bolton (twice), Newcastle, Everton, Liverpool, Blackburn, Manchester United and Wigan in the league cup semi-final.

It took a hat-trick from Henry in the final game at Highbury against Wigan and an outbreak of gastroenteritis in the Tottenham dressing room to ensure Arsenal finished above Spurs on the last day of the season.

Disappointingly the rumour that this divine attack of the runs was brought on by a consignment of dodgy lasagne at Canary Wharf hotel turned out to be a myth but while the whole episode neatly symbolised just what a Mickey Mouse outfit the N17 mob were, it was a disconcertingly close finish. While it partially lifted the pressure ahead of the Champions League final with Barcelona it didn't dispel the feeling that this might be the last chance Arsenal would get for a while to win the trophy.

In the final itself Henry missed two clear chances. The first, in the opening minutes, might not have been pivotal, but the second, midway through the second half with Arsenal clinging to a 1-0 lead, probably was.

After three minutes he controlled Eboue's cross and just needed to knock it to either side of Victor Valdes to give Arsenal the lead, only to hit it straight at him.

From the resulting corner he had a decent effort from the edge of the box, but it was one that Valdes comfortably dealt with and from the moment Lehmann was sent off he was forced to endure what must have been one of the most difficult and frustrating nights of his career.

Effectively forced to carry the attack on his own, Henry had to run even more than usual, while dealing with the dark arts Barcelona consistently deployed to reduce his effectiveness.

Rafael Marquez exaggerated the slightest contact to draw a foul from a legitimate challenge and Henry then suffered a tap on the ankle from the same player, that was designed to look like an accident (straight from the Keown and Adams textbook).

He was the victim of an over-the-ball tackle from Deco that wasn't punished by a yellow card and then made a challenge on Marc Van Bommel that saw him win the ball but take a booking for the follow-through.

He was subjected to constant niggling from Captain Caveman himself, Carles Puyol and while all this was going on he found the time to put in the cross for Campbell's goal and politely hand back the shirt "Jimmy Jump" had tried to give him at the start of the second period. It was a great pity he didn't ram it up his arse.

Midway through the second half Puyol went in on Henry with both feet off the ground and was left on his arse after Henry eluded him and stayed on his feet.

Marquez was next to try to "do" him and he too was left on his backside, but Puyol had by then recovered his position and was able to limit the damage to the concession of a corner, an isolated moment of relief.

The key moment came with 20 minutes left when Hleb put him through on goal. Henry hard a yard on the covering defender Marquez and was about 15 yards out when he shot. Valdes narrowed the angle, but Henry had scored from far more difficult positions. This time his shot was poorly placed and went straight into the keeper's midriff.

A goal then would not, contrary to some claims, have guaranteed victory but it's impossible to guess what psychological effect chasing a two-goal lead would have had on Barcelona and how it would have affected their belief.

Given it was a European final the siege would probably have resumed and it's worth remembering they scored twice in the closing minutes, but dejection and fear can have a powerful effect on the human mind.

Henry had reasonable grounds to feel hard done by after the final whistle, but his haranguing of the officials couldn't mask the fact the better side had won.

Yet his anger at this supposed persecution seemed to play a part in his decision to stay at Arsenal and sign a new deal.

With his contract having expired he could have walked out on the club to join Barcelona and pocketed a staggering signing on fee, as every newspaper in Britain had been pointing out on a daily basis, though the Sun briefly took time out from its core purpose of generally ruining innocent lives to give us the "Thierry In June" headline, saying he would sign a new deal.

And when he did, a few days after the final, it was an immense relief.

Henry cited the team's performance, its potential and the response he got from the fans at the final whistle as one reason why he'd decided to stay: "The love that the fans showed me was amazing."

He might have felt otherwise if he'd been on the Metro train I'd been on, when an Arsenal fan was on the phone to his friend saying: "Naaaah mate, it's full of Spanish cunts," referring to the carriage we were in.

When he realised he was sitting opposite a female Barcelona fan he immediately apologised for his language.

"Fuck, sorry love," he said, before adding: "You want Thierry Henry? After tonight, you can have him."

Wenger said Arsenal had wanted three things going into the end of the season - to qualify for the Champions League, keep Henry and win the final. He said he was happy with two of those but historically it would probably have been better if Arsenal had won the final and Henry had gone.

It would have been desperately disappointing had he left, but the 2006-07 season was a sour affair, in more than one sense and the mere act of signing a four-year deal only put a temporary stop the to the stories about an eventual departure (in a similar situation Tottenham fans were laughably naïve when stories ran about Gareth Bale "ending speculation" about his future when he signed a new deal).

There was a hiatus for the World Cup however, where France, more by accident than design, reached the final.

The French of 2006 could be seen as an experiment in how far a team can go without a coach. On paper they had a superb squad of players, certainly the strongest they'd had since 2000, but they were unimpressive in qualifying and gave little or no impression they were responding to anything Raymond Domenech was telling them.

The team for the first game was Barthez, Sagnol, Thuram, Gallas, Abidal, Vieira, Makelele, Ribery, Zidane, Wiltord and Henry.

There were no weak links, but they were still held to a 0-0 draw by a Swiss defence that included Philippe Senderos.

If that was bad enough, in the next game they blew a 1-0 lead Henry had given them against a keen but limited South Korean side.

That 1-1 draw meant they needed to beat Togo in the final group game to avoid a first-round exit, and while they did that comfortably enough, Vieira and Henry scoring in a 2-0 win, their route to the final looked treacherous.

By coming second in the group they were paired with an improving Spain side instead of the Ukraine, pitting Henry against Puyol barely a month after the Champions League final.

The score was 1-1, Ribery having equalised a penalty from David Villa before half-time when, with eight minutes, left Puyol baulked Henry as he chased a through ball. The free-kick was given, but Henry had gone down clutching his face, which gave the impression the offence was more serious than it actually was.

It was largely forgotten that Puyol had started it, that it was a clear foul and that Spain could hardly complain when, having failed to defend the free-kick properly, Vieira put France ahead.

Complain they did however, as did an army of posturing knee-jerk moralists like the ever-sanctimonious James Lawton, who were more offended by the victim's actions than the perpetrator's.

The referee, Italy's Roberto Rosetti, was one of very few judges to actually get the incident in any kind of proportion, showing Puyol the yellow card his cynicism deserved.

When Zidane scored again in stoppage time France were into the last eight and, almost by accident, just two games from the final. At this point an England team would have imploded, while a German one would have somehow scratched its way through. France took the German path.

Against Brazil in the quarter-finals they were underdogs, but only marginally so, and for reasons of sentimentality and history rather than cold logic.

Just as in 1986, when they met at exactly the same stage, Brazil lacked the kind of players they'd had in 1970 or 1982, whose presence alone could help to outpsyche the opposition.

Ronaldinho was the exception, but Ronaldo was already passing his use by date and Cafu and Roberto Carlos had both exceeded theirs long ago.

Unlike 1986, one of the most free-flowing and exhilarating games in living memory, this was a flat affair, with the most clear cut chances coming from set-pieces.

Vieira and Makele locked down the centre, while Henry, Ribery and Zidane tried to stretch Brazil.

A minute after half-time Zidane floated in a free-kick Henry couldn't quite finish. His header went wide, but ten minutes into the second period, this time from the left, Zidane tried again. This time he aimed for the far post, where Henry had inexplicably been allowed to run into an unmarked spot barely two yards from goal.

The static Brazilian keeper Dida stayed on his line and Henry scored with a simple volley, for the game's only goal.

"A side everyone was laughing at doesn't suddenly become favourites," Henry cautioned, but having been paired with Portugal in the last four they were now expected to reach the final.

They did, with an uninspiring 1-0 win in Munich. Henry was brought down for a penalty and Zidane scored. The Portuguese (their Brazilian manager Luiz Felipe Scolari included) again disgraced themselves with their gamesmanship and histrionics, and to general relief even from neutrals France were through - and just 90 minutes from repeating their 1998 triumph.

The French starting line-up didn't look noticeably weaker than the 98 vintage and the Italians were arguably less talented than the Brazil side that played in St Denis.

They were, however, united. Italy were far better organised than Brazil had been and they also had the unquantifiable advantage that none of their players had suffered a fit before kick-off.

Just as he had in Rotterdam, Henry had a frustrating final, the Italian defenders again offering no more joy for him than they had in his six months in Serie A.

He managed a snap-shot that Buffon comfortably parried, but he was subbed for Wiltord three minutes before Zidane's extra-time meltdown and unable to alter the course of the shoot-out.

It was another final failure and things were now going wrong off the field, which may explain why Henry seemed so tetchy during the 06-07 season.

After the Brazil quarter-final the cameras had homed in on Henry, who was kissing a stunning-looking woman in the crowd.

"There's Thierry Henry with his wife. Or at least I hope it's his wife," Gary Lineker said, with the laughter of a man who knew a thing or two about a failing marriage.

It was Henry's wife, but trouble was brewing. Part of the attraction of Arsenal for Henry was his stable, settled family life with Nicole Merry and the daughter he clearly adored (not necessarily a given for a professional footballer).

The two had met while filming an advert for the kind of car no self-respecting footballer would be seen dead driving. The "va va voom" motif was popular with the kind of simpletons who spout catchphrases from advertising campaigns and it gave journalists an alternative to the phrase "je ne sais quoi" to the delight of whichever nefarious agency dreamt it up.

The attractions of Merry were a lot more obvious than those of the car she advertised, so when it was reported Henry had had an affair, it was difficult to understand why he'd risked breaking up his family for the sake of the kind of woman who frankly looked no different to the kind a shelf-stacker might pull at a Sheerness night club five minutes from closing time.

As Charles Wheeler once observed of John F Kennedy and Bill Clinton, the former was forgiven by some because they could understand someone having an affair with Marilyn Monroe.

The latter never was because, Wheeler somewhat ungallantly claimed, there was "the whiff of the trailer park" about Monica Lewinsky.

Top-level sportsmen attract women even when they look like Shane Warne so it was no surprise Henry had had offers, but by succumbing he lost something he could never get back.

Whoever was to blame there was something desperately sad about an interview he gave in his first season with Barcelona: "I'm not happy because a father that only sees his daughter five times in the last eight months cannot be. If you know what it is to have a daughter then you can imagine what it is like. I'm not asking you to cry for me, only that people don't talk for me."

His last season with Arsenal was by far the unhappiest, for everyone concerned.

If results against the other "big four" sides decided the title Arsenal would have been champions, but a squad that could rouse itself for the big occasions was found wanting against supposedly lesser opposition, particularly at the new stadium.

Henry scored brilliant goals at Liverpool and Blackburn, but his only real moment of glory that year came in stoppage time against Manchester United at the Emirates.

Having trailed until the final ten minutes, Arsenal turned the game on its head, Henry heading in an Eboue cross to complete a 2-1 win.

It was said, somewhat optimistically as it turned out, that this might be the moment Arsenal finally grew into the new ground. It was the first time the Emirates had really erupted, but it was also Henry's last goal at the ground for five years.

He scored once more, an equaliser in a 1-1 draw at Middlesbrough, before his Arsenal career seemed to have been extinguished. Niggling hamstring, back and foot injuries kept him out of the side until Wenger gambled on throwing him on as a sub as Arsenal tried to overturn a 1-0 deficit from the first leg with PSV Eindhoven in the Champions League second round.

There were 25 minutes left and the score was 1-1 on aggregate. After three minutes he went down in a heap, clutching his calf. He had a couple of half-chances, but by the time PSV had scored he was almost reduced to walking pace and his season was over.

So, it seemed, was his Arsenal career. As his private life disintegrated, the stories linking him to Barcelona resurfaced.

It wasn't a great time to be an Arsenal fan. There was a dawning realisation that this would never end, that the best players would be almost permanently unsettled by tabloid journalists with the translation bar on their computers enabled and by broadsheet writers told to fill 400 words even if they didn't have a single fact to play with.

The departure dragged on for months, yet when the end came the club's media department managed to spin it as merely the latest instalment in a beautiful friendship and a remarkable number of fans seemed to agree.

The assertion that Henry needed to go somewhere he could win the Champions League went largely unchallenged.

Henry spoke of how much he loved Arsenal and always would, but this merely begged the question: if you love us that much why are you leaving?

When the news of his divorce broke, granted on the grounds of "his unreasonable behaviour", everything became clear. The life he'd loved in London was over and a new, far more troubling chapter was starting.

He was still injured when he agreed to join Barcelona and for several months it looked as though Wenger had pulled another masterstroke in the transfer market.

Without the brooding presence of Henry on the field, castigating them for their mistakes, Arsenal's young players initially seemed liberated, while Henry's form, stuck out on the wing at Barcelona was so indifferent he grew defensive and started referring to himself in the third person, which was always a worrying sign: "Stop comparing the Henry of Barcelona to the Henry of Arsenal. If you want to see him, buy a Gunners DVD."

He seemed almost neutered in his first season in Catalonia during the dog days of Frank Rijkaard's regime, but his second saw him win a treble, including the Champions League medal he coveted after a 2-0 win over Manchester United in the Rome final (a game which not a single non-plastic football supporter I knew wanted the English side to win).

He was, for the final time in his career, a great player in a great team, part of a front three with Messi and Eto'o that effectively ended the 4-4-2 era.

Pep Guardiola's Barcelona team from that season played a style of football never attempted before.

It was relentless, high-speed and intricate all at once. Only players of the highest technical ability could cope with this so-called "tika taka" style. The passing had to be in exactly the right place all the time and the movement off the ball telepathic, a word usually deployed in football to describe a pass that just happened to go to the right place.

Yet arguably the most interesting aspect of all was in the work rate. Usually work rate was a leveller - the most reliable way a less gifted team could combat superior opposition through sheer athleticism and desire. Arsenal's football during this era was a decent imitation and it was certainly wonderful to watch, but the players were never quite on the same level as Barcelona and physically they were significantly weaker.

Guardiola had somehow managed to combine the Total Football of Rinus Michaels' Dutch side, with the will to win and physicality of pre-Milton Keynes Wimbledon.

It was almost unbeatable. United were flattered by the 2-0 scoreline in the 2009 final, yet Henry's contribution was that of a single cog in the machine. He once again failed to score in a final and the match represented a watershed.

The following season he became a fringe player for Barcelona, moving the Finacial Times' Simon Kuper to describe him as "almost completely clapped out."

That was an exaggeration, but Kuper, a rare example of a journalist who doesn't genuflect when writing about a great player, argued that Henry had been in decline from the moment Wenger had sold him in 2007, comparing it to "the moment the surgeon invites his patient into the office for a private chat" and saying that he moved like "somebody's Dad with back problems".

Kuper's profile appeared after the most notorious episode of Henry's career, the handball that ensured France qualified for South Africa 2010.

It was November 2009 and France were on the brink of their worst humiliation since the Bulgarian fiasco 16 years earlier.

They had won the first leg of their play-off with Ireland 1-0 in Dublin and at this level of football it was almost unheard of for a team to lose a tie after winning the first leg away from home, but the French, playing with the same level of fear that saw them eliminated in 1993, were 1-0 down at the end of normal time in the Stade de France.

13 minutes into extra-time they were awarded a free-kick just inside the Irish half. Florent Malouda lofted the ball towards the far post, but marginally overhit it and Henry reached out a hand to stop it from going out of play.

The ball hit the lower part of his wrist and then the tips of his fingers. Having controlled the ball, manifestly illegally but crucially on the blindside of the referee, he steered it back across goal, where William Gallas stooped to head in from all of a yard.

It was one of the most high-profile and successful attempts at cheating ever witnessed in sport. The act itself wasn't that unusual. Players often handle if they think there's a chance they can get away with it and Henry could cite the FA Cup final from 2001 as the proof that they sometimes succeed.

Nor was Robbie Keane, who'd scored the Irish goal, averse to trying it on. It was largely forgotten that the Irish were only in a position to eliminate the French because they had been awarded a penalty for a non-existent handling offence by Georgia in a qualifier just eight months beforehand.

The only strange aspect to Henry's handball was that he wasn't caught. His profile and the relative stature of the game meant he was immediately put in the same league as Diego Maradona.

The reaction in both the short and long term was instructive.

In Argentina Maradona's goal was seen as some kind of divine retribution imposed on the English for having the temerity to win a war they hadn't even started.

In the immediate aftermath of Gallas's goal the French fans in the crowd understandably erupted, in relief as much as jubilation. Some might have seen the handball, but hardly any would have had a good enough view to have been sure. The Irish players, equally understandably, were livid. If ever there was a moment that dispels the idea a player should unquestioningly accept a referee's decision this was it. Why be gracious when someone has just done this to you?

Just as England's players had hared after the Tunisian referee who allowed the Hand of God in 1986, so the Irish sprinted after Martin Hansson. Shay Given incredulously pointed to his hand, just as Terry Fenwick had done 23 years earlier but with the same effect.

The French meanwhile were wheeling away. Henry's initial body language betrayed no sense of guilt, only ecstasy. Gallas wore an altogether stranger expression. He looked almost angry but that was nothing unusual. He locked foreheads with Henry and Anelka then walked back to his half, taking what seemed to be furtive glances at the scoreboard.

Television footage of the incident makes Gallas look like someone who can't quite believe what he's gotten away with.

Hansson gestured to the Irish players, pointing to the part of the chest he was trying to claim Henry had controlled the ball with, but as he tried to wave them back to the centre circle he looked like a man who'd realised he'd just made the mother of all errors in front of an audience of millions.

Ireland had 17 minutes to respond and couldn't. After the final whistle Henry sat with the Irish players, none of whom seemed to show him any animosity. Unlike the unrepentant Maradona, he seemed genuinely contrite, but when he was interviewed on live television he tried to claim that his handling hadn't been deliberate, which appeared disingenuous at best.

A man of Henry's intelligence knew full well a shitstorm was on its way. The rush to apportion blame saw some blame Hansson and others criticise FIFA for refusing to countenance the use of television replays - something which in this instance could have resolved the issue within seconds and seen play resume far earlier than it eventually did once the Irish protests had subsided.

But the real culprit was Henry and about the only credit he could salvage from the situation was to admit he was responsible - which stopped short of saying he was guilty.

"I have said at the time and I will say again that yes I handled the ball," he said, before insisting: "I am not a cheat and never have been. It was an instinctive reaction to a ball that was coming extremely fast in a crowded penalty area.

"It is impossible to be anything other than that. I have never denied that the ball was controlled with my hand. I told the Irish players, the referee and the media this after the game. Naturally I feel embarrassed at the way that we won and feel extremely sorry for the Irish who definitely deserve to be in South Africa. There is little more I can do apart from admit that the ball had contact with my hand leading up to our equalising goal and I feel very sorry for the Irish."

He said a replay would be the fairest suggestion, though there was almost no danger of this being officially sanctioned.

The French were embarrassed. Pires said he wouldn't celebrate: "You cannot say it's unintentional. That would be lying and hypocritical."

Bixente Lizarazu called the display a catastrophe and said: "We're going to go to the World Cup, but we go to the locker room with our heads bowed. It was not something to be proud of. I'm not going to party."

Irish politicians demanded a replay and were predictably ignored. Wenger, who had offered Sheffield United a replay after Arsenal had beaten them in similarly nefarious circumstances in 1999 advised Henry to say sorry, but Domenech, almost inevitably, said he "didn't understand why we have been asked to apologise," proving that just when it seemed he had no credibility left to lose, he still managed to surrender a little more from somewhere.

Nicolas Sarkozy by contrast realised there was little political mileage to be gained from defending the indefensible and apologised to his Irish counterpart, Brian Cowen, at an EU summit.

Sarkozy was however, an accountable politician. The unaccountable, crooked cabal that governs FIFA did exactly what they were expected to do, which was nothing at all.

Two months after the incident, they released the kind of pompous, hand-washing statement Pontius Pilate himself could have drafted, saying that Henry would not even be suspended because: "Handling the ball cannot be regarded as a serious infringement as stipulated in the FIFA disciplinary code."

As Ireland's Sean St Ledger pointed out: "it promotes 'if you can get away with it, do it'," an ethos that accurately summed up FIFA's attitude to a lot more than football.

France, and Henry, had gotten away with it, but the karmic retribution was heading their way. It would surely have been better for them to have been knocked out than to endure what followed in South Africa, where Henry was left on the bench to watch on in a kind of stupor as the French floundered.

He was by now a second-choice player for club and country. When he returned to the Emirates with Barcelona in the Champions League quarter-final he came on late in the second half and was given a warm reception, but nothing more than that.

There was a certain gratitude that he didn't score, but in truth his return was a mere sideshow as Arsenal fought back from 2-0 down to earn a draw.

The mood afterwards was euphoric, but nobody was seriously fooled.

Barcelona had just produced the best football I had ever seen, but the best player I had ever seen in an Arsenal shirt hadn't played any significant part in it. They might easily have won by three or four goals and the recovery meant Arsenal's chances of winning the tie were merely wafer-thin, as opposed to non-existent.

Henry was an unused sub for the second leg, his time at the Nou Camp all but over. He played no part at all in the semi-final with Inter Milan and then had to endure the debacle in South Africa before finally making his long-rumoured escape to the USA.

"This marks an exciting new chapter in my career and life," he said, reading from the script all players who are being put out to pasture read from. "It is an honour to play for the New York Red Bulls. I am fully aware of the team's history and my sole goal during my time here is to help win the club its first championship."

New York didn't have a great deal of history for him to be aware of, but Henry was one of the few players who you could actually believe would have researched his new club, a man so devoted to the game he would watch French third division matches in his spare time.

For over 12 seasons Henry had been operating at the very top of the game. To the fan it's sometimes difficult to understand why anyone would want to leave such a stage, but after a while even the strongest characters can burn out.

The West Indies cricketer Richie Richardson once told me why he'd decided to play for a village cricket team, when he was still at his physical peak. The body was still willing, he explained, but the constant pressure of having to live up to everyone's expectations had finally ground him into submission. His form deteriorated so badly, even at county level, that he'd basically stopped enjoying the game, something he only remembered how to do when he resumed in the Kent village leagues, where he was easily the best player, by a very wide margin.

The drop from Barcelona to the New York Red Bulls was hardly less pronounced, even allowing for the progress the US league had made, but it allowed Henry to enjoy himself again.

In America Henry was still reasonably well known, but he was no-longer an A-list property, particularly in a country where "soccer" was only ever a minor television sport.

His career there is almost irrelevant in the context of his wider achievements. Two goals from 11 games in his first season didn't represent much of a return for several million dollars in wages and although 14 from 26 in his second season represented an improvement, the act of qualifying for the MLS play-offs still seemed like an a footnote in his career, as did New York's subsequent Conference semi-final defeat to the side habitually-referred to as "David Beckham's LA Galaxy".

Yet when the Red Bulls arrived in England for the Emirates Cup, Henry was greeted like a messiah.

Context is everything. When he'd returned with Barcelona Arsenal were still in with a theoretical chance of winning both the Champions League and English League title without him.

In the summer of 2011 the club was at its lowest ebb since the dog days of the Graham regime and Henry's return offered what felt like a last chance to say a proper goodbye until a few months later, when it was announced Henry would be training with Arsenal, supposedly with a view to maintaining his match fitness during the MLS's off-season.

That at least was the cover story and it's quite possible that both parties actually meant it when they said it, but it was a bit like inviting a former partner round for a platonic bottle of wine and whacking on Marvin Gaye's "Let's Get It On."

While he was in London the club unveiled a statue in his honour outside the ground and the ceremony moved him to tears.

Henry clearly fancied a "bonus night" and Wenger, about to lose Gervinho and Chamakh to the Africa Cup of Nations, knew you could still play a good tune on an old piano.

To nobody's surprise, a loan deal was announced 48 hours before the January transfer window opened. Henry was to be used as cover for Robin van Persie, who, having miraculously managed to stay free of injury for nearly a year, was in the form of his life, though the same could not be said for the team, which was well off the pace in the league

"I am not coming here to be a hero or to prove anything, I am just coming here to help," he said. "I'll be on the bench most of the time, if I can make the bench that is. Even if it is just five seconds, one second or just talking in the dressing room, I will give my best, whatever it is."

Simon Kuper's theory about players essentially being businessmen holds a large amount of truth, but most players develop an affection for their clubs and this was a player who genuinely and unquestionably loved Arsenal.

His first spell in London was quite possibly the happiest time of his life. The end of his marriage meant that was something he would never be able to recapture, which would explain his tears at the statue ceremony, but he'd unexpectedly been handed the chance to put something right, even though both he and Arsenal had fallen some distance in the intervening years.

The manner of his departure was still a raw wound: the way he trudged round the pitch against PSV too injured to carry on, the ruinous media saga, the photoshoot at Arsenal station in the new away kit that rival fans gleefully pointed out showed him next to an arrow that said "exit".

Now there was a chance for the final sight of Henry in an Arsenal shirt - the number 12 he'd wanted to wear when he joined the club only to find it was taken by Christopher Wreh - to mean something better.

His second debut came in an FA Cup tie with Leeds. At 34 years of age he wasn't deemed fit enough to start, but after 68 minutes of watching Marouane Chamakh struggle to make any kind of impression on a very poor Leeds side, Wenger threw him on. It could have been interpreted as an act of desperation, but it worked.

With a replay looming Henry, his head shaved to hide a receding hairline and a full beard giving him an almost piratical look, ghosted into space behind the Leeds back four.

Alex Song knew exactly where he was going and threaded a pass just as Bergkamp would once have done, through two defenders.

Henry's first touch controlled the ball, his second planted it in the bottom corner and he wheeled away, his arms spread wide and his mouth gaping, celebrating as if he'd just scored the winner he never managed in a European cup final.

Do the google test on this moment and you'll get 1,290,000 results that include the word "fairytale".

For a man who'd been interviewed hundreds if not thousands of times during his career, Henry was almost always unfailingly polite in press conferences and interviews, often apologising for the fact he'd said precisely the same thing several hundred times.

Strangely, or perhaps not, some of the most revealing things he ever said in an interview were coaxed out of him by Dermot O'Leary, a television presenter who managed to retain a fair amount of credibility despite working on a number of lowest-common denominator programmes.

O'Leary had been asked to interview one of his heroes for a special edition of the Independent in aid of Sport Relief. It was quite revealing about O'Leary too - he earned vast sums of money from sticking microphones under the noses of talentless wannabe pop stars and reality tv non-entities, but here he was, coaxing insights from Henry even some of the best football writers never had.

"I don't think I ever felt what I felt when I scored against Leeds," Henry said. "I don't think I'll ever feel that again because that will never come back. I'm not saying I'll never do another comeback.

"I mean you can never have another first goal on a first comeback. That can never be done again. It was kind of weird because everyone was hoping it would happen. You know you dream about something that will never happen? And it did happen. It's weird."

The next game was a reality check. Arsenal lost 3-2 at Swansea and Henry became embroiled in an argument with a fan, telling him to: "support your team" after the final whistle and gesturing with his hand that he should keep his mouth shut.

It was another example of a defeat being treated as some kind of moral failing and while it was undeniably depressing to watch, much of this stemmed from a perception that Swansea, because they were a small club from Wales, somehow didn't even deserve to be on the same pitch as Arsenal when they were in fact one of the most vibrant, exciting and technically gifted sides in the league.

Henry made seven substitute appearances during his loan spell, scoring three times, two of them decisively. Against Blackburn he scored in injury time when Arsenal were already 6-1 ahead and his team mates were trying to tee him up, just as he'd gifted Francis Jeffers a charity goal against Everton a decade before.

But at Sunderland a week later, in his final league appearance, he again scored in stoppage time, winning a game Arsenal might easily have lost.

In his last significant contribution for Arsenal, Andre Arshavin scooped the ball to Henry, who almost kung-fu kicked it into the goal.

That would have been an ideal way to end his second career, but instead he played the final 45 minutes of a 4-0 defeat to AC Milan in the San Siro, unable to stop an already listing ship from going under.

It didn't matter, because something had changed.

His interview with O'Leary took place a month after he'd returned to the Red Bulls and another revelation was that he'd flown all the way from New York to visit the former Arsenal youth player Fabrice Muamba, who days earlier had collapsed while playing for Bolton at White Hart Lane and would almost certainly have died but for the actions of Tottenham's medical staff and a heart surgeon who happened to be in the crowd.

Henry knew a player who hadn't survived a heart-attack in Marc-Vivien Foe and had played with another, Lilian Thuram, who had spent his entire career playing with a hidden defect that could have been fatal.

He too knew the wisdom of John Arlott's take on what did and didn't matter. That was a far more nuanced argument than simply saying football was unimportant, but he was not entirely comfortable about being considered worthy of a statue.

"My friends tell me to embrace it and be happy. And I am. But at the time (he paused here) … but that's the guy I am. I know about the fun you give to people when you play but for me, the statue is like, a war hero. But I embrace it. What a place to have it. I love Arsenal and to have it right there in front of the stadium. I'm still speechless."

When I started writing this book I was tempted to write a heretical view of Thierry Henry, to attempt a revisionist comparison of his parallel career with the misunderstood Anelka. In the end it was impossible.

Just watching the goals he scored and the way he celebrated them demonstrated why Henry was loved at Arsenal in a way Anelka never could have been anywhere he played.

As O'Leary pointed out, the spine of Arsenal's greatest ever team was French, but they were also Londoners. "London is home for me," Henry said. "And that's where I consider home, now and forever." At the last count, 300,000 thousand French citizens felt the same way and a part of London, like Arsenal, will be forever France, well after Wenger has gone.

APPENDICES
GUILLAME WARMUZ

ALTHOUGH he never actually played for Arsenal, Guillame Warmuz provides an interesting footnote to the club's history.

A goalkeeper from the Saone-et-Loire region, Warmuz spent two seasons with OM as an understudy during the Tapie era and two more with Louhans-Cuisaux where he became a French youth international, before joining Lens in 1992.

At Lens he became part of a side that grew together and won the French title in 1998, and it was Warmuz who kept goal at Wembley a few months later when the "sang et or" eliminated Arsenal from the Champions League.

Unfortunately he developed a reputation for being prone to gaffes and after he made two blunders worthy of David James in a UEFA cup defeat to Porto eyebrows were raised when he joined Arsenal midway through the 2002-03 season, following an injury to Rami Shaaban.

"It was a wonderful experience," he said. "Arsenal arrived at the right moment for me and it remains an exceptional memory thanks to the group of French players and the fraternal atmosphere among the goalkeepers, like David Seaman, Stuart Taylor, and Bob Wilson. I left enriched, having learned what daily life was like with a big club."

That testimony, from Warmuz's official website, was accompanied by a photo of Warmuz with Taylor, Wilson and Seaman and the FA Cup. All seem elated, but Wilson later wrote that Warmuz's arrival had a significantly negative impact on Taylor's career.

Wilson clearly rated the English keeper, who had performed with distinction the year before when both Seaman and Richard Wright were injured, but he also felt that an incident on the training ground showed Wenger favoured Warmuz and that Taylor's career never really recovered. He became a serial bench warmer at Aston Villa and Manchester City.

In the summer of 2003 Warmuz left for Borussia Dortmund - with Jens Lehman coming in the opposite direction.

ARSENAL FRANCE

In the end, it was all down to "arsehole". The most lucid analysis of Arsenal's peerlessly depressing 2010-11 season came from neither Arsene Wenger, nor his playing staff but from a fan I overheard on the train to the home game with Blackburn, on the day I'd arranged to watch a match with members of the Arsenal France Supporters Club.

From his age and accent I deduced the fan in question was one of the many London emigrés who found their way to Kent sometime after the second world war.

This was an afternoon that would epitomise almost all the frustrations of the 2010-11 season. When I left my house in Maidstone, it was half-time in the early kick-off and West Ham United were leading Manchester United 2-0.

On the car radio Geoffrey Boycott, who was supposed to be commentating on the cricket World Cup final at the time, veered off at a tangent and berated 'Sir' Alex for failing to listen to the advice he had given him two years beforehand:

"I told 'im that midfield wasn't good enough!"

Reasoning that things could only go wrong from there and that I didn't want to listen to them when they did, I switched off the radio during the drive to Ebbsfleet, but I turned it on again near Cobham, to hear a snatch of commentary from Mike Ingham that confirmed everything I'd feared would go wrong had indeed gone wrong.

On a train packed with Arsenal fans someone asked how the game had finished and there was a tangible sense of deflation when the answer "4-2" came back.

Someone mentioned that Vidic should have been sent off. I was inwardly stewing over the injustice that Wayne Rooney had been allowed to play at all, given that he'd elbowed James McCarthy with impunity in United's previous game with Wigan.

(The FA said they "couldn't punish Rooney retrospectively for this - ironically they did ban him retrospectively for swearing furing the West Ham game).

There was an understandable reluctance to give United any credit at all, except from the London émigré, who swatted aside all attempts at mitigation by saying:

"Yes, but they've got arsehole."

To the untrained ear that wouldn't sound like a compliment, but that was the intention and we all knew what he meant. He wasn't saying that United were arseholes, but that they had arsehole, meaning that they had a visceral loathing of defeat that partly stemmed from their manager. That they would do anything, on either side of the laws of the game, to make sure they didn't lose.

Like any self-respecting British rail user (not an easy status to maintain given the continual degradation passengers have suffered since privatisation) I usually abhorred any attempts at making conversation with strangers, but this monologue, targeted at the man opposite him in the replica shirt but broadcast to a far wider audience, was more entertaining than anything we would witness on the field that afternoon.

"That Denilson is the worst player in the Premiership," he said, launching into a merciless deconstruction of a team nominally at least still in with a chance of winning the title.

"Look at Nasri, Clichy and Sagna, they're just little boys. Rosicky's lost it and who can blame Cesc for wanting to go back to Barcelona? Then there's that Eduardo. You can't just pick' im because you feel sorry for him."

I'd been offered a ticket to this game by Francis Peyrat, chairman of the Arsenal France Supporters Club.

I had wanted to watch a game with the club and its members, to test a number of preconceived ideas I had about the club's burgeoning French fan base.

In the pre-Wenger era Arsenal were still a well-known club in France, but they had nothing like the profile they now enjoy. Television exposure was minimal, limited to a fleeting presence on a Sunday night highlights package. League games were never shown live, so unless Arsenal had made a cup final the only way to see them if you were based in France was to physically go to Highbury, or hope they drew French opposition in a European cup, which happened infrequently in the years after the ban on English clubs was lifted.

The epic semi-final with PSG was followed a year later by a less enthralling but equally fraught quarter-final with Auxerre, then successive seasons in which Arsenal played "derbies" with Lens.

The written media in France was several years ahead of its British counterpart in attaching importance to European games, if you agree with the principle that devoting multiple pages to a single match represents some kind of an advance.

Both L'Equipe and France Football would devote far more attention to their club's opponents than the essentially inward-looking British press, where newspapers (then) usually limited themselves to a single article preview.

I'd already noticed the unifying affect European games had on the French during my year in Strasbourg, with the otherwise uninitiated taking a surprising amount of interest in the progress or otherwise of their clubs across the three competitions of that era.

Perhaps because of the glut of success before Heysel, English fans had taken European success for granted, but equally it may have had something to do with a lingering post-war superiority complex, as if winning the European Cup was somehow expected.

This was reinforced when Manchester United marked the end of England's exile with victory in the 1991 Cup Winners Cup, but the following decade was almost barren.

Arsenal's 1994 win the same competition represented the exception to the rule that the continent had left the English game behind, until United belatedly and fortuitously bridged the gap in the most implausible circumstances against Bayern Munich in 1999.

By contrast, 1990-1999 was and remains the most successful decade in French club football history, even if you discount Marseilles' "victory" in 1993 and runners-up slot in 1991. Paris St Germain's win in the 1996 Cup Winners Cup remains, to this day, France's only ever win in any European cup and it was greeted with far more enthusiasm in the country at large than Arsenal's success was in England two years earlier.

I used to support English teams as a matter of course in Europe, but this waned over the years. When Heysel happened in 1985 I was too young to fully understand what was going on, but the five-year exile clearly had an effect. It's embarrassing to admit it now, but when Tottenham won the UEFA cup in 1984 I was genuinely excited. United's win in 1991 pleased me, but as the decade went on my allegiance weakened, the tipping point coming at Villa Park in 1999, when Gary Neville reacted to United's injury-time win over Arsenal in an FA Cup semi-final replay by sprinting over to the Holte End to goad us in a manner he would repeat in front of various rival fans down the years.

Whether Neville would have been as brave had there not been barriers and hundreds of police officers in the way is another matter, but the sight of him and thousands of other Mancs invading the pitch marked the moment I started to actively support anyone United were playing against in Europe, even the German sides I previously had an automatic aversion to.

A dozen years down the line, and contrary to my expectations, the view that we "lacked arsehole" was almost universally shared by the French fans I spoke to outside the Tollington, even if the limits of my fading French meant I couldn't quite translate the concept of arsehole.

"We need more players like Jack Wilshere, players who get up as soon as they've been knocked over," said Regis Kerguen, who was one of the few who supported the club before Wenger's arrival.

I also expected the French fans to show a natural sympathy to their compatriots, but there was little. They were not members of the prawn sandwich brigade, too awestruck by the spectacle of actually being at the Emirates to grasp the gravity of the situation. They had flown to England to see Arsenal win and were uninterested in the nationalities of the players who did it. The most strident critic was Dylan Flynn and he also spoke the best English, as a result of having a property in Margate and an Irish grandparent.

"Yes I know, you're probably thinking we're all pikeys down there in our caravans," he said, before telling me at length that £10 to watch Margate FC was a rip-off and then turning his fire the centre of Arsenal's defence.

"Everyone said Laurent Koscielny had a great game against Barcelona," he said, almost stupefied. "But that's because they never once played the ball in the air!"

"Mais il est jeune," Peyrat said, trying to defend him, though at 25 he was older than the average age of the squad and far older than the likes of Vieira and Anelka had been when they first won trophies with Arsenal.

"And then there's Squilacci," Flynn continued, undeterred. "Who was responsible for scouting him?"

Nobody disagreed with this and everyone was scathing about the new generation of facebook Gooners from the far corners of the globe, who greeted every defeat and setback with a barrage of barely literate comments on the club's official site, demanding the sacking of everyone from Wenger down.

For a club that guards and protects its image so successfully it seemed incredible that Arsenal tolerate this kind of online sedition.

"They don't seem to realise what supporting a team means," Flynn told me. "It's about supporting them whether you win or lose."

He was an extremely arch observer and while this wasn't the most profound insight he offered that afternoon it mirrored exactly what I and most sane observers felt.

I walked the few hundred yards to the ground with Kerguen, who told me what it was like supporting Arsenal in France before Wenger's arrival.

In the pre-satellite tv and internet era it meant looking out for results in the papers and catching a few seconds of highlights L'Equipe du dimanche".

Now it was exponentially easier, both to attend games and keep up with the club's news given that l'Equipe and France Football gave Arsenal almost as much coverage as they did their domestic sides.

Another fan, who I knew only as Loic, told me it was only an hour and a half from where he lived in Toulouse on a plane to Heathrow.

Ease of transport was clearly a factor. Almost absurdly, thanks to the Eurostar, it was now easier to get from Arsenal to Paris, than Hastings on England's south coast.

When the game began the French fans were all seated together in the Clock End, next to a block who had flown in from Sweden.

There were a handful of Koreans behind us who, in accordance with the stereotype, were diffident and seemingly overawed, but for the French contingent the mission was clear: cheer Arsenal to victory.

Among themselves they were critical of individual players and while there were one or two audible groans during an incrementally exasperating 90 minutes, this never turned into any kind of orchestrated booing of individuals.

That didn't mean they didn't have a dry sense of humour. At half-time Flynn told me of his rebuffed suggestions to help "Arsenalise" the stadium.

"They want us to put up banners, but it's a bit totalitarian," he said. "I wanted to put one up that said 'There's Only One Marouane Chamakh … thank God!'"

That reflected a general lack of faith that we would get a happy ending. Several journalists had adopted the line that Arsenal had "at one stage been on course for the quadruple and were now faced with another trophyless season," but this was a revisionist fantasy.

I didn't know a single Arsenal supporter who thought we would win four trophies that season.

Nor did it necessarily bother me that we would be trophyless as since the 2005 FA Cup success the only teams to have won anything of any consequence - Liverpool, Chelsea, United and Portsmouth - had all done so against a backdrop of some kind of financial or political uncertainty.

I did think we would win the Carling Cup however and would probably have been happy with that. By the time we played Blackburn I thought we might just nick the league with a bit of luck.

That feeling grew progressively fainter as the second half wore on and Nicklas Bendtner began warming up.

Flynn and the two French fans in front of me immediately rose to their feet and started signing: "Super, Super Nick, Super Nick, Super, Super Nick, Super Nickklas Bendtner," but they were both laughing as they did so.

In the closing stages Chamakh lived down to his billing by missing the kind of chance an Henry or Anelka would probably have buried seven or eight times out of ten and the nagging feeling that had been growing for weeks was all but confirmed.

They were trying, but they weren't good enough. Not good enough to break down defensively minded teams down and not good enough to keep offensively minded teams from scoring, at least not on a consistent enough basis to win the title.

Unlike Henry, Wiltord, Pires and Vieira, this crop of players lacked "arsehole" and it was nothing to do with their nationality.

Peyrat, sitting alongside me, was suffering precisely the same agonies I was going through, throwing his head back in exasperation, then burying it in his hands, shaking it, exhaling in agony.

There was more than one cry of "puuutaaaaain," but every attack floundered and it was of no consolation that a Frenchman, Christophe Samba, was the chief architect of this rearguard action.

In common with most Arsenal fans, they were downcast but not inconsolable. For all journalists talk of "broken hearts" and "devastation" when a team fails, most supporters are well adjusted enough to realise that the game, while not merely a game, is not life itself.

And for most of the members of the French supporters club they could console themselves that their trip home was likely to be a lot easier than mine. They only lived a couple of thousand miles away. I was at the mercy of the Southeastern Rail network.

ARSENAL v FRENCH CLUB SIDES

BOTH before and after Arsene Wenger's arrival in 1996, Arsenal's record against French sides in competitive fixtures has been excellent.

The first ever European tie between Arsenal and a French club came in the 1969-70 European Fairs Cup.

Writing in the Times, Norman Fox praised Arsenal for "exemplary conduct in the face of crude tactics by a Rouen team who were outclassed," during a first leg that ended 0-0.

Geoffrey Green's report of the second leg also comes close to peddling the stereotype of the foreigner who resorts to skulduggery and negativity because he's unable to compete with fine upstanding English players like Peter Storey.

"Rouen committed totally to an eight and often nine men defence and were not over fussy how they achieved it ... (they) all but achieved their limited object, using every device in the book from blatant body checking to undisguised force... the unemployed Wilson might just as well have installed a television set in his undisturbed parish."

A goal from Jon Sammels, two minutes from time, gave Arsenal a 1-0 win and a place in the quarter-finals of a competition they would eventually win.

Arsenal didn't play another French side until 1994 and the semi-final of the Cup Winners Cup with Paris St. Germain, which is dealt with elsewhere.

The following year a superb goal by Ian Wright saw Auxerre beaten 2-1 in the quarter-finals of the same competition, after a disappointing 1-1 draw in the first leg at Highbury and the subsequent expansion of the Champions League meant cross-Channel fixtures became far more frequent.

In 1998 the Gunners drew 1-1 in Lens and then suffered a 1-0 defeat at Wembley which, at the time of writing, remains one of only two competitive defeats to French opposition.

The following year, having been demoted to the UEFA Cup, Arsenal beat Nantes and Lens on the way to the final and in 2000-01 they took four points from Lyon in the second group stage of the Champions League, winning 1-0 away and drawing 1-1 at home.

In 2002-03 they won 1-0 in Auxerre in the group stages but lost the return match 2-1, a result that traumatised Arsene Wenger, who locked himself in his office and refused to attend a birthday celebration in his honour.

Surprisingly it was nearly a decade before they next played a French team, winning 1-0 in Marseilles in 2011, before drawing 0-0 with the same opponents at the Emirates.

As of the end of the 2011-12 season, the overall record against French opposition is played 18, won nine, drawn seven, lost two.

Under Wenger it's played 12, won six, drawn four, lost two, but his teams play significantly better on French soil, where the record is played six, won four, drawn two.

If there is a logical explanation for this, it's that Arsenal's French players are even more motivated than usual when playing on home turf, while the club's profile in France has grown to the extent that when Lens came to Wembley in 1999 they were equally fired up.

Or it could just be down to luck.

Arsenal have lost two competitive games in France, both in European finals against Spanish teams: 2-1 to Real Zaragoza in the 1995 Cup Winners Cup and 2-1 to Barcelona in the 2006 Champions League.

ARSENAL 2 FRANCE 0

On Valentine's day 1989 Arsenal played the French national team in a friendly at Highbury at the behest of their new manager Michel Platini, who wanted to test his players against British opposition before a key World Cup qualifier with Scotland.

The fact the match took place at all shows how much the game has changed in just over two decades. The idea of Wenger sanctioning a friendly in the middle of a title run-in is beyond laughable, but Arsenal were out of the cups and with English teams banned from Europe it gave a young side a rare chance to play against foreign opposition.

George Graham said he wanted to "soften the French up" ahead of the Scotland game and given the way his tenure at Arsenal developed perhaps he had other, entirely altruistic reasons for agreeing to the game.

Scotland's manager Andy Roxburgh took umbrage, but Graham's possibly tongue-in-cheek approach worked.

With a noisy 20,000 watching at Highbury Martin Hayes swept a Paul Merson miskick into the top corner in the first half and Alan Smith steered in a cross from Perry Groves in the second for a 2-0 win against a side who, Laurent Blanc aside, were flattered by just a two-goal margin.

Three weeks later a demoralised French side lost 2-0 at Hampden Park to a Mo Johnston double and Scotland qualified for Italia 90 at France's expense.

Years later I had to interview Hayes on a fairly regular basis when he was managing Dover Athletic. It wasn't the high watermark of either of our careers, but Hayes was at least working in football, having apparently been a car salesman at one point and Dover, in Kent terms, are a "big" club.

They have a small but an atmospheric stadium high up on the North Downs and a healthy band of around 800 hardcore supporters who occasionally sing moronic songs about Slovakian immigrants but are predominantly sane.

They are the nearest British football club to French soil, but what's striking about Dover is how it's almost completely devoid of any French influence at all.

Even though thousands of passengers and vehicles pass through it every day, there is almost nothing in the town that would make a casual visitor think France was a mere 22 miles away.

The town's population is largely monoglot, only a handful of road signs are written in French and the town centre itself has more in common with Scunthorpe or Motherwell than Calais, demonstrating just how profoundly different Britain and France still remain.

Although I spoke to Hayes around a dozen times, I never once met him in person. This was the era of churnalism, when papers decreed it was no longer cost effective to send reporters to games, so interviews were conducted according to a formula: how did the last game go, were there any new signings, injuries, team news etc.

Hayes uncomplainingly talked me and my colleagues through it all every week.

In his time at the Crabble he took Dover on their best ever run in the FA Cup, knocked Gillingham out to widespread rejoicing around the rest of the county and narrowly missed out on a play-off place at the end of the season.

Hayes and Wenger didn't have a lot of common on the face of it, but one problem both faced was that they were forever asked to explain the game to people who knew far less about it than themselves. Like Wenger, Hayes was also unable to hang on his best players, in this case the former Arsenal youth striker Adam Birchall, who after "weeks of speculation about his future" joined Gillingham, just as Cesc Fabregas was signing for Barcelona.

A little over a year after taking the job, Hayes was sacked.

All the while my four-year-old daughter kept saying "whopsadaisy Martin-Hayesey" at home every time she fell over, having once heard me use the phrase, which had popular on the North Bank 25 years beforehand. Reasoning this wouldn't be much of a consolation to him, when I spoke to him for the final time, I didn't bother telling Hayes about this.

TERMS, REFERENCES AND SOURCES

For the purposes of this book, a "French" player is someone who chooses to represent the French national team, regardless of where they were born, raised or how far back they can trace their ancestry.

Thus Patrick Vieira was born in Senegal but chose to play for France, merits a chapter while Armand Traore was born in Paris but opted for Senegal, the country of his parents gets a passing reference.

A number of other players like Alex Song and Johan Djorou have strong French connections and are fluent in the language but aren't actually French and for reasons of space have been left out.

The players are detailed in chronological order. Although Remi Garde was the first French player to sign for Arsenal by a couple of hours, Vieira was the first Frenchman to actually play for the club and given their respective contributions he was the most obvious starting point. As Thierry Henry was, at the time of writing, the last Frenchman to sign for Arsenal, albeit for the second time and on loan, he was a logical choice to close the story.

The word count devoted to each player isn't a reflection on either their status or their abilities. Pressed to choose Arsenal's best French players I would select Henry, Vieira, Petit and Pires in that order, but of these only Petit was among the most interesting character studies, alongside Nicolas Anelka and William Gallas, both of whom were fascinating for very different reasons.

The chapter on Arsene Wenger had to be slightly truncated, partly because, at two decades older than everyone else concerned there was that much more to write about, but also because much of the story can be told through his players and there's little point in covering the same ground twice - especially as Jasper Rees and Xavier Rivoire have both written compelling biographies of the man already.

One day, we can at least hope that Wenger will sit down and write his own story. It could be a classic of the genre and he is unlikely to need a ghostwriter, although the same can't be said of the players. The autobiographies of Emmanuel Petit, William Gallas and Robert Pires are entertaining to a point because of the source material and as first-hand accounts, but they also represent severely wasted opportunities.

Usually written after "conversations with" an author, players' autobiographies are typically slim, slight volumes designed to cash in on a player's popularity, usually at the height of his career before there is any chance for considered reflection - if, in the case of Theo Walcott, whose "Growing Up Fast" was released when he'd barely emerged from adolescence, there's anything to reflect on.

They can be read in an afternoon and give the impression of having been written in under a week. The players themselves are often hazy on matters of fact and their ghosts regularly betray their own superficial knowledge of their subjects by failing to either check or correct these errors.

"False Memory Syndrome" is common in autobiographies, but even allowing for the fact that players play hundreds of games in their careers it still seems incredible to a fan that William Gallas can't remember the score from his first ever FA Cup final, or that Robert Pires describes the goal that kick-started his Arsenal career at Lazio as a "winner" when it in fact earned Arsenal a draw, albeit one that felt like a win.

In both cases a fact checker or editor could have spotted these errors before committing them to print, but it does illustrate the difference between those who earn a living from the game and those who follow it and still, whatever arrogant financiers might claim, pay their wages in a variety of ways.

I read around a dozen autobiographies while researching this book, with Ashley Cole's "My Defence" costing 3p from Amazon. My publisher, Greg Adams, tells me I overpaid.

One of many interesting themes in Simon Kuper's book "The Football Men" is that the moment you cross the line between fan and professional, you are unable to look at the game and the people who play it in the same way ever again.

I found this partially true. As a journalist specialising in cricket and cycling, my experience of covering the English top-flight is limited, but on the rare occasions I covered Arsenal as a reporter I found it was surprisingly easy to become dispassionate when professional requirements compelled me to do so.

When I saw Thierry Henry equalise with a direct free-kick at The Valley I would have erupted had I been in the away end, but instead I took a bland note of what happened and breathed an inward sigh of relief.

On another occasion, covering a game with Newcastle at the Emirates, I was simultaneously trying to monitor six other matches, write a round-up of the Scottish Premier League and crib a report from the Rugby League Cup final at Wembley, so any tension I felt was down to trying to juggle so many balls at once rather than anything happening on the field.

Watching Arsenal as a supporter, however, usually left me in a state of almost permanent agitation. Oddly when we were losing I felt least nervous because at least the worst had already happened. If we were level I feared we'd concede and if we were ahead I dreaded an equaliser. Nick Hornby wrote that he was never comfortable unless Arsenal had a 2-0 lead, though to me even that seemed complacent, particularly after the 4-4 debacle at

Newcastle in 2011. By the latter years of Wenger's reign even a four goal advantage seemed brittle.

While researching this book I watched footage from hundreds of old matches to check if my own memories of them were accurate.

In some cases they weren't. Refereeing decisions I was convinced bordered on the criminal turned out to have been correct as I grudgingly had to concede watching the Champions League final of 2006. I'm now embarrassed to admit I stayed behind to boo the Norwegian referee for his harsh but perfectly correct decision to send off Jens Lehman. I was equally convinced Didier Drogba was offside when he equalised in the 2007 League Cup final and he wasn't.

By contrast the 2001 FA Cup final, when Stephane Henchoz stopped Henry's shot on the goal line with his hand and the 2004 debacle at Old Trafford remain inexplicable and a sense of injustice lingers years after the event.

Whether my memories were correct or not, what was impossible was trying to recreate the feeling of watching a live match, with the absurd surges in heart rate every time the opposition attacked.

This in turn made it easier to be dispassionate and see things I'd missed or failed to fully appreciate first time around.

When football is at its most intense it's possible to feel that life outside the stadium has ceased to exist, but watching an old match what strikes you is the sheer banality of much of what's happening in even the biggest games.

A classic example is the Euro 2000 final, which predated my journalistic career and took place while I was teaching at a language school in Hastings. My students were all French (even if most of them were, like the Arsenal 23, dual-nationality) and they were completely consumed by the match, even if they usually had no interest in football.

Watching the game 11 years on, what was striking was the relative lack of action and crowd noise, even after what at the time seemed like a heart-stopping goal by Sylvain Wiltord.

For me at least however, the inner fan can never be completely buried. The only time I ever saw experienced journalists experience a fan's level of anxiety while covering a live sporting event was on the final day of the first Ashes test at Cardiff in 2009, when England batted out the entire day to see out a draw with Australia.

As a purely visual spectacle it wasn't that engrossing, but with every delivery in the final hour the anxiety increased. I was sat alongside Matthew Engel, a former editor of Wisden and a man who had seen absolutely everything it was possible to see on a cricket field, yet even he was a ball of tension, quoting John Cleese's famous line from the film Clockwise: "It's not the despair. I can take the despair. It's the hope I can't stand."

For the only time in my career I found it physically difficult to write (I can imagine it might have been difficult at Anfield in 1989). Having to file as soon as the match finished I had to keep updating two stories, one in the event of the draw and the other for an Australian win, then remember which one to send. That sounds pretty basic but just over 12 months later CBS announced that Holland had won the World Cup, after the wrong report had been put on the wires.

At moments like these, when a sports field appears to be the centre of the universe, it's easy to forget these men are merely human.

Jimmy Anderson, Monty Panesar and Andrew Strauss all walked into the press room like any other sportsmen who'd just finished their day's work, with Anderson in particular looking distinctly underwhelmed.

Australia's then-captain Ricky Ponting is loathed by many English fans, but it isn't possible to hate him (or indeed 99.9 percent of people) if you've met him in person and this is another paradox of the relationship between players and fan and that of player and journalist.

Unlike fans, journalists can see at close quarters that the men they write about are flesh and blood, yet many elevate and excoriate them and describe them in apocalyptic language, talking of heroism, treachery, cowardice and shame as if they were soldiers risking their lives rather than people who just happen to be slightly better than average at games.

The author Gideon Haigh, covering the 2011 Ashes series, wrote of Australian reporters being ordered by their editors to crucify players who in many cases they had excellent working relationships with and whose only crime was that weren't quite good enough to win a cricket match.

This partly explains why clubs are so protective of their image.

When I asked Arsenal for help with this book they put me in touch with Francis Peyrat of the Arsenal France Supporters Club (who was fantastically helpful), but told me they "wouldn't be able to accommodate" an interview with any players or Arsene Wenger.

I could understand why. Perry Groves once said Arsenal's media department was like Pravda, but their job was to portray the club in the best possible light, which wasn't easy given the agenda pursued by some of the reporters they had to work with.

And it's still preferable to following a club like Tottenham, where information leaks into the papers from multiple sources, concerning everything from managerial sackings the manager doesn't even know about (Martin Jol) to their latest fantastical transfer targets (too many to list, though the moment Glenn Hoddle revealed the "thank you for your interest" letter he received from Rivaldo remains one of my fondest memories in football).

In any case, by then twitter had changed almost everything. Around the year 2000 a website company called Icons provided a foretaste of what would happen when they gave players the chance to run their own websites and say exactly what they wanted to their fans.

It failed because too few fans signed up for the sites and the papers pilfered and twisted the stories, but by the time twitter swept the globe players realised they could not only talk directly to the fans again - for the first time in a generation - they could then skewer any journalists who'd misquoted them.

There are honourable exceptions in the fourth estate, though in my opinion some of the best books written about the Arsenal were produced by an author who wasn't a journalist at all, but a teacher from Faversham in Kent called Jon Spurling.

There were only a few occasions when writing this book that I struggled to empathise with the subjects, and most of them involved Nicolas Anelka. When I did, I asked myself the question: put in that situation would I honestly have done things differently? At all times I tried to remember the human factor and I hope that's reflected in the text.

Most translations from French to English are my own, although in some cases I have quoted from sources who had already translated the copy.

In a limited number of cases I translated quotes that I suspect but can't confirm were originally in English, from French sources.

Inevitably some phrases don't translate very easily. French is far more flowery than English and some of the resulting imagery sounds clunking when translated.

Profanity is also tricky to convert. The French word "con" directly translates as the far stronger English "cunt" but it's so commonly and widely used in French that it's been variously translated as "dickheads," "twats" or even the innocuous "shmucks".

SOURCES

For general fact-checking sources included the Rothmans/Sky Sports Year Book, www.soccerbase.com, www.arsenal.com, www.arseweb.co.uk, the French Football Federation wesbite and bbc.co.uk

Newspapers (print and online)

The Times, The Guardian, The Independent, Le Soir, L'Equipe, Daily Mail,

The Sun, The Mirror

Books:
Jon Spurling's Rebels for the Cause
The French Revolution: 10 years of English football after Cantona by Alex Hayes and Daniel Ortelli, with Xavier Rivoire
David O'Leary: My Story
George Graham: The Glory and the Grief
Wenger - Jasper Rees
Arsene Wenger - The Biography - Xavier Rivoire
Mutzig website
Simon Kuper - Ajax, the Dutch, The War
Official RC Strasbourg website
My Defence: Ashley Cole
Mr Wright - the autobiography of Ian Wright
Emmanuel Petit - A Fleur de Peau
Paul Merson: How not to be a professional footballer
Why England Lose, by Simon Kuper and Stefan Szymanski
Le Foot - edited by Christophe Kuhn
Anelka, by Arnaud Ramsey and Nicolas Anelka
Le Parole est a la Defense- William Gallas
The Football Grounds of South East London – Mike Floate
Alex Fynn and Kevin Whitcher: Arsenal, the Making of a Modern Superclub

Websites
Gap Hautes-Alpes Football Club official website
La Derniere Heure website (for quotes from David Grondin)
MLS website (For interview with Gilles Grimandi)
Four-Four-Two website (interview with Robert Pires)
Mail Online (interview with Abou Diaby)
Liberation

Plus:
Associated Press (Jerome Pugmire's interview with William Gallas)
Arsenal Club Magazine

Also by the author:

Tour de Kent

The Arsenal Book of Quotations
(available on Amazon)

Exodus: Maidstone United 1988 to 2012

PLUS: COMING SOON
Welcome to Kent (Sorry About The Racists)

Printed in Poland
by Amazon Fulfillment
Poland Sp. z o.o., Wrocław